# TRANSFORMING
# GRACE

### LIVING CONFIDENTLY IN GOD'S UNFAILING LOVE
### SMALL-GROUP CURRICULUM

# JERRY BRIDGES

**NAVPRESS**

Discipleship Inside Out™

**NAVPRESS**
Discipleship Inside Out™

NavPress is the publishing ministry of The Navigators, an international Christian organization and leader in personal spiritual development. NavPress is committed to helping people grow spiritually and enjoy lives of meaning and hope through personal and group resources that are biblically rooted, culturally relevant, and highly practical.

**For a free catalog go to www.NavPress.com
or call 1.800.366.7788 in the United States or 1.800.839.4769 in Canada.**

ISBN-13: 978-1-61521-571-3

Cover design by Arvid Wallen
Cover image by Paul Edmondson/Digital Vision

Some of the anecdotal illustrations in this book are true to life and are included with the permission of the persons involved. All other illustrations are composites of real situations, and any resemblance to people living or dead is coincidental.

Unless otherwise identified, all Scripture quotations in this publication are taken from the *Holy Bible, New International Version®* (NIV®). Copyright © 1973, 1978, 1984 by International Bible Society. Used by permission of Zondervan. All rights reserved. Other versions used include: the New American Standard Bible® (NASB), Copyright © 1960, 1962, 1963, 1968, 1971, 1972, 1973, 1975, 1977, 1995 by The Lockman Foundation. Used by permission; the *Williams New Testament* (WMS) by Charles B. Williams, © 1937, 1965, 1966, by Edith S. Williams, Moody Bible Institute of Chicago; and the King James Version (KJV).

Printed in the United States of America

1 2 3 4 5 6 7 8 / 14 13 12 11 10

# Contents

# Preface

The grace of God is one of the most important subjects in all of Scripture. At the same time it is probably one of the least understood.

All Christians by definition believe in grace. Many of us frequently quote Paul's well-known words in Ephesians 2:8-9: "For it is by grace you have been saved, through faith — and this not from yourselves, it is the gift of God — not by works, so that no one can boast." And John Newton's beloved hymn "Amazing Grace" is said to be the all-time favorite hymn in the United States. Why then do I say the grace of God is one of the least understood subjects in the Bible?

When we think of grace, we almost always think of being saved by grace. That is why Ephesians 2:8-9 is so familiar to us. Even Christian literature available on the subject of grace seems to deal almost exclusively with salvation. But the Bible teaches we are not only saved by grace, but we also live by grace every day of our lives. It is this important aspect of grace that seems to be so little understood or practiced by Christians.

My observation of Christendom is that most of us tend to base our personal relationship with God on our performance instead of on His grace. If we've performed well — whatever "well" is in our opinion — then we expect God to bless us. If we haven't done so well, our expectations are reduced accordingly. In this sense, we live by works rather than by grace. We are saved by grace, but we are living by the "sweat" of our own performance.

Moreover, we are always challenging ourselves and one another to "try harder." We seem to believe success in the Christian life (however we define success) is basically up to us: our commitment, our discipline, and our zeal, with some help from God along the way. We give lip service to the attitude of the apostle Paul, "But by the grace of God I am what I am" (1 Corinthians 15:10), but our unspoken motto is, "God helps those who help themselves."

The realization that my daily relationship with God is based on the infinite merit of Christ instead of on my own performance is a very freeing and joyous experience. But it is not meant to be a one-time experience; the truth needs to be reaffirmed daily. That is what this book is all about.

I often study some important topic of Scripture using what I call the "Crock Pot" or slow cooker method. That is, I let it "cook" slowly over the back burner of my mind for months, even years. That has been true with the subject of God's grace. It has been on my "back burner" for more than ten years. I've written three other books during that time, but my mind and heart have kept coming back to God's grace.

As I've studied this subject, and more particularly in recent months as I have focused my thoughts into the material for this book, I've frequently felt like a child trying to dip all the water out of the ocean. The grace of God is so inexhaustible and at times overwhelming. I trust I have been able to express something of that feeling in the message of this book, and that you, too, will come to appreciate more the vast riches of God's grace given to us through Christ.

Several people have played an important role in the writing of this book. My pastor, Rick Fite, read the complete manuscript and affirmed and encouraged me in this emphasis on grace. Another friend, Don Simpson, also read the manuscript and gave me valuable feedback and suggestions. Jon Stine, a very exacting editor, constantly challenged me to clarify my thoughts and to present a biblically balanced message. A number of friends across the country have prayed regularly for this work, but "senior saint" Grace Peterson has again been my Moses on the top of the hill while I have been fighting the "Amalekites" of concepts and thoughts, which often would just not come together. (Refer to Exodus 17:8-13 if you're not familiar with the Bible analogy I'm using.)

Jessie Newton, my administrative assistant, has put my handwritten manuscript on a computer, ready to be typeset. This is the second book Jessie has typed for me, and she has done a superb job.

My dear wife, Jane, has been a constant encourager and never complained, either in word or attitude, about being a "writer's widow" during the months when I devoted all my free time to writing this book.

Most of all, God Himself has poured out His mercy and grace on me. I trust my efforts will not be in vain and, through the message of this book, many will "grow in the grace and knowledge of our Lord and Savior Jesus Christ. To him be glory both now and forever! Amen" (2 Peter 3:18).

# Before You Begin

Grace. It truly is amazing. But why do so few Christians experience the joy of knowing God and His infinite grace? Since it is by God's grace that we are saved, and by His grace that we grow, what is our part in this process? In this study you will explore these and other questions about grace. In the end, we hope you will come away with a deeper understanding and a fuller experience of the amazing grace of our Lord.

Each session in this combined book and group study guide contains the text of one or more chapters of *Transforming Grace* followed by study and discussion questions. Please notice that some of the book chapters are combined in the sessions. We created the study guide this way so as to compress it into a shorter amount of time (eight weeks, if you do one per week) than the book would allow (thirteen chapters). Also, while this guide is written to stimulate group discussions, you can use it for individual study. The section at the back of the book called "Help for Group Leaders" gives practical suggestions about how to lead a group through this study.

Each session contains the following sections:

*Text.* Group members should read this chapter or chapters before getting together.

*Central Idea.* This states the main point of the session. It will be helpful to keep this in mind while you prepare and during group discussions.

*Warm-up.* This ice-breaker question will introduce the topic of discussion and help you and other group members connect at the beginning of the sessions.

*Exploring Grace.* These questions help you grapple with the ideas in the text as you look at relevant Scripture passages. They will challenge you to think about how these truths relate to your particular circumstances. Please read and answer these questions before the group meets together.

*Closing Prayer.* These suggestions are designed to help your closing prayer time relate to the lesson. Also, at this time the group should intercede for personal needs people shared during the discussion.

*Going Deeper.* These are extra questions for additional study and discussion if time allows. Your group leader might draw from these questions if more material is needed. You can also complete these on your own after the session.

*Pondering Grace.* These quotes are for personal reflection and for stimulating further thought. They may also help broaden the discussions.

God's grace is not something abstract and theoretical in the life of faith. It is the essential and pervasive means by which God impacts our lives. To know God's grace is to see His hand at work transforming our lives. May His grace draw you deeper into fellowship with Him.

# The Performance Treadmill

Read the following portion of *Transforming Grace*. In the margins, record observations, illustrations, or questions that come to mind as you read. Then answer the study questions that follow the reading.

---

### Chapter One: The Performance Treadmill

*Are you so foolish? After beginning with the Spirit, are you now trying to attain your goal by human effort?*
GALATIANS 3:3

*B*ankrupt! The word has a dreadful ring to it. In fact, it is more than a word, it's an expression. It means failure, insolvency, inability to pay one's debts, perhaps financial ruin. Even in our lax and permissive society, being bankrupt still conveys some degree of disgrace and shame. Can you imagine a boy bragging to his buddies that his father has just declared bankruptcy?

In the moral realm, the word *bankrupt* has an even more disparaging connotation. To say a person is morally bankrupt is to say he or she is completely devoid of any decent moral qualities. It is like comparing that person to Adolph Hitler. It is just about the worst thing you can say about a person.

Now, you may have never thought of it this way, but you are bankrupt. I'm not referring to your financial condition or your moral qualities. You may be financially as solid as the Rock of Gibraltar and the most upstanding person in your community, but you are still bankrupt. So am I.

You and I and every person in the world are *spiritually* bankrupt. In fact, every person who has ever lived, except for Jesus Christ — regardless of his or her moral or religious state — has been spiritually bankrupt. Listen to this declaration of our

9

bankruptcy from the pen of the apostle Paul:

> There is no one righteous, not even one;
>     there is no one who understands,
>     no one who seeks God.
> All have turned away,
>     they have together become worthless;
> there is no one who does good,
>     not even one. (Romans 3:10-12)

No one righteous, no one who seeks God, no one who does good, not even one. This is spiritual bankruptcy in its most absolute state. Usually in a bankrupt business, the company still has a few assets that can be sold to partially pay its debts. But we had no assets, nothing we could hand over to God as partial payment of our debt. Even "our righteous acts are like filthy rags" in His sight (Isaiah 64:6). We were spiritually destitute. We owed a debt we could not pay.

Then we learned salvation is a gift from God; it is entirely by grace through faith — not by works, so that no one can boast (see Romans 6:23; Ephesians 2:8-9). We renounced confidence in any supposed righteousness of our own and turned in faith to Jesus Christ alone for our salvation. In that act we essentially declared spiritual bankruptcy.

But what kind of bankruptcy did we declare? In the business world, financially troubled companies forced into bankruptcy have two options, popularly known as chapter 7 and chapter 11, after the respective chapters in the federal bankruptcy code. Chapter 11 deals with what we could call a temporary bankruptcy. This option is chosen by a basically healthy company that, given time, can work through its financial problems.

Chapter 7 is for a company that has reached the end of its financial rope. It is not only deeply in debt, it has no future as a viable business. It is forced to liquidate its assets and pay off its creditors, often by as little as ten cents on the dollar. The company is finished. It's all over. The owners or investors lose everything they've put into the business. No one likes chapter 7 bankruptcy.

## TEMPORARY OR PERMANENT BANKRUPTCY?

So what kind of bankruptcy did we declare? To use the business analogy, did we file under chapter 7 or chapter 11? Was it permanent or temporary? I suspect most of us would say we declared permanent bankruptcy. Having trusted in Jesus Christ alone for our salvation, we realized we could not add any measure of good works to what He has already done. We believe He completely paid our debt of sin and secured for us the gift of eternal life. There is nothing more we can do to earn our salvation, so using the business analogy, we would say we filed permanent bankruptcy.

However, I think most of us actually declared temporary bankruptcy. Having trusted in Christ alone for our salvation, we have subtly and unconsciously reverted to a works relationship with God in our Christian lives. We recognize that even our best efforts cannot get us to heaven, but we do think they earn God's blessings in our daily lives.

After we become Christians we begin to put away our more obvious sins. We also start attending church, put money in the offering plate, and maybe join a small group Bible study. We see some positive change in our lifestyle, and we begin to feel pretty good about ourselves. We are now ready to emerge from bankruptcy and pay our own way in the Christian life.

Then the day comes when we fall on our face spiritually. We lapse back into an old sin, or we fail to do what we should have done. Because we think we are now on our own, paying our own way, we assume we have forfeited all blessings from God for some undetermined period of time. Our expectation of God's blessing depends on how well we feel we are living the Christian life. We declared temporary bankruptcy to get into

His kingdom, so now we think we can and must pay our own way with God. We were saved by grace, but we are living by performance.

If you think I am overstating the case, try this test. Think of a time recently when you really fell on your face spiritually. Then imagine that immediately afterward you encountered a terrific opportunity to share Christ with a non-Christian friend. Could you have done it with complete confidence in God's help?

We are all legalistic by nature; that is, we innately think so much performance by us earns so much blessing from God. The apostle Peter thought this way. After listening to Jesus' conversation with the rich young man, he said to Jesus, "We have left everything to follow you! What then will there be for us?" (Matthew 19:27). Peter had already added up his merit points, and he wanted to know how much reward they would buy.

Not only are we legalistic by nature, our Christian culture reinforces this attitude in us. We are exhorted to attend church regularly, have a daily quiet time, study our Bibles, pray, memorize Scripture, witness to our neighbors, and give to missions — all of which are important Christian activities. Though no one ever comes right out and says so, somehow the vague impression is created in our minds that we'd better do those things or God will not bless us.

Then we turn to the Bible and read that we are to work out our salvation, to pursue holiness, and to be diligent to add to our faith such virtues as goodness, knowledge, self-control, and love. In fact, we find the Bible filled with exhortations to do good works and pursue the disciplines of spiritual growth. Again, because we are legalistic by nature, we assume our performance in these areas earns God's blessings in our lives.

I struggle with these legalistic tendencies even though I know better. Several years ago I was scheduled to speak at a large church on the West Coast. Arriving at the church about fifteen minutes before the Sunday morning service, I learned that one of the pastoral staff had died suddenly the day before. The staff and congregation were in a state of shock and grief.

Sizing up the situation, I realized the "challenge to discipleship" message I had prepared was totally inappropriate. The congregation needed comfort and encouragement, not challenge, that day. I knew I needed a totally new message, so I silently began to pray, asking God to bring to my mind a message suitable for the occasion. *Then I began to add up my merits and demerits for the day:* Had I had a quiet time that morning? Had I entertained any lustful thoughts or told any half-truths? I had fallen into the performance trap.

I quickly recognized what I was doing, so I said, "Lord, I don't know the answer to any of those questions, but none of them matters. I come to You today in the name of Jesus and, by His merit alone, ask for Your help." A single verse of Scripture came to my mind and with it a brief outline for a message I knew would be appropriate. I went to the pulpit and literally prepared the message as I spoke. God did answer prayer.

Why did God answer my prayer? Was it because I had a quiet time that morning or fulfilled other spiritual disciplines? Was it because I hadn't entertained any sinful thoughts that day? No, God answered my prayer for only one reason: Jesus Christ had already purchased that answer to prayer two thousand years ago on a Roman cross. God answered on the basis of His grace alone, not because of my merits or demerits.

One of the best kept secrets among Christians today is this: *Jesus paid it all. I mean all. He not only purchased your forgiveness of sins and your ticket to heaven, He purchased every blessing and every answer to prayer you will ever receive.* Every one of them — no exceptions.

Why is this such a well-kept secret? For one thing, we are afraid of this truth. We are afraid to tell even ourselves that we don't have to work anymore, the work is all done. We are afraid that if we really believe this, we will slack off in our Christian duties. But the deeper core issue is that we don't really believe we are still bankrupt. Having come into God's kingdom by grace alone solely on the merit of Another, we're now trying to pay our own way by our performance. We declared only temporary bankruptcy; we are now trying to live by good works rather than by grace.

The total Christian experience is often described in three distinct phases: justification, sanctification, and glorification.

*Justification* — being declared righteous before God through faith in Jesus Christ — is a point-in-time event. It is the time in our lives when we are saved. It is the Ephesians 2:8 experience: "For it is by grace you have been saved, through faith."

*Sanctification* is our growth in Christlikeness. It is a progressive experience covering our entire Christian lives from salvation to glorification. *Glorification* occurs at the time we depart from this life to be with Christ. (Glorification actually achieves its complete fulfillment at the resurrection, of course, but even now those who are with Christ are described as "the spirits of righteous men made perfect" [Hebrews 12:23].)

All true Christians readily agree that justification is by grace through faith in Christ. And if we stop to think about it, we agree that glorification is also solely by God's grace. Jesus purchased for us not only forgiveness of sins (justification) but also eternal life (glorification). But sanctification — the entire Christian experience between justification and glorification — is another story. At best, the Christian life is viewed as a mixture of personal performance and God's grace. It is not that we have consciously sorted it all out in our minds and have concluded that our relationship with God, for example, is based on 50 percent performance and 50 percent grace. Rather it is a subconscious assumption arising from our own innate legalism — reinforced and fueled by the Christian culture we live in.

Accordingly, our view of the Christian life could be illustrated by the following timeline:

| Justification<br>Based on Grace | Christian Life<br>Based on Works | Glorification<br>Based on Grace |
|---|---|---|

According to that illustration, our concept of the Christian life is a grace-works-grace sequence. The principal thesis of this book, however, and the truth I hope to demonstrate is that the illustration should look like this:

| | | |
|---|---|---|
| Justification Based on Grace | Christian Life Based on Grace | Glorification Based on Grace |

That is, the entire Christian life from start to completion is lived on the basis of God's grace to us through Christ.

Now let's return to the bankruptcy analogy. As devastating as permanent bankruptcy is, there is a bright side. The beleaguered businessman is finally free. He doesn't owe anyone anything anymore. His debts were not fully paid, but at least they were canceled. They no longer hang over his head; he is free from the phone calls and the demands and threats of his creditors. They can't harass him anymore. This businessman may be humiliated, but at least he is free.

Meanwhile the businessman who filed for temporary bankruptcy is still scrambling to make a go of it. He has a reprieve from his creditors for a period of time, but he has to work extra hard to try to turn his business around. Eventually his creditors must be paid. This businessman isn't free. Instead, he's on a performance treadmill.

All human analogies of spiritual truth, however, ultimately fall short of the truth. They can never tell the whole story, as we see in the bankruptcy analogy. The businessman who declared permanent bankruptcy is not totally free. He is free of his past debts, but not any he incurs in the future. His slate is wiped clean for the past, but starting all over again, he has to try to keep it clean in the future. In the business world, then, there really isn't a permanent bankruptcy in the sense of freedom from future performance.

But the good news of the Bible is that, in the spiritual realm, there really is total, permanent bankruptcy. It doesn't work like commercial bankruptcy; it is much better in two significant ways.

First of all, in the business world the debts of the permanently bankrupt business are never paid in full. The creditors accept the meager amount they receive from the sale of the company's assets. Neither the bankrupt businessman nor his creditors are satisfied. The businessman, if he is conscientious at all, feels guilty about the debts he did not pay; and the creditors are unhappy about the payments they did not receive.

Conversely, the Christian's total debt has been paid by the death of Christ. The law of God and the justice of God have been fully satisfied. The debt of our sins has been marked "Paid in Full!" God is satisfied and so are we. We have peace with God, and we are delivered from a guilty conscience (see Romans 5:1; Hebrews 10:22).

Second, not only has the debt been fully paid, *there is no possibility of going into debt again.* Jesus paid the debt of all our sins: past, present, and future. As Paul said in Colossians 2:13, "[God] forgave us all our sins." We don't have to start all over again and try to keep the slate clean. There is no more slate. As Stephen Brown wrote, "God took our slate and He broke it in pieces and threw it away."[1] This is true not only for our justification, but for our Christian lives as well. God is not keeping score, granting or withholding blessings on the basis of our performance. The score has already been permanently settled by Christ. We so often miss this dimension of the gospel.

We are brought into God's kingdom by grace; we are sanctified by grace; we receive both temporal and spiritual blessings by grace; we are motivated to obedience by grace; we are called to serve and enabled to serve by grace; we receive strength to endure trials by grace; and finally, we are glorified by grace. The entire Christian life is lived under the reign of God's grace.

## WHAT IS GRACE?

What, then, is the grace by which we are saved and under which we live? *Grace* is God's free and unmerited favor shown to guilty sinners who deserve only judgment. It is the love of God shown to the unlovely. It is God reaching downward to people who are in rebellion against Him.

Grace stands in direct opposition to any supposed worthiness on our part. To say it another way: Grace and works are mutually exclusive. As Paul said in Romans 11:6, "And if by grace, then it is no longer by works; if it were, grace would no longer be grace." Our relationship with God is based on either works *or* grace. There is never a works-plus-grace relationship with Him.

Furthermore, grace does not first rescue us from the penalty of our sins, furnish us with some new spiritual abilities, and then leave us on our own to grow in spiritual maturity. Rather, as Paul said, "He who began a good work in you [by His grace] will [also by His grace] carry it on to completion until the day of Christ Jesus" (Philippians 1:6). John Newton captured this idea of the continuing work of grace in our lives when he wrote in the hymn "Amazing Grace," "Tis grace hath brought me safe thus far, and grace will lead me home."

The apostle Paul asks us today, as he asked the Galatian believers, "After beginning with the Spirit, are you now trying to obtain your goal by human effort?" (Galatians 3:3). Although the issue of circumcision was the specific problem Paul was addressing, notice that he did not say, "Are you trying to attain your goal by circumcision?" He generalized his question and dealt, not with the specific issue of circumcision, but with the broader problem of trying to please God by human effort, any effort — even good Christian activities and disciplines performed in a spirit of legalism.

## THE MERIT OF CHRIST

The apostle Paul sometimes used the grace of God and the merit of Christ almost interchangeably — as I do in this book. For example, Paul said,

> Mark my words! I, Paul, tell you that if you let yourselves be circumcised, Christ will be of no value to you at all. Again I declare to every man who lets himself be circumcised that he is obligated to obey the whole law. You who are trying to be justified by law have been alienated from Christ; you have fallen away from grace. (Galatians 5:2-4)

Notice the parallel statements Paul used, "Christ will be of no value to you"; "You . . . have been alienated from Christ; you have fallen away from grace."

In Ephesians 2:4-7, Paul wrote,

> But because of his great love for us, God, who is rich in mercy, made us alive with Christ even when we were dead in transgressions — it is by grace you have been saved. And God raised us up with Christ and seated us with him in the heavenly realms in Christ Jesus, in order that in the coming ages he might show the incomparable riches of his grace, expressed in his kindness to us in Christ Jesus.

Again note the close connection between Christ and grace. We are made "alive with Christ . . . it is by grace you have been saved." And God wants to "show the incomparable riches of his grace, expressed in his kindness to us in Christ Jesus."

Though the grace of God and the merit of Christ are not the same, they always go together in our relationship with God. We cannot experience one without the other. In terms of order, God's grace comes first. It was because of His grace that God the Father sent His only Son to die in our place. To say it another way, Christ's death was the result of God's grace; grace is not the result of Christ's death.

But it is also true that our experience of God's grace is made possible only by the death of Christ. God is gracious, but He is also just in an absolute sense; that is, His justice cannot overlook the least infraction of His holy law. Because Christ completely satisfied the justice of God, we can now experience the grace of God. Years ago I heard a simple acronym of grace expressing this relationship: GRACE is God's Riches At Christ's Expense. This is why I have stated in this chapter —and will repeat it over and over again in this book—that Jesus Christ has already paid for every blessing you and I will ever receive from God the Father.

There is a beautiful story in the life of King David illustrating God's grace to us through Christ. Mephibosheth was the son of David's bosom friend, Jonathan, son of Saul. He had been crippled in both feet at age five. After David was established as king over all Israel, he desired to show kindness to anyone remaining of Saul's house "for Jonathan's sake." So Mephibosheth—crippled and destitute, unable to care for himself and living in someone else's house—was brought into David's house and "ate at David's table like one of the king's sons" (2 Samuel 9:11).

Why was Mephibosheth treated like one of David's sons? It was for Jonathan's sake. We might say Jonathan's loyal friendship with David "earned" Mephibosheth's seat at David's table. Mephibosheth, in his crippled and destitute condition, unable to improve his lot and wholly dependent on the benevolence of others, is an illustration of you and me, crippled by sin and unable to help ourselves. David, in his graciousness, illustrates God the Father, and Jonathan illustrates Christ.

Just as Mephibosheth was elevated to a place at the king's table for Jonathan's sake, so you and I are elevated to the status of God's children for Christ's sake. And just as being seated at the king's table involved not only daily food but other privileges as well, so God's salvation for Christ's sake carries with it all the provisions we need, not only for eternity but for this life as well.

As if to emphasize the special privilege of Mephibosheth, the inspired writer mentions four times in one short chapter that Mephibosheth ate at the king's table (see 2 Samuel 9:7,10,11,13). Three of those times he says he *always* ate at the king's table. But the account both begins and ends with the statement that Mephibosheth was crippled in both feet (see verses 3,13). Mephibosheth never got over his crippled condition. He never got to the place where he could leave the king's table and make it on his own. And neither do we.

---

## Chapter Two: Grace — Who Needs It?

*This righteousness from God comes through faith in Jesus Christ to all who believe. There is no difference, for all have sinned and fall short of the glory of God, and are justified freely by his grace through the redemption that came by Christ Jesus.*
ROMANS 3:22-24

S am and Pam, two friends, both arrived in the United States as immigrants from the country of Quadora. Each one wanted to buy a house, and it so happened they each found one for sale by a certain wealthy man. Both houses were priced at $100,000. Sam arrived with 500,000 quadros, the currency of Quadora, and Pam arrived with 1,000,000 quadros.

They knew quadros were not worth one dollar apiece, but they assumed they would be able to exchange the quadros for at least enough to buy a house. However, Quadora had been ravished by hyperinflation, and the quadro had been debased until it was virtually worthless. The bank would not accept their quadros in exchange for any dollars.

To compound the problem, Sam and Pam both discov-

SESSION ONE: The Performance Treadmill

ered that the wealthy man from whom they hoped to buy their houses was not unknown to them. They'd each had business transactions with the man while still in Quadora, and were heavily in debt to him. Sam owed him about a million dollars, and Pam owed him $500,000. Since their quadros were worthless, neither could even begin to pay his or her debt, let alone buy a house from him.

Then a strange thing happened. The wealthy man — hearing Pam and Sam were now in this country and knowing they would have arrived with only their worthless quadros — sought them out. Despite the fact they were heavily in debt to him, he canceled the debts, gave them each the house they desired, completely furnished, with utilities and maintenance paid for life.

That is a picture of how God's grace operates. The "currency" of our morality and good deeds is worthless in God's sight. Furthermore, we all are so heavily in debt to Him because of our sin that there is no question of our even partially paying our way with God.

## A BIBLICAL VIEW OF GRACE

I once heard a definition of grace as God's making up the difference between the requirements of His righteous law and what we lack in meeting those requirements. No one is good enough to earn salvation by himself, this definition said, so God's grace simply makes up what we lack. Some receive more grace than others; but all receive whatever they need to obtain salvation. No one ever need be lost because whatever grace he needs is his for the taking.

This definition of grace sounds very generous of God, doesn't it, making up whatever we lack? The problem with this definition, though, is that it isn't true. It represents a grave misunderstanding of the grace of God and a very inadequate view of our plight as sinners before a holy God. We need to be sure we have a biblical view of grace, for grace is at the very heart of the gospel. It is certainly not necessary for someone to understand all the theology of grace to be saved, but if a person does have a false notion of grace, it probably means he or she does not really understand the gospel.

Although this is a book about *living* by grace, we need to be sure we first understand *saving* grace, for two reasons. First, all that I say about the grace of God in subsequent chapters assumes you have experienced the *saving* grace of God — that you have trusted in Jesus Christ alone for eternal salvation. It would be a fatal injustice if I allowed you to believe that all the wonderful provisions of God's grace we will see in the following chapters are yours apart from salvation through Jesus Christ.

Second, although this is a book about living by grace, grace is always the same, whether God exercises it in saving us or in dealing with us as believers. In whatever way the Bible defines saving grace, that same definition applies in the arena of living the Christian life day by day.

## GOD'S OFFER OF GRACE

God says to us,

> Come, all you who are thirsty,
>    come to the waters;
> and you who have no money,
>    come, buy and eat!
> Come, buy wine and milk
>    without money and without cost.
>    (Isaiah 55:1)

The gospel is addressed to those who have *no* money or good works. It invites us to come and "buy" salvation without money and without cost. But note the invitation to come is addressed to those who have *no* money — not to those who don't have *enough*. Grace is not a matter of God's making up the difference, but of God's providing all the "cost" of salvation through His Son, Jesus Christ.

The apostle Paul spoke to this issue in Romans 3:22 when he said, "There is no difference." There is no difference between Jew and Gentile, between the religious and the irreligious, between the most decent moral person and the most degenerate. There is no difference between us, because we all have sinned and fall short of the glory of God.

To say the grace of God makes up the difference of what God requires of us is like comparing two people's attempts to leap across the Grand Canyon. The canyon averages about nine miles in width from rim to rim. Suppose one person could leap out about thirty feet from the edge while another can leap only six feet. What difference does it make? Sure, one person can leap five times as far as the other, but relative to nine miles (47,520 feet!), it makes no difference. Like the quadros in my parable, both leaps are absolutely worthless for crossing the canyon. And when God built a bridge across the "Grand Canyon" of our sin, He didn't stop thirty feet or even six feet from our side. He built the bridge all the way.

Even the comparison of trying to leap across the Grand Canyon fails to adequately represent our desperate condition. To use that illustration we have to assume people are *trying* to leap across the canyon; that is, most people are actually trying to earn their way to heaven and, despite earnest effort, are falling short of bridging the awful chasm of sin separating them from God.

Nothing could be further from the truth. Almost no one tries to earn his way to heaven (Martin Luther, prior to his conversion, being a notable exception). Rather, almost everyone *assumes* that what he or she is *already* doing is sufficient to merit heaven. Almost no one is making a sincere effort to increase the length of his "leap" across the canyon. Instead, in our minds, we have narrowed the width of the canyon to what we can comfortably cross without any additional effort beyond what we are already doing. The person whose moral lifestyle might be equivalent to thirty feet sees the distance as narrowed to a comfortable twenty-nine feet; and the person who can leap only six feet has narrowed his canyon to five. Everyone expects that God will accept what he is already doing as sufficient "currency" to "buy" a house in heaven.

Like the first audience who heard Jesus' famous parable of the Pharisee and the tax collector, most people are confident of their own righteousness (Luke 18:9-14). They may, at a moment of serious reflection, concede they are not perfect by any means, but they consider themselves to be basically good.

One great problem today is that most of us really don't believe we're all that bad. In fact, we assume we're good. In 1981, a book addressing the difficult subject of pain and heartache was published and rapidly became a best seller. Its title: *When Bad Things Happen to Good People.* The book is based, as the title reveals, on the assumption that most people are "good." The definition by author Harold Kushner of good people is, "ordinary people, nice friendly neighbors, neither extraordinarily good nor extraordinarily bad."[2]

By contrast, the apostle Paul said we are all bad. Consider again Romans 3:10-12, noting the words I have emphasized:

> There is *no one* righteous, *not even one;*
>> there is no one who understands,
>> *no one* who seeks God.
> All have turned away,
>> they have together become worthless;
> there is *no one* who does good,
>> not even one.

These words were written to support Paul's answer to the question, "Are we [Jews] any better [than the Gentile pagans]?" To which he answered, "Not at all! We have already made the charge that Jews [the religious people of the day] and Gentiles [the 'sinners' of the day] alike are all under sin" (Romans 3:9).

The difference between Harold Kushner's appraisal of most people as basically "good" and the apostle Paul's of *all* people as basically "bad" arises from a totally different orientation. To Rabbi Kushner, you are good if you're a nice, friendly neighbor. To the apostle Paul (and the other Scripture writers), all people are bad because of our alienation from God and our rebellion against Him.

## GOING OUR OWN WAY

One of the most damning indictments of mankind is found in Isaiah 53:6: "We all, like sheep, have gone astray, each of us has turned to his own way." *Each of us has turned to his own way.* That is the very essence of sin, the very core of it—going our *own* way. Your way may be to give money to charity, while another person's way may be to rob a bank. But neither act is done with reference to God; both of you have gone your own way. And in a world governed by a sovereign Creator, that is rebellion, that is sin.

Consider a particular territory in a country rebelling against the central government of the nation. The citizens of that territory may be generally decent people, basically upright and caring in their dealings with one another. But all their goodness among themselves is totally irrelevant to the central government. To those authorities there is only one issue: the state of rebellion. Until that issue is resolved, nothing else matters.

This illustration is in danger of losing its force if we think in terms of present-day realities. Some central governments are so obviously corrupt and unjust, we may applaud a rebellious territory. We might, in some cases, consider their rebellion a just course of action.

But God's government is perfect and just. His moral law is "holy, righteous and good" (Romans 7:12). No one ever has a valid reason to rebel against the government of God. We rebel for only one reason: We were born rebellious. We were born with a perverse inclination to go our own way, to set up our own internal government rather than submit to God.

It is not that some of us *become* sinful because of an unfortunate childhood environment, while others are blessed with a highly moral upbringing. Rather we are *all* born sinners with a corrupt nature, a natural inclination to go our own way. As David wrote, "Surely I was sinful at birth, sinful from the time my mother conceived me" (Psalm 51:5). Here is an amazing statement from David that he was sinful while still in his mother's womb, even during the period of pregnancy when as yet he had performed no actions, either good or bad.

A Christian writer, in a magazine article, asked the question, "How could I go on believing in a God who picked on innocent children?" Setting aside her problem about the relationship of a righteous God to suffering in our lives, note her reference to *innocent* children. I single out this writer's question, not to criticize but to illustrate, because I believe she expressed the view of the vast majority of people, both believers and unbelievers: that children are born innocent and are corrupted by their environment.

But this is not the view of Scripture. According to Psalm 51:5, there are no innocent children. Rather, all of us were sinful at birth, even from the time of conception. Because of Adam's rebellion, we are all born with a sinful, perverse nature, an inclination to go our own way. Whether it is the way of the decent individual or the way of the obvious transgressor, it makes no difference. We were all born in a state of rebellion against God.

The Bible says we have all sinned, and almost everyone would agree with that statement. The problem is our shallow view of sin. The man on the street would simply shrug his shoulders at that charge and say, "Sure, no one's perfect." Even we Christians talk about *failures* and *defeats*, but the Bible uses other terms. It speaks of *wickedness* and *rebellion* (Leviticus 16:21).[3] The Bible speaks of King David as *despising* God (2 Samuel 12:9-10). It charges another man of God with *defying* the Word of the Lord, when all he did was eat and drink in a place forbidden to him by God (1 Kings 13:21). It is evident by these descriptive synonyms for sin — rebellion, despising, defying — that God takes a far more serious view of sin than the man on the street or even most Christians.

Sin, in the final analysis, is rebellion against the sovereign Creator, Ruler, and Judge of the universe. It resists the rightful prerogative of a sovereign Ruler to command obedience from His subjects. It says to an absolutely holy and righteous God that His moral laws, which are a reflection of His own nature, are not worthy of our wholehearted obedience.

Sin is not only a series of actions, it is also an attitude that ignores the law of God. But it is even more than a rebellious attitude. Sin is a state of heart, a condition of our inmost being. It is a state of corruption, of vileness, yes, even of filthiness in God's sight.

This view of sin as corruption, vileness, and filth is symbolically portrayed in Zechariah 3:1-4:

> Then he showed me Joshua the high priest standing before the angel of the LORD, and Satan standing at his right side to accuse him. The LORD said to Satan, "The LORD rebuke you, Satan! The LORD, who has chosen Jerusalem, rebuke you! Is not this man a burning stick snatched from the fire?"
>
> Now Joshua was dressed in filthy clothes as he stood before the angel. The angel said to those who were standing before him, "Take off his filthy clothes."
>
> Then he said to Joshua, "See, I have taken away your sin, and I will put rich garments on you."

Note who is described here. It is not a portrayal of the prodigal son, but of Joshua the high priest — the person holding the highest religious office in all Israel. Yet he is shown dressed in filthy clothes, a pictorial representation of both his sins and the sins of the people he represented as high priest. The filthiness of his garments depicts not the guilt of his sin but its pollution. Like Joshua, all of us are, in a spiritual sense, dressed in filthy clothes. We are not just guilty before God; we are also corrupted in our natures, polluted and vile before Him. We need forgiveness and cleansing.

For this reason the Bible never speaks of God's grace as simply making up our deficiencies — as if salvation consists in so much good works (even a variable amount) plus so much of God's grace. Rather the Bible speaks of "a God who justifies the wicked" (Romans 4:5) who is found by those who do not seek Him, who reveals Himself to those who do not ask for Him (see Romans 10:20).

The tax collector in Jesus' parable did not ask God to simply make up his deficiencies. Rather, he beat his breast — a sign of his deep anguish — and said, "God, have mercy on me, a sinner" (Luke 18:13). He declared total spiritual bankruptcy, and on that basis, he experienced the grace of God. Jesus said the man went home justified — declared righteous by God (see Luke 18:9-14).

Like the tax collector, we do not just need God's grace to make up for our deficiencies; we need His grace to provide a remedy for our guilt, a cleansing for our pollution. We need His grace to provide a satisfaction of His justice, to cancel a debt we cannot pay.

It may seem that I am belaboring the point of our guilt and vileness before God. But we can never rightly understand God's grace until we understand our plight as those who need His grace. As Dr. C. Samuel Storms has said,

> The first and possibly most fundamental characteristic of divine grace is that it presupposes sin and guilt.
>
> Grace has meaning *only* when men are seen as fallen, unworthy of salvation, and liable to eternal wrath. . . .
>
> Grace does not contemplate sinners merely as *un*deserving but as *ill*-deserving. . . . It is not simply that we do not deserve grace; we *do* deserve hell![4]

## RESPONDING TO GRACE

Earlier in this chapter, I told of a true incident in which an individual gave a very inadequate, perhaps even a fatally wrong, definition of grace. I suspect most readers responded negatively to the suggestion that God's grace merely makes up what we lack in an acceptable righteousness before God. You probably responded as one person did, "No, that's not right. Even our righteous deeds are as filthy rags in God's sight."

I did not mention that incident merely to set up a "straw man" to be easily refuted. I used that incident because *I believe it is the way most Christians live the Christian life.* We act as if God's grace only makes up what our good works lack. We believe God's blessings are at least partially earned by our obedience and our spiritual disciplines. We know we are saved by grace, but we think we must live by our spiritual "sweat."

So who needs grace? All of us, the saint as well as the sinner. The most conscientious, dutiful, hardworking Christian needs God's grace as much as the most dissolute, hard-living sinner. All of us need the same grace. The sinner does not need more grace than the saint, nor does the immature and undisciplined believer need more than the godly, zealous missionary. We all need the same amount of grace because the "currency" of our good works is debased and worthless before God.

Neither our merits nor our demerits determine how much grace we need, because grace does not supplement merits or make up for demerits. Grace does not take into account merits or demerits at all. Rather, grace considers all men and women as totally undeserving and unable to do anything to earn the blessing of God. Again, as C. Samuel Storms has so aptly written,

> Grace ceases to be grace if God is compelled to bestow it in the presence of human merit. . . . Grace ceases to be grace if God is compelled to withdraw it in the presence of human demerit. . . . [Grace] is treating a person

29

without the slightest reference to desert whatsoever, but solely according to the infinite goodness and sovereign purpose of God.[5]

Note that Dr. Storms' description of God's grace cuts both ways: It can neither be earned by your merit nor forfeited by your demerit. If you sometimes feel you deserve an answer to prayer or a particular blessing from God because of your hard work or sacrifice, you are living by works, not by grace. But it is just as true that if you sometimes despair of experiencing God's blessing because of your demerits — the "oughts" you should have done but didn't or the "don'ts" you shouldn't have done but did — you are also casting aside the grace of God.

Frankly, the second of Dr. Storms' statements is most helpful to me. I seldom think of merit on my part, but I'm often painfully aware of my demerits. Therefore, I need to be reminded frequently that my demerits do not compel God to withdraw His grace from me, but rather He treats me without regard to deserts whatsoever. I'd much rather stake my hope of His blessing on His infinite goodness than on my good works.

John Newton, the debauched and dissolute slave trader, after his conversion wrote the wonderful old hymn "Amazing Grace." He never tired of contemplating with awed amazement the wonder of a grace that would reach even to him. But the person who grew up in a godly Christian family, who trusted Christ at an early age, and who never indulged in any so-called "gross" sins should be just as amazed at the grace of God as was John Newton.

Here is a spiritual principle regarding the grace of God: *To the extent you are clinging to any vestiges of self-righteousness or are putting any confidence in your own spiritual attainments, to that degree you are not living by the grace of God in your life.* This principle applies both in salvation and in living the Christian life. Let me repeat something I said in chapter 1. Grace and good works (that is, works done to earn favor with God) are mutually exclusive. We cannot stand, as it were, with one foot on grace and the other on our own works of merit.

If you are trusting to *any* degree in your own morality or religious attainments, or if you believe God will somehow recognize any of your good works as merit toward your salvation, you need to seriously consider if you are truly a Christian. I realize I risk offending some with that statement, but we must be absolutely clear about the truth of the gospel of salvation.

Over two hundred years ago Abraham Booth (1734–1806), a Baptist pastor in England, wrote,

> The most shining deeds and valuable qualities that can be found among men, though highly useful and truly excellent, when set in their proper places, and referred to suitable ends, are, as to the grand article of justification treated as nonentities. . . .
>
> For divine grace disdains to be assisted in the performance of that work which peculiarly belongs to itself, by the poor, imperfect performances of men. Attempts to complete what grace begins, betray our pride and offend the Lord; but cannot promote our spiritual interest. Let the reader, therefore, carefully remember, that grace is either absolutely free, or it is not at all: and, that he who professes to look for salvation by grace, either believes in his heart to be saved entirely by it, or he acts inconsistently in affairs of the greatest importance.[6]

The thoughts of Abraham Booth are just as valid and needful today as they were two hundred years ago. Those who are truly saved are those who have come to Jesus with the attitude expressed in the words of an old hymn, "Nothing in my hand I bring, simply to thy cross I cling."[7]

# The Performance Treadmill

## (Chapters 1 and 2)

## STUDY QUESTIONS

### CENTRAL IDEA

God's grace alone saves us, helps us grow, meets our daily needs, and guarantees our future in heaven. These blessings are never given to us based on our performance.

### WARM-UP

Tell about a time when someone (a parent, teacher, or friend) treated you with grace instead of treating you as your behavior deserved.

### EXPLORING GRACE

1. a. What do the following verses say about your spiritual condition apart from Christ?

   • Isaiah 53:6

   • Romans 3:10-20

b.   Relate an experience that made you keenly aware of your spiritual "bankruptcy" apart from Christ.

2.   Why is it important to focus on your spiritual condition apart from Christ in order to understand God's grace?

3.   In Philippians 3:1-14 Paul contrasts the attitude of legalism with a true understanding of the transforming grace of God. In the following chart, contrast a legalist trying to earn God's favor and a person trusting in God's grace.

|  | Legalist | One Trusting in Grace |
|---|---|---|
| Basis of a relationship with God |  |  |
| Feelings toward God |  |  |
| Motivation for good behavior |  |  |
| Reasons for feeling bad about failures |  |  |
| Treatment of others who have fallen short |  |  |
| Basis of strength during trials |  |  |
| Basis of strength to serve the Lord |  |  |

4. Many Christians believe that their justification is based on grace, the blessings in their Christian life are based on works, and their future glorification will be based on grace. Where is the error in this thinking? (See Galatians 3:3 and Philippians 1:6.)

5. Look at the following verses. What do they teach about trying to mix grace and works as the basis for a relationship with God?

    • Romans 11:6

    • Galatians 5:2-6

6. What do you think makes it so hard for a person to rely on God's grace rather than his own efforts?

7. Give an example of a recent time when you were tempted to think that God's blessings in your life depended on your performance. For example:

    • You missed your quiet time. When things went wrong during the day, you attributed it to God's disappointment with you for missing your time with Him.
    • You had an especially worshipful time with the Lord, reading His Word, praising Him, and interceding for your friends. When you needed the Lord's help with a particular problem, you felt He owed you this favor.

8. Do you ever experience feelings of self-righteousness and spiritual pride creeping into your life? In what circumstances do you find yourself most vulnerable to these kinds of thoughts?

9. How can you guard against these attitudes of self-righteousness and spiritual pride? Decide on one specific thing you plan to do this week to guard against depending on your performance to earn God's favor. For example:

- For one day, keep a running tally on a three-by-five-inch card of the times you think sinful thoughts. Each time you make a mark on the card, stop and thank God that your forgiveness was procured at Calvary, and that by His grace you are growing in Him.
- Make a list of God's blessings in your life in the last year. Put a check beside anything on your list that you earned through your behavior.
- Make a list of some of your accomplishments in life. Put a check beside any that you achieved on your own efforts, without any help from God.

## CLOSING PRAYER

At this time, pray for any personal needs mentioned during the discussion. Praying for one another's needs will bind your group closer together. Spend some of your prayer time thanking God for His boundless grace in your lives.

## GOING DEEPER (Extra questions for further study)

1. What insights do the following verses give us about God's view of our sin?

- Leviticus 16:1-34

- 2 Samuel 12:9-10

- 1 Kings 13:21-22

2. Sometimes the word *sin* doesn't mean anything to a nonbeliever. How would you explain the concept of sin without using the word? (You might want to look up the word *sin* in a Bible dictionary or a thesaurus.)

3. What is the relationship between the grace of God and the righteousness of Christ?

- Romans 3:22-24

- Galatians 5:2-4

- Ephesians 2:4-7

4. Which person needs God's grace more: the conscientious, dutiful, hardworking Christian, or the most decadent, hard-living sinner? Explain your answer.

## Pondering Grace (For personal reflection)

*The first and possibly most fundamental characteristic of divine grace is that it presupposes sin and guilt. Grace has meaning only when men are seen as fallen, unworthy of salvation, and liable to eternal wrath. . . . Grace does not contemplate sinners merely as undeserving but as ill-deserving. . . . It is not simply that we do not deserve grace; we do deserve hell.*

C. Samuel Storms, *The Grandeur of God*

*Let grace be the beginning, grace the consummation, grace the crown.*

Bede

*Grace is love that cares and stoops and rescues.*

John R. W. Stott

*Grace ceases to be grace if God is compelled to bestow it in the presence of human merit. Grace ceases to be grace if God is compelled to withdraw it in the presence of human demerit. Grace is treating a person without the slightest reference to desert whatsoever, but solely according to the infinite goodness and sovereign purpose of God.*

C. Samuel Storms, *The Grandeur of God*

*Divine grace disdains to be assisted in the performance of that work which peculiarly belongs to itself, by the poor, imperfect performances of men. Attempts to complete what grace begins, betray our pride and offend the Lord; but cannot promote our spiritual interest. Let the reader therefore, carefully remember, that grace is either absolutely free, or it is not at all: and, that he who professes to look for salvation by grace, either believes in his heart to be saved entirely by it, or he acts inconsistently in affairs of the greatest importance.*

Abraham Booth, *The Reign of Grace*

# Grace — It Really Is Amazing

Read the following portion of *Transforming Grace*. In the margins, record observations, illustrations, or questions that come to mind as you read. Then answer the study questions that follow the reading.

---

### Chapter Three: Grace — It Really Is Amazing

*But where sin increased, grace increased all the more,*
*so that, just as sin reigned in death, so also grace might*
*reign through righteousness to bring eternal life*
*through Jesus Christ our Lord.*
ROMANS 5:20-21

Notes and Observations

A study of the grace of God is a study in contrast, a contrast between the desperate plight of mankind and the abundant and gracious remedy God has provided for us through Christ Jesus. This contrast is beautifully described in the words of an old hymn:

Guilty, vile and helpless we,
Spotless Lamb of God was He;
Full atonement! Can it be?
Hallelujah, what a Savior!¹

In session 1 (chapter 2), we saw that all of us are indeed guilty, vile, and helpless. We recognized that all of us are equally in need of the grace of God. In this chapter, we will consider God's gracious provision for our desperate plight.

When an engaged couple goes into a jewelry store to shop for that special diamond, the jeweler will often set a dark, velvet-covered pad on his counter, then carefully lay each diamond on the pad. The contrast of the dark velvet provides the background that enhances the sparkle and beauty of each diamond.

Our sinful condition hardly qualifies as a velvet pad, but against the dark background of guilt and moral pollution, God's grace in salvation sparkles like a beautiful, clear, and flawless diamond.

## OUR RUIN, GOD'S REMEDY

The apostle Paul used a contrasting background when he described God's gracious remedy for our ruin in a series of Scriptures I like to call God's wonderful "buts."

We already saw the dark background Paul painted in his indictment of all mankind, both religious and irreligious, in Romans 3:10-12. In verses 13-20, he elaborated on that indictment, finally concluding in verse 20, "Therefore no one will be declared righteous in his sight by observing the law; rather, through the law we become conscious of sin."

Having painted the dark background of our ruin, Paul proceeds to set before us the clear, sparkling diamond of God's remedy. Notice how he begins: "But now a righteousness from God, apart from law, has been made known, to which the Law and the Prophets testify" (verse 21). We are all found to be in a state of ruin, *but now* God has provided a remedy: a righteousness that comes from God through faith in Jesus Christ. This righteousness is said to be "apart from law," that is, apart from any consideration of how well or not so well we have obeyed the law of God.

Under God's grace, the extent or quality of our law-keeping is not an issue. Instead, those who have faith in Jesus Christ "are justified freely by his grace" (verse 24). To be justified means more than to be declared "not guilty." It actually means to be declared *righteous* before God. It means God has *imputed* or charged the guilt of our sin to His Son, Jesus Christ, and has *imputed* or credited Christ's righteousness to us.

Note, however, that we are justified *by His grace*. It is because of God's grace we are declared righteous before Him. We are all guilty before God — condemned, vile, and helpless. We had no claim on God; the disposition of our case was wholly up to Him. He could with total justice have pronounced us all guilty, for that is what we were, and consigned us all to eternal damnation. That is what He did to the angels who sinned (see 2 Peter 2:4), and He could have with perfect justice done the same to us. He owed us nothing; we owed Him everything.

Notes and Observations

But, because of His grace, God did not consign us all to hell; instead, He provided a remedy for us through Jesus Christ. Romans 3:25 says, "God presented him as a sacrifice of atonement, through faith in his blood." What is a sacrifice of atonement? A footnote of the New International Version gives an alternate reading of "the one who would turn aside his wrath, taking away sin."

The meaning of Christ as a sacrifice of atonement, then, is that Jesus by His death turned aside the wrath of God from us by taking it upon Himself. As He hung on the cross, He bore our sins in His body and endured the full force of God's wrath in our place. As Peter said, "He himself bore our sins in his body," and suffered, "the righteous for the unrighteous" (1 Peter 2:24; 3:18). By His death Jesus completely satisfied the justice of God, which required eternal death as the penalty for sin.

It is important that we notice who presented Christ as this sacrifice of atonement. Romans 3:25 says God presented Him. The whole plan of redemption was God's plan and was undertaken at God's initiative. Why did He do this? There is only one answer: *because of His grace*. The atonement was God's extending favor to people who deserved not favor but wrath. The atonement was God's bridging the awful "Grand Canyon" of sin to reach people who were in rebellion against Him. And He did this at infinite cost to Himself by sending Jesus to die in our place.

Another of God's wonderful "buts" is found in Ephesians 2:1-5:

As for you, you were dead in your transgressions and sins, in which you used to live when you followed the ways of this world and of the ruler of the kingdom of the air, the spirit who is now at work in those who are disobedient. All of us also lived among them at one time, gratifying the cravings of our sinful nature and following its desires and thoughts. Like the rest, we were by nature objects of wrath. But because of his great love for us, God, who is rich in mercy, made us alive with Christ even when we were dead in transgressions — it is by grace you have been saved.

Again we see the contrast drawn so sharply between our ruin and God's remedy. In verses 1-3, Paul described us as dead in our sins, under the sway of Satan, captivated by the world, prisoners of our own sinful lusts, and objects of God's holy wrath. Could any picture be more dark, any background more contrasting? But against this dark background Paul once again presented the flawless diamond of God's grace.

*But God intervened!* We were dead in our transgressions, but God intervened. We were in bondage to sin, but God intervened. We were objects of wrath, but God intervened. God who is rich in mercy intervened. Because of His great love for us, God intervened and made us alive with Christ, even when we were dead in our transgressions and sins. All this is summed up in one succinct statement: "It is by grace you have been saved." Our condition was hopeless, but God intervened in grace.

A third instance of God's wonderful "buts" occurs in Titus 3:3-5:

At one time we too were foolish, disobedient, deceived and enslaved by all kinds of passions and pleasures. We lived in malice and envy, being hated and hating one another. But when the kindness and love of God our

Savior appeared, he saved us, not because of righteous things we had done, but because of his mercy.

Again Paul draws a gracious contrast between our ruin and God's remedy. The contrast could not be more bold and complete. Our foolishness, disobedience, and enslavement to all kinds of sinful passions are met by God's kindness, mercy, and love. The utterly unrighteous are declared righteous (justified) *by His grace* (see Titus 3:7). God's grace really is amazing.

God's grace, then, does not supplement our good works. Instead, His grace overcomes our *bad* works, which are our sins. God did this by placing our sins on Christ and by letting fall on Him the wrath we so richly deserved. Because Jesus completely paid the awful penalty of our sins, God could extend His grace to us through complete and total forgiveness of our sins. The extent of His forgiveness is vividly portrayed to us in four picturesque expressions in the Old Testament.

## AS FAR AS THE EAST IS FROM THE WEST

Psalm 103:12 reads, "As far as the east is from the west, so far has he removed our transgressions from us." How far is the east from the west? If you start due north at any point on earth, you would eventually cross over the North Pole and start going south, but that is not true when you go east or west. If you start west and continue in that direction you will always be going west. North and south meet at the North Pole, but east and west never meet. In a sense, they are an infinite distance apart. So when God says He removes our transgressions from us as far as the east is from the west, He is saying they have been removed an infinite distance from us. But how can we get a "handle" on this rather abstract truth in such a way that it becomes meaningful in our lives?

When God uses this metaphorical expression describing the extent of His forgiveness of our sins, He is saying His forgiveness is total, complete, and unconditional. He is saying He is not keeping score with regard to our sins. The psalmist clarifies this idea: "He does not treat us as our sins deserve or repay us according to our iniquities" (Psalm 103:10). Yes, God actually says that! I know it seems too good to be true. I confess I almost hesitate to write those words because they are so foreign to our innate concepts of reward and punishment.

But those gracious words are right in the Bible, and they are God's words. How can God possibly do this? How can He so completely disregard our transgressions as to say He removes them an infinite distance from us? The answer is by His grace through Jesus Christ. As we saw in an earlier part of this chapter, God laid our sins on Christ and He bore the penalty we should have borne. Because of Christ's death in our place, God's justice is now completely satisfied. God can now, without violating His justice or His moral law, forgive us freely, completely and absolutely. He can now extend His grace to us; He can show favor to those who, in themselves, deserve only wrath.

## BEHIND HIS BACK

Isaiah 38:17 gives another pictorial expression to describe the extent of God's forgiveness of our sins. The prophet said of God, "You have put all my sins behind your back." When something is behind our back, it is out of sight. We can't see it anymore. God says He has done that with our sins. It is not that we haven't sinned or, as Christians, do not continue to sin. We know we sin daily—in fact, many times a day. Even as Christians our best efforts are still marred with imperfect performance and impure motives. But God no longer "sees" either our deliberate disobedience or our marred performances. Instead He "sees" the righteousness of Christ, which He has already imputed to us.

Does this mean God ignores our sins like an overindulgent, permissive father who lets his children grow up undisciplined and ill-behaved? Not at all. In His relationship to us as our heavenly Father, God does deal with our sins, but only in such a way as for our good. He does not deal with us as our sins deserve, which would be punishment, but as His grace provides, which is for our good.

In His relationship to us as the moral Governor and Judge of mankind, God has put our sins behind His back. In His relationship to us as the Supreme Sovereign dealing with His rebellious subjects, He no longer "sees" our sins. And note that our sins do not just happen to be behind God's back. The Scripture says He has *put* them there. How can He do this and still be a just and holy God? Again, the answer is that Jesus Christ paid the penalty we should have paid. As another hymn put it, "What can wash away my sin? Nothing but the blood of Jesus."[2]

## HURLED INTO THE SEA

Another striking metaphor expressing the completeness of God's forgiveness occurs in Micah 7:19. There the prophet Micah said of God, "You will tread our sins underfoot and hurl our iniquities into the depths of the sea." When I was a naval officer I had an experience where equipment was lost in the depths of the sea through a small boat accident. I know what it is to drag grappling hooks across the bottom of the sea all day in a vain effort to recover the equipment. That ship's gear was lost forever.

So it is with our sins. God has hurled them into the depths of the sea to be lost forever, never to be recovered, never to be held against us. Again, just as God said He *put* our sins behind His back, so here He says He will hurl them into the depths of the sea. They will not "fall overboard"; God will *hurl* them into the depths. He wants them to be lost forever, because He has fully dealt with them in His Son, Jesus Christ.

Do you begin to get the picture? Are you realizing that God's forgiveness is complete and irreversible? Have you started to understand that regardless of how "bad" you've been or how many times you've committed the same sin, God completely and freely forgives you because of Christ? Do you see that, because God has already dealt with your sins in Christ, you do not have to do penance or fulfill some probationary term before God can bless you or use you again?

I once heard someone say he felt he could no longer claim God's gracious promise of forgiveness in 1 John 1:9: "If we confess our sins, he is faithful and just and will forgive us our sins and purify us from all unrighteousness." He reasoned that he had sinned so many times he had used up all his "credit" with God. I believe many Christians think that way because we do not entirely comprehend the fullness of God's forgiveness in Christ. But if we insist on thinking in terms of "credit" before God, we must think only of Christ's credit, for we have *none* on our own. And how much does He have? An infinite amount. That is why Paul could say, "But where sin increased, grace increased all the more" (Romans 5:20).

## BLOTTED FROM THE RECORD

The fourth passage emphasizing the complete and absolute forgiveness of our sins is Isaiah 43:25:

> I, even I, am he who blots out
> your transgressions, for my own sake,
> and remembers your sins no more.

Here God uses two expressions: He *blots out* our transgressions — that is, He removes them from the record — and He *remembers them no more.*

A friend of mine, because of a teenage "prank," had a felony conviction in Canada. Later, he received a Queen's pardon. Now, if his past is ever investigated for criminal activity, the response given is, "We have no record of this person." His record has not just been marked "pardoned," it has been completely removed from the file and destroyed. It has been blotted out, never to be seen again. This is what God does with our sins. When you trust in Jesus Christ as your Savior, God removes your record from the file. He doesn't keep it there or daily add the long list of sins you continue to commit even as a Christian.

God not only blots our sins from His record, He also remembers them no more. This expression means He no longer holds them against us. The blotting out of our transgressions is a *legal* act. It is an official pardon from the Supreme Governor. The remembering them no more is a *relational* act. It is the giving up by an injured party of all sense of being offended or injured. It is a promise never to bring up, either to Himself or to you, your sins.

Jay Adams, in his book *From Forgiven to Forgiving*, helpfully pointed out the difference between *not remembering* and *forgetting*:

> Forgetting is passive and is something that we human beings, not being omniscient, do. "Not remembering" is active; it is a promise whereby one person (in this case, God) determines not to remember the sins of another *against him*. To "not remember" is simply a graphic way of saying, "I will not bring up these matters to you or others in the future."[3]

Consider a rebellious, recalcitrant student in a classroom. His acts of defiance toward the teacher may have both legal and relational consequences. Legally, he may be expelled from school. Relationally, the teacher may feel a deep sense of hostility toward the student. Even if the student is allowed to return to school (the equivalent of a pardon), the teacher may continue to hold hostility toward the student, "remembering" his rebellion and defiance. In order to gain a good standing in the classroom, the rebellious student needs to be both pardoned by the school authorities and forgiven by the teacher. He needs to have the teacher give up all sense of being offended and agree "not to remember" — not to bring up — his poor behavior. (Obviously, for this to happen, the student's attitude and future conduct must change. But, still, the teacher must decide to not remember the past.)

This, then, is similar to what God does when He blots out our transgressions and remembers our sins no more. As the Supreme Governor and Judge, He *pardons* us. As the offended party, He *forgives* us and He promises never to bring up our sins again. Through His death, Jesus not only secured our pardon with God, He also reconciled us to God. But as Paul said, "All this is *from God, who reconciled us to himself* through Christ" (2 Corinthians 5:18, emphasis added). God, acting in grace through the giving of His Son to die for us, was the initiator of reconciliation.

If you have trusted in Jesus Christ alone for your salvation, you are both justified (a legal act) and reconciled (a relational act). You are no longer condemned by God. As Paul said, "Therefore, there is now *no* condemnation for those who are in Christ Jesus" (Romans 8:1, emphasis added). In addition, you are no longer estranged from God. God is no longer against you; He is now for you. Again as Paul said, "If God is for us, who can be against us?" (8:31). Both of these wonderful changes occurred because of God's grace and despite our sin and guilt: "[For] where sin increased, grace increased all the more" (5:20).

## FREE FROM ACCUSATION

The New Testament is replete with assurances of God's forgiveness to those who have trusted in Jesus Christ. Just one Scripture will suffice to show again the contrast between our dreadful condition and God's love, mercy, and grace in reaching out to us. It is, incidentally, another instance of God's wonderful "buts."

> Once you were alienated from God and were enemies
> in your minds because of your evil behavior. But now

he has reconciled you by Christ's physical body through death to present you holy in his sight, without blemish and free from accusation. (Colossians 1:21-22)

I want to call your attention to the last phrase of this passage, "*free from accusation.*" Does this phrase describe the way you think about yourself? Or do you often, in your mind, find yourself standing in the dock of God's courtroom hearing His pronouncement, "Guilty"? If the latter is true, you are not living by grace.

If you have never received the free gift of salvation by trusting in Christ Jesus, then of course you are guilty. You certainly are not living by grace; rather, you are under the wrath of God, and you will eventually experience the full force of His wrath. This wrath is not that of a hot tempered tyrant who has lost control of his emotions; rather, it is the calm, objective, legal wrath of the Judge who is meting out the stiffest sentence possible to the most violent and recalcitrant criminal. Your greatest need is to trust in Jesus Christ for your salvation, for the forgiveness of your sins, and for the free gift of eternal life.

On the other hand, if you have trusted Christ as your Savior, then all the expressions of God's forgiveness are true of you. He has removed your sins as far as the east is from the west. He has put them behind His back and hurled them into the depths of the sea. He has blotted them out of His record book and promised never to bring them up again. You are free from accusation, not because of anything whatsoever in you, but because of His grace alone through Jesus Christ.

Are you willing to believe this wonderful truth and live by it? You probably reply, "I do believe it. I do believe my sins are forgiven and I will go to heaven when I die." But are you willing to *live* by it today, in this life? Will you accept that God not only saves you by His grace through Christ but also *deals* with you day by day by His grace?

Do you accept the fact that the Bible's definition of

grace — God's unmerited favor shown to people who are totally undeserving of it — applies to you not only in salvation but in your everyday life? This meaning of grace never changes. As I've said, grace is always the same, whether God is exercising it in salvation or in His dealings with us as His children.

Jesus said, "I have come that [you] may have life, and have it to the full" (John 10:10). Do you have life, that is, eternal life? Have you renounced all confidence in your own moral or religious efforts and turned in faith completely to Jesus to be clothed with *His* righteousness? If so, you do have eternal life. But do you have it to the full? Are you experiencing both the *peace* of God that comes with salvation and the *joy* of God that comes with living by grace each day? If not, you may be saved by grace, but you are living by works.

## GRACE TO OTHERS

Grace is not only to be received by us, it is, in a sense, to be extended to others. I say "in a sense" because our relationship to other people is different from God's relationship to us. He is the infinitely superior Judge and moral Governor of the universe. We are all sinners and are on an equal plane with one another. So we cannot exercise grace as God does, but we can relate to one another as those who have received grace and who wish to operate on the principles of grace.

In fact, we will not experience the peace with God and the joy of God if we are not willing to extend grace to others. This is the point of Jesus' parable of the unmerciful servant in Matthew 18:23-34. He told the story of a man who was forgiven a debt of ten thousand talents (millions of dollars), but who was unwilling to forgive a fellow servant who owed him a hundred denarii (a few dollars). The unstated truth in the parable, of course, is that our debt of sin to God is "millions of dollars," whereas the debt of others to us is, by comparison, only a few dollars.

The person who is living by grace sees this vast contrast between his own sins against God and the offenses of others against him. He forgives others because he himself has been so graciously forgiven. He realizes that, by receiving God's forgiveness through Christ, he has forfeited the right to be offended when others hurt him. He practices the admonition of Paul, in Ephesians 4:32: "Be kind and compassionate to one another, forgiving each other, just as in Christ God forgave you."

Notes and Observations

---

## Chapter Four: The Generous Landowner
*He who did not spare his own Son, but gave him up*
*for us all — how will he not also, along with him,*
*graciously give us all things?*
ROMANS 8:32

The fact that God deals with His children on the basis of grace without regard to merit or demerit is a staggering concept. It is opposed to almost everything we have been taught about life. We have been generally conditioned to think that if we work hard and "pay our dues" in life, we will be rewarded in proportion to our work. "You do so much, you deserve so much" is a commonly accepted principle in life.

But God's grace does not operate on a reward for works basis. It is much better than that. God is generous beyond all measure or comparison. The Scripture says, "God so loved the world that he *gave* his one and only Son"; and Paul spoke of this as God's "*indescribable* gift" (John 3:16; 2 Corinthians 9:15, emphasis added). God's inexpressible generosity, however, does not stop at saving us; it provides for all our needs and blessings throughout our entire lives. As Paul said in Romans 8:32,

He who did not spare his own Son, but gave him up for us all — how will he not also, along with him, graciously give us all things?

51

Paul used the argument of the greater to the lesser to teach us God's generosity. He said if God gave His Son for our salvation (the greater), will He not also give us all blessings (the lesser)? No blessing we will ever receive can possibly compare with the gift of God's Son to die for us. God demonstrated His gracious generosity to the ultimate at the cross. And Paul based the assurance that we can expect God to meet all our other needs throughout life on the fact that God has already met our greatest need.

Note that Paul said God will *graciously* or *freely* give us all things. Just as salvation is given freely to all who trust in Christ, so all blessings are given freely to us, also through faith in Christ. Just as you cannot earn your salvation but must receive it as a gift, so you cannot earn the blessings of God but must receive them also as gifts given through Christ.

## A PARABLE OF GRACE

For a number of years I have been drawn to Jesus' parable of the workers in the vineyard as one of the best illustrations of the grace of God in the life of believers. Though all titles given to this parable consistently refer to the workers, I believe the emphasis of the parable is on the landowner and his generosity to his workers. I would title the parable "The Gracious Landowner."

To help us learn from this parable, I quote it here in its entirety:

> For the kingdom of heaven is like a landowner who went out early in the morning to hire men to work in his vineyard. He agreed to pay them a denarius for the day and sent them into his vineyard.
>
> About the third hour he went out and saw others standing in the marketplace doing nothing. He told them, "You also go and work in my vineyard, and I will

pay you whatever is right." So they went.

He went out again about the sixth hour and the ninth hour and did the same thing. About the eleventh hour he went out and found still others standing around. He asked them, "Why have you been standing here all day long doing nothing?"

"Because no one has hired us," they answered.

He said to them, "You also go and work in my vineyard."

When evening came, the owner of the vineyard said to his foreman, "Call the workers and pay them their wages, beginning with the last ones hired and going on to the first."

The workers who were hired about the eleventh hour came and each received a denarius. So when those came who were hired first, they expected to receive more. But each one of them also received a denarius. When they received it, they began to grumble against the landowner. "These men who were hired last worked only one hour," they said, "and you have made them equal to us who have borne the burden of the work and the heat of the day."

But he answered one of them, "Friend, I am not being unfair to you. Didn't you agree to work for a denarius? Take your pay and go. I want to give the man who was hired last the same as I gave you. Don't I have the right to do what I want with my own money? Or are you envious because I am generous?"

So the last will be first, and the first will be last. (Matthew 20:1-16)

This parable grew out of Jesus' encounter with the rich young man, when Jesus told him to sell his possessions, give to the poor, and follow Him (Matthew 19:16-22). Peter, reflecting on all this, said to Jesus, "We have left everything to follow you!

What then will there be for us?" Like the other Jews of his day, Peter thought he was operating on the basis of merit, and he was already adding up his merit points.

Jesus does not rebuke Peter for his merit mentality. Instead, He assures him there will indeed be a reward for him and the other disciples. Not only that, everyone who has sacrificed for Jesus' sake will receive "a hundred times as much." Expressed as a percentage, a hundred times as much is ten thousand percent. In the financial world, an investment that doubles itself in a few years is considered an excellent investment. Yet that is only a hundred percent gain. Jesus promises us not one hundred but ten thousand percent return.

Why does Jesus use such an astonishing amount as ten thousand percent? He is telling us that God's reward is out of all proportion to our service and sacrifice. He is telling us that in the kingdom of heaven God's reward system is based not on merit but on grace. And grace always gives far more than we have "earned."

As R. C. H. Lenski wrote,

> The generosity and the magnanimity of God are so great that he accepts nothing from us without rewarding it beyond all computation. . . . The vast disproportion existing between our work and God's reward of it already displays his boundless grace, to say nothing of the gift of salvation which is made before we have even begun to do any work.[4]

The landowner of Jesus' parable, who obviously represents God, was a very gracious and generous man. From the very beginning he was as concerned for the welfare of the workers as he was for his vineyard. He readily agreed to pay the first workers a day's wages — a fair amount. In the labor culture of that day, the workers needed the money to buy food for their families. They lived a day-to-day existence. That is why landowners were instructed to pay a hired man "his wages each day before sunset, because he is poor and is counting on it" (Deuteronomy 24:15).

The landowner was not only fair with his workers; he was progressively more generous with each group of workers he hired throughout the day. Each worker, regardless of how long he had worked, received a day's wages. He received, not what he had earned on an hourly basis, but what he *needed* to sustain his family for a day. The landowner could have paid them only what they had earned, but he chose to pay them according to their need, not according to their work. He paid according to grace, not debt.

The parable focuses particularly on those workers who were hired at the eleventh hour. They were treated extremely generously, each one receiving twelve times what he had earned on a strict hourly basis. Why did the landowner hire these workers at the eleventh hour? Perhaps it was because an extra push was needed to complete the work by the end of the day. More likely, since Jesus was not teaching about Jewish agriculture but about the kingdom of heaven, *those eleventh-hour workers were hired because they needed to receive a day's wages.* They had been standing all day waiting for someone to hire them so they could earn money to support their families. They needed to work more than the landowner needed their work. He hired them, not because of his need, but because of their need. He represents God in His gracious awareness of our needs and His continuous work to meet them. God calls us to serve Him, not because He needs us, but because we need Him. Then His reward for our service is always out of proportion to our efforts — as Jesus said to Peter, "a hundred times as much" (Matthew 19:29).

## GRACIOUS AND GENEROUS

Over and over again the Bible portrays God as gracious and generous, blessing His people freely without regard to their demerits, rather than because of their merits. (I use the word *gracious* not in its commonly accepted meaning of kindness and courtesy, but in the biblical sense of one disposed to deal with others on the basis of grace.) We see God's gracious disposition even before the Fall in the Garden of Eden when as yet there were no merits or demerits. The Scripture says, "And the LORD God made all kinds of trees grow out of the ground — trees that were pleasing to the eye and good for food" (Genesis 2:9).

It wasn't just the tree of the knowledge of good and evil that was good for food and pleasing to the eye (see 3:6). God didn't place only one desirable tree in the garden with a "look but don't eat" sign hung on it just to tempt Adam and Eve. Rather He placed *all kinds* of trees in the garden that were delightful to see and to eat from. I enjoy fresh fruit, and I like to go to the supermarket in the summer when all the peaches, plums, pears, strawberries, and cantaloupes are on display. I am dazzled. I want some of all of them. Think what it must have been like for Adam to have all kinds of trees that not only produced delectable food but were also beautiful to behold. If I am dazzled today, think of what Adam's reaction must have been.

But God did still more for Adam. God said, "It is not good for the man to be alone. I will make a helper suitable for him" (2:18). God knew Adam needed a companion, and He graciously met that need, because it is His disposition to be generous. God anticipated and provided for every need Adam could possibly have.

Then Adam sinned. What would happen now to the gracious and generous disposition of God? Would God cease to be gracious? Would God say, "I was generous to you, giving you everything you needed, and yet you disobeyed Me. From now on you are on your own. Fend for yourself"? God didn't say that. Instead He dealt mercifully and graciously with Adam and Eve. Yes, today we are still living with the eternally cataclysmic consequences that came out of the Fall; God did judge Adam as He had said He would. But in the midst of all that, God did one more thing: "The LORD God made garments of skin for Adam and his wife and clothed them" (3:21). Right in the midst of fulfilling His role as Judge, God took note of Adam and Eve's need for clothes, and for a little while, He assumed the role of a tailor.

Why, in the midst of all the weighty and eternal issues, did God take time to make clothes for two people who had just flagrantly disobeyed Him, and who through that had brought sin and misery upon the whole human race? God did it because it is His nature to be gracious and to meet our needs without regard to our deserts. Neither Adam's innocence nor his sin was the cause of God's grace. God was gracious because it is part of His eternal nature to be so.

## GOD DELIGHTS TO DO GOOD

When my first wife — who is now with the Lord — and I were married, we asked that the following Scripture, which we felt God had given us as a promise, be read at our wedding:

> They will be my people, and I will be their God. I will give them singleness of heart and action, so that they will always fear me for their own good and the good of their children after them. I will make an everlasting covenant with them: I will never stop doing good to them, and I will inspire them to fear me, so that they will never turn away from me. I will rejoice in doing them good and will assuredly plant them in this land with all my heart and soul. (Jeremiah 32:38-41)

Note the expressions of God's goodness. He will give us singleness of heart for *our own good* and the *good* of our children. He will *never stop doing good* to us, in fact He will *rejoice* in doing us good. This sounds appropriate, doesn't it, for two young people committed to serving God full time?

But this assurance of God's goodness was not originally

given to people who were serving God or who "deserved" His goodness. Instead it was given to a group of people who were described by God as those who "have done nothing but evil in my sight from their youth" (verse 30). These people were in captivity in Babylon because of their sins over many generations.

Just a few chapters before in Jeremiah, God had said to these people:

> This is what the LORD says: "When seventy years are completed for Babylon, I will come to you and fulfill my gracious promise to bring you back to this place. For I know the plans I have for you," declares the LORD, "plans to prosper you and not to harm you, plans to give you hope and a future." (Jeremiah 29:10-11)

The *goodness* of God is demonstrated in His assurance of plans to prosper them and not to harm them. Note in verse 10 that God refers to His *gracious* promise, that is, a promise given freely without regard to the fact that they obviously did not deserve it. Here we see a vivid illustration of the truth of Samuel Storms' statement that grace is no longer grace if God is compelled to withdraw it in the presence of human demerit. If anyone qualified for demerits, surely the Israelites in captivity did. Yet God promised to prosper them, to *rejoice* in doing them good.

Another insight into God's gracious disposition is found in the prophecy of Joel. Joel prophesied judgment through a tremendous invasion of locusts that would devour all the trees and plants, resulting in widespread famine in the land. Then Joel looked forward to a day of restoration, a day when the trees would again bear fruit, the threshing floor would again be filled with grain, and the vats would overflow with new wine and oil. In the midst of this prophecy of restoration, God made the following promise:

> I will repay you for the years the locusts have eaten —
>> the great locust and the young locust,
>> the other locusts and the locust swarm —
>> my great army that I sent among you. (Joel 2:25)

Consider the amazing generosity of God. He does not limit His promise merely to restoring the land to its former productivity. He says He will *repay* them for the years the locusts have eaten, years that they themselves forfeited to the judgment of God. God could well have said, "I will restore your land to its former productivity, but it's too bad about those years you lost. They are gone forever. That is the price you pay for your sin." He would have been generous just to have restored them, but He went beyond that. He would cause their harvests to be so abundant they would recoup the losses from the years of famine. He says He will *repay* them, though He obviously owes them nothing.

From time to time I have opportunity to minister individually to people who in some way have really "blown it" in life. For some, it may have been before they became Christians; for others it occurred while they were believers. Usually these people lament their "lost" years, the years when they served sin instead of God, or years that were wasted as Christians.

I try to encourage these people about the grace of God. I cannot promise them God will "repay" those lost years as He did the Israelites, but I can assure them that it is God's nature to be gracious. I encourage them to pray to this end and to realize, as they pray, that they are coming to a God who does not withhold His grace because of demerits.

## THE GOD OF ALL GRACE

God is just and holy. He judges sin and disciplines His children. But He is also "the God of all grace" (1 Peter 5:10). No one knew that better than the apostle Peter. He had a history of "blowing it" even before the night when he denied Jesus. Simon Peter didn't exactly get started on the right foot with Jesus.

One day Jesus was teaching, and the people were crowding around Him on the shore of a lake. Because of the press of the crowd, Jesus got into Peter's boat and from it He taught the people. Afterward,

> He said to Simon Peter, "Put out into deep water, and let down the nets for a catch."
>
> Simon answered, "Master, we've worked hard all night and haven't caught anything. But because you say so, I will let down the nets."
>
> When they had done so, they caught such a large number of fish that their nets began to break. (Luke 5:4-6)

Can you hear the doubt, skepticism, and reluctance in Peter's response? In effect he said, "Master, You don't realize we've just fished all night, but if You say so, we'll do this to humor You." Not exactly an auspicious beginning of their relationship, is it?

Then there was the day Peter miraculously walked on water only to find himself sinking and having to cry out for help (see Matthew 14:29-30). With their competitive spirits, the other disciples probably watched with envious awe as Peter walked on the water (they even argued on the eve of Christ's betrayal over which of them was considered to be the greatest [see Luke 22:24]). But their awe no doubt changed to derision as Peter began to sink beneath the waves. I suspect they didn't let him forget that incident very quickly.

Another time Peter, in loyalty, protested Jesus' prediction of His coming death, only to be put down with the severe rebuke, "Get behind me, Satan! You are a stumbling block to me; you do not have in mind the things of God, but the things of men" (Matthew 16:23).

Again, on the night of Christ's betrayal, Peter rushed to defend his Lord with the sword, only to be rebuked by Him (see John 18:10-11). Then, of course, there is Peter's oft-retold denial of Jesus coming right on the heels of his vehement protest, "Even if I have to die with you, I will never disown you" (Matthew 26:35). Undoubtedly Peter's bitter grief at denying his Lord was aggravated by the reminder of his own proud and foolish boast (26:69-75).

It begins to look as if Peter couldn't do anything right, doesn't it? Even today he is held up in sermons as the ultimate example of someone who was proud, impetuous, and boastful; someone who, to use a colloquial expression, was always "sticking his foot in his mouth."

But whom did God select to be the primary spokesman for the apostles on the day of Pentecost? Who has the privilege of preaching that first sermon when three thousand people were saved? It is Peter, who couldn't seem to do or say anything right (see Acts 2:14-41). Whom did God choose to be the preacher when He opened wide the door of salvation to the Gentiles? It was Peter at the house of Cornelius (see 10:34-44). Who made the decisive statement at the council of Jerusalem that turned the tide against the Pharisee believers who were demanding that the new Gentile believers be circumcised and obey the law of Moses? It was Peter (see 15:6-11). It seems as if Peter's failures and foibles are all behind him, doesn't it? But they are not.

Some time later Peter again "blows it." At Antioch he compromised himself in fear of the circumcision group and played the hypocrite, thereby gaining a justified *public* rebuke by the apostle Paul (see Galatians 2:11-14). The man who could do nothing right, who had seemingly become the man who could do no wrong, falls flat on his face again. But the story doesn't end there. God chooses Peter to be the inspired writer of two books of the New Testament. Is it any wonder Peter refers to God as "the God of all *grace*" (1 Peter 5:10, emphasis added)? Is it any wonder his last word of instruction is to "grow in the *grace*

61

and knowledge of our Lord and Savior Jesus Christ" (2 Peter 3:18, emphasis added)?

Peter had personally experienced what Paul described: "But where sin increased, grace increased all the more" (Romans 5:20). The translation "increased all the more" probably does not capture completely the contrast Paul was seeking to convey between the results of sin and the effects of grace. Noted Bible commentators R. C. H. Lenski and John Murray both use the term *superabounding* to describe the riches of God's grace as Paul represented it in Romans 5:20.[5] So, a good translation would be, "But where sin abounded, grace superabounded." Let me illustrate.

A few drops of a dark-colored ink in a glass of water will turn the water dark. But put the glass under a kitchen faucet and turn on the water full force, and the pressure of the water will soon flush out all the dark color, leaving a glass full of clear water. The ink "abounds" in its effect on the water, turning it dark. But the clean water from the faucet "superabounds." It flows so abundantly and with such force, it erases all the effects of the ink.

That is what Peter experienced. His failures and his sins abounded. There is no question about that. But however much his sin increased, God's grace increased all the more. It superabounded. God blessed Peter, not in spite of his sins, but *without regard to his sins*. That's the way His grace operates. It looks not to our sins or even to our good deeds but only to the merit of Christ.

What's the point of all this discussion about Peter and his failures and his experience of the grace of God? It is this: Most of us can identify with Peter. Regardless of how outwardly "successful" in the Christian life we may appear to others, in our hearts we know the truth. We know that in one way or another we're like Peter. We've "blown it" and fallen on our spiritual faces too many times. Just like Peter, we need to be convinced in our hearts that God is the God of all grace, that He is going to bless us and use us, not according to our deserts, but as Samuel Storms said, "according to [His] infinite goodness and sovereign purpose."[6]

## ONE BLESSING AFTER ANOTHER

The apostle John wrote that Jesus was "full of grace and truth," and "From the fullness of his grace we have all received one blessing after another" (John 1:14,16). The idea portrayed in verse 16 is analogous to the ocean waves crashing upon the beach. One wave has hardly disappeared before another arrives. They just keep coming from an inexhaustible supply. So it is with the grace of God through Christ. He is full of grace and truth, and it is from His inexhaustible fullness that we receive one blessing after another.

In his commentary on the gospel of John, William Hendriksen translated verse 16 as follows: "For out of his fulness we have all received grace upon grace."[7] Notice we did not receive just grace, but grace upon grace. Hendriksen wrote,

> The meaning of verse 16 is that believers are constantly receiving grace *in the place of grace*. One manifestation of the unmerited favor of God in Christ is hardly gone when another arrives; hence *grace upon grace*. . . .
>
> The concept *grace upon grace*, an incessant supply of grace, harmonizes better with the idea *from his fulness* than does the simple term grace. The limitless supply or reservoir indicated by the words *his fulness* would seem to suggest a limitless outflow: *grace upon grace*.[8]

## EXPERIENCING GOD'S GRACE

Why then do we not experience more of this endless supply of God's grace? Why do we so often seem to live in spiritual poverty instead of experiencing life to the full as Jesus promised (see John 10:10)? There are several reasons that may or may not apply to a particular believer, but for the purposes of our study on grace, I'd like to look at two that probably apply to most of us.

First, is our frequent misperception of God as the divine equivalent of Ebenezer Scrooge; the God who demands the last ounce of work out of His people and then pays them poorly. That may sound like an overstatement of our perception of God, but I believe it is a fairly accurate representation of how many Christians think.

Consider the following words from one of John Newton's hymns:

> Come, my soul, thy suit prepare:
> Jesus loves to answer prayer;
> He himself has bid thee pray,
> Therefore will not say thee nay.

> Thou art coming to a King,
> Large petitions with thee bring;
> For his grace and power are such,
> None can ever ask too much.[9]

How many Christians really believe those words? How many of us really believe Jesus *loves* to answer prayer? How many of us believe His grace and power are such that *we can never ask too much*? Rather, we tend in the direction of believing God is reluctant to answer prayer and His grace and power aren't sufficient to fulfill our needs, let alone our requests.

We should not forget that Satan's very first temptation of mankind was based on questioning the goodness and generosity of God (see Genesis 3:1-5). And his vicious attack on the patriarch Job was designed to cause Job to question God's goodness so that he would then curse God (see Job 1:6-11). Satan has not changed his strategy today. This perception of God as the reluctant giver comes right from Satan and must be resisted by us if we are to experience the fullness of God's grace.

I remember from my college days a story my pastor told about an aged former slave. This old man's former master had died and left him an inheritance of $50,000, an enormous sum in those days. The old man was duly notified of his inheritance and told that the money had been deposited in an account for him at the local bank. After weeks went by, and he had failed to withdraw any of his money, the banker called the man in and again explained to him that he had $50,000 available to him. The old slave — who had no comprehension of how much $50,000 was — asked, "Sir, do you think I can have fifty cents to buy a sack of corn meal?"

Many believers live like the old slave. Because we do not comprehend the superabundance of God's grace and generosity, we ask Him for paltry blessings, the fifty-cent variety, when we could be drawing on the abundance of His riches. The apostle Paul told us that God "has blessed us in the heavenly realms with every spiritual blessing in Christ," and "[He] will meet all your needs according to his glorious riches in Christ Jesus" (Ephesians 1:3; Philippians 4:19). Within the scope of these two Scriptures, God promises to meet every one of our needs, both spiritual and temporal.

The God who was gracious to Adam and Eve both before and after the Fall, who rejoiced in doing good to the Jewish nation in captivity, who was the "God of all grace" to Peter, is the same gracious and generous God today. Grace is part of the very nature of God, and He cannot change. He is indeed the generous landowner of the parable, continually going to the marketplace of life to find those in need of "a day's wages" so that He can bring them into His vineyard and then reward them out of all proportion to their labors.

Perhaps the larger reason why we do not experience more of God's grace is our misconception that, having been saved by grace, we must now, at least to some degree, "pay our own way" and earn God's blessings in our daily lives. An accepted maxim among people today, "There is no such thing as a free lunch" (which may be true in our society), is carried by us into our relationship with God.

In fact this misconception that we must pay our own way is more than a mistaken theological notion. It actually springs from the perverse disposition of our hearts — the disposition of pride.

Noted theologian R. C. Sproul wrote,

> Perhaps the most difficult task for us to perform is to rely on God's grace and God's grace alone for our salvation. It is difficult for our pride to rest on grace. Grace is for other people — for beggars. We don't want to live by a heavenly welfare system. We want to earn our own way and atone for our own sins. We like to think that we will go to heaven because we deserve to be there.[10]

Although Dr. Sproul was writing on the subject of the grace of God in salvation, the problem of pride he described is applicable to living the Christian life. Not only do we think we must pay our own way, at least to some degree, we subtly *insist* on paying our own way. As Dr. Sproul said, "Grace is for other people — for beggars," but not for us.

Let me illustrate from my own experience. After the death of my first wife, Eleanor, God very soon brought into my life another charming and godly lady whom Eleanor and I had known for a number of years. Just over a year after Eleanor's death, Jane and I were married.

A few months later I began to realize I was experiencing a vague sense of guilt despite confidence that God had guided in our marriage. One day I realized my sense of guilt was due to the feeling that I had not "paid my dues" in long months of grief and loneliness unlike some of my friends who have lost their spouses. I felt I didn't "deserve" such a tremendous blessing from God so soon after Eleanor's death. In fact, I discovered I was unconsciously not allowing myself to enjoy the full riches of the blessing God had so obviously given me. I had lapsed into the world's way of thinking that we somehow must earn God's blessings through our suffering or sacrifice or hard work.

It can be humbling, sometimes humiliating, to realize we have not paid our own way. Think of the workers in the parable who worked only one hour. How did they feel when they realized they had received as much pay as those who had worked twelve long hours through the heat of the day? Did they feel grateful for the generous *gift* they had received, or guilty that they had not earned their *pay*? If they were living by a philosophy of works as we so often do, they would have felt guilty. They would have *experienced* the gracious generosity of the landowner, but they would not have *enjoyed* it.

You and I actually experience the grace of God in our lives far more than we realize. But all too often we do not enjoy His grace because we are trying to live by merit, not by grace. In looking for our own goodness by which we hope to earn the blessing of God, we fail to see the superabundance of the goodness and grace of God in our lives.

# Grace — It Really Is Amazing

## (Chapters 3 and 4)

## STUDY QUESTIONS

### CENTRAL IDEA

In His infinite grace, God does not treat us as we deserve, but rather offers us forgiveness through faith in Christ. Christ removes our guilt and puts in its place His righteousness. The blessings we receive come to us through faith in Jesus Christ, not because of anything we have done.

### WARM-UP

Imagine for a moment that next time you pray you will have to come into God's presence based on your own merit. What things would you be able to say you have accomplished? Do they outweigh the times you have failed God? Now, give each person a chance to answer this question: "How does trying to come into God's presence on your own merits make you feel?"

### EXPLORING GRACE

1.  Read Romans 3:19-26. There are two aspects to our justification. First, God removes our guilt from us and places it upon Jesus. Second, He credits Jesus' righteousness to us. What practical difference does it make to your life that God has removed your sin and given you Jesus' righteousness? How should this fact affect the way you feel? The way you live?

2. It's easy to believe this doctrine of justification intellectually, but many people find it hard to let this truth strongly affect their lives. Why do you suppose that's the case?

3. Read Ephesians 2:1-9. Fill in this chart to help show the contrast Paul makes between what we deserve and what God has done for us.

| Our spiritual condition before we have faith in Christ | What God has done for us in Christ |
|---|---|
|  |  |
|  |  |
|  |  |
|  |  |
|  |  |
|  |  |
|  |  |

4. What do the following verses show us about God's forgiveness?

- Psalm 103:12

- Isaiah 38:17

- Isaiah 43:25

- Micah 7:19

5. Sometimes we know that God has forgiven us but we have trouble forgiving ourselves. Why do you think this is true?

## Barriers to Experiencing God's Forgiveness

- *A mistaken feeling that we must somehow suffer or pay for our own sins, at least to some degree.* We often act like we think God's forgiveness only kicks in after we have reached some mysterious level of suffering for our own sins.
- *A desire to hold on to our guilt so that we don't have to change our behavior.* If I consider myself a terrible and guilty person then of course I will continue to sin. But if I know I am forgiven then I am truly free to go forward and improve, however slowly, in my behavior (see Hebrews 9:14).
- *Failure to cultivate our relationship with God.* If we are not growing in our knowledge of who God is, through time in His Word and in conversation with Him, then we will also be out of touch with the forgiveness He is so ready to offer (see Philippians 3:7-10).

6. Are there any areas of your life where you are not experiencing God's forgiveness? What factors in the list above may be part of why you are not experiencing God's forgiveness?

7. Believers fail to experience God's grace on a daily basis for many reasons. Two of these are:

   • A misconception of God as a hard taskmaster who meets our needs begrudgingly.
   • The belief that while we were saved by grace we must now "pay our own way" and earn God's blessings in our daily lives.

   It is possible to know that the above beliefs are lies and still to operate as though they were true. Share a time when you were tempted to operate according to one of these misconceptions.

8. Decide to do one of the following things or else come up with your own plan to help you experience God's forgiveness more fully.

   a. Memorize one of the verses about God's forgiveness in question 4.

   b. Write a letter to the Lord confessing once and for all the things that you still feel He has not forgiven. Then burn the letter and thank Him that "He himself bore our sins in his body on the tree, so that we might die to sins and live for righteousness; by his wounds you have been healed" (1 Peter 2:24).

c.  Ask a close friend to get together with you for a time of prayer. Turn your past sins over to the Lord, once and for all. When doubts come in, dispel them with the memory of that specific time when your sins were confessed and forgiven.

d.  Write down the lie you are tempted to believe about God (see question 7). Tell God you know it's a lie and ask Him to do whatever He needs to do to teach your heart the truth about this.

## CLOSING PRAYER

Thank the Lord that He "does not treat us as our sins deserve or repay us according to our iniquities" (Psalm 103:10).

## GOING DEEPER (Extra questions for further study)

1.  What does it mean when we say that Christ made atonement for our sins? Look at the following verses and see how they help you understand atonement.

    •   John 3:36

    •   Romans 3:25

    •   Hebrews 2:17

- 1 John 2:2; 4:10

2.  Fill in the following chart based on Titus 3:3-7.

| Characteristics of man and what he has done | Characteristics of God and what He has done |
| --- | --- |
|  |  |
|  |  |
|  |  |
|  |  |
|  |  |
|  |  |
|  |  |
|  |  |

3.  Is it possible to go beyond the point where God can forgive? Explain how a person might feel he has sinned one too many times to receive God's forgiveness, and why those feelings are wrong.

4.  Read Colossians 1:21-22. Does the phrase "free from accusation" describe the way you think about yourself? Why, or why not?

5.   What do the following verses say about how God wants to treat us?

•   Jeremiah 29:10-11

•   Jeremiah 32:38-41

### Pondering Grace (For personal reflection)

*Guilty, vile and helpless we; Spotless Lamb of God was he; Full atonement! Can it be? Hallelujah! What a Savior!*

Philip P. Bin

*The generosity and the magnanimity of God are so great that he accepts nothing from us without rewarding it beyond all computation. . . . The vast disproportion existing between our work and God's reward of it displays his boundless grace, to say nothing of the gift of salvation which is made before we have even begun to do any work.*

R. C. H. Lenski, *The Interpretation of St. Matthew's Gospel*

*Perhaps the most difficult task for us to perform is to rely on God's grace and God's grace alone for our salvation. It is difficult for our pride to rest on grace. Grace is for other people — for beggars. We don't want to live by a heavenly welfare system. We want to earn our own way and atone for our own sins. We like to think that we will go to heaven because we deserve to be there.*

R. C. Sproul

# Does God Have a Right?

Read the following portion of *Transforming Grace*. In the margins, record observations, illustrations, or questions that come to mind as you read. Then answer the study questions that follow the reading.

---

## Chapter Five: Does God Have a Right?

Notes and Observations

*"These men who were hired last worked only one hour,"*
*they said, "and you have made them equal to us who have*
*borne the burden of the work and the heat of the day."*
*But he answered one of them, "Friend, I am not being*
*unfair to you. Didn't you agree to work for a denarius?*
*Take your pay and go. I want to give the man who was*
*hired last the same as I gave you. Don't I have the*
*right to do what I want with my own money? Or*
*are you envious because I am generous?"*
MATTHEW 20:12-15

A t a certain state university there was a freshman English class with the typical variety of students. On the one hand there were a few conscientious and well-disciplined students who had learned good study habits in high school. They consistently did assignments, studied well for tests, and turned in well-prepared term papers on time. At the opposite end of the spectrum were the typical "party boys" who did just enough work to get by. They rarely did assignments, hardly studied for tests, and never turned in a term paper on time. And as is typical in such a class, the vast majority of students were somewhere in between.

At last final exam day arrived. As expected, the disciplined students all did well, and the party boys all did poorly. After a couple of days, the professor posted the grades outside his office door. As the students crowded around to see what grade they had received, they were all stunned to see that everyone in the class had received an A. The party boys could hardly believe their good fortune, and the good students were outraged to realize that those who deserved to fail had received the same top grade as they had.

If you saw any credibility in this story you probably shared in the outrage of the hardworking students. It certainly does seem unfair that the class "goof-offs" should receive the same grade as those who actually earned an A. But what you have read is simply a modern-day version of the parable of the generous landowner we considered in session 2 (chapter 4). Although I have recast the story in terms of a present-day setting, the essential elements of the two stories are identical. In both versions a group of people got far more than they deserved and received as much reward as those who had actually worked for theirs.

The message even of the biblical parable strikes many people as unfair. On some speaking occasions, I have actually asked for a show of hands on the issue, and the vast majority of people have felt the landowner was unfair. People agree with those workers who labored a full twelve hours, right through the heat of the day, that they should be paid more than those who worked only one hour. In the strict context of labor relations (or of class grades in the modern parable), they are right. A person should be paid in proportion to his work. The landowner and the English professor both seem unfair.

But Jesus was not teaching principles of labor relations. He was teaching principles of grace. He said, "The kingdom of heaven is like . . ." and proceeded to tell the parable. In effect, He said to Peter, "In the kingdom of heaven the operative principle is not merit but grace."

One group of people didn't think the landowner was unfair: the laborers who worked only one hour. Jesus didn't tell us their reaction, but we can easily assume they were elated and grateful. As the day had worn on, leaving them standing unemployed in the marketplace, their hope for any pay and hence any food for their families for the day had gradually eroded. At five o'clock in the afternoon they faced an evening with no supper. Finally they were given an opportunity to earn what they assumed would be a mere pittance, one-twelfth of a day's wages — not nearly enough to buy food for their families. It's not hard to imagine, then, their joy upon receiving a full day's wages, enough to feed their families that day. They didn't think about any unfairness on the part of the landowner; they considered him very generous.

## AN ATTITUDE OF DESERVING

Why do so many people stumble over this parable and consider the landowner to be unfair? I believe it is because we Christians instinctively identify with the workers who had worked all day. We place ourselves in their shoes instead of in the shoes of those who worked only one hour. We look at society around us, instead of at Jesus Christ, and we begin to feel pretty good about ourselves. We consider ourselves to be twelve-hour workers, and we expect to be rewarded accordingly.

That is the way Peter felt and that is the way many people feel today. I was talking one day with a man whose mother, a faithful servant of God for over forty years, was dying of painful cancer. He said, "After all she's done for God, this is the thanks she gets." Such a statement sounds irreverent to us, but the man didn't intend it to be that way. He simply thought God owed his mother a better life. He only verbalized what many people feel in their hearts.

There are other occasions when we remind God of the sacrifices we have made to serve Him. "Lord, I've done this sacrificial service for You, and now I'm in need of this special answer to prayer." When we assume such an attitude, we are putting ourselves in the position of the twelve-hour workers. We suggest to God that we *deserve* this answer to prayer because of our sacrificial service. With such an attitude we may grumble about

77

blessings not received instead of being grateful for those we have received.

We need to adopt the attitude of the Roman centurion described in Luke 7. The man sent some of the Jewish elders to Jesus asking Him to come and heal his sick servant. When the elders came to Jesus, they pleaded earnestly with Him: "This man deserves to have you do this, because he loves our nation and has built our synagogue" (verses 4-5). Notice the Jewish elders' emphasis on *deserving*.

The centurion surely was a remarkable man. He was an officer in the Roman occupation army, yet he served the occupied people by building a synagogue for them. Think of an occupying army in today's culture and ask yourself how many "enemy" officers would do such a thing.

But the centurion's attitude about himself is even more remarkable than his deeds. Instead of thinking of what he should receive because of what he deserved, he freely confessed he didn't deserve anything. He sent word to Jesus, saying, "I do not deserve to have you come under my roof. That is why I did not even consider myself worthy to come to you" (verses 6-7). The centurion placed himself in the shoes of the eleventh-hour workers. Because of this he not only experienced the joy of having his request granted, but also the added joy of knowing he had received what he did not deserve. He experienced the joy of knowing he had received a gift — not a repayment of a debt.

## WE CAN NEVER OBLIGATE GOD

We can never obligate God by our obedience or our sacrificial service. Even if we were perfectly obedient in all our Christian duties, we would still be forced to say, "We are unworthy servants; we have only done our duty" (Luke 17:10).

Suppose you perfectly obey all the traffic laws of your state. You *always* stay within the speed limit, *always* come to a complete stop at stop signs, *always* drive in the proper lane, *always* use your turn signals — *always* obey every traffic rule. Do you receive any reward? Not at all, that is what you are supposed to do. You have only done your duty. You do not, by perfect obedience of the traffic laws, obligate the state to reward you in any manner. All you can say is, "I have only done my duty."

As the Sovereign Ruler of the universe, God has the right to require perfect obedience and faithful service from all of us without in the least obligating Himself. We *owe* Him such obedience and service. If we were to perfectly obey every command God has given and faithfully perform every duty — which, of course, we never do — we still could only say, "I have merely done my duty." We cannot obligate God in any way.

God Himself asserted His freedom from any obligation when He said to Job, "Who has a claim against me that I must pay? Everything under heaven belongs to me" (Job 41:11). God was not stating a mere abstract, theological principle. He was rebuking an attitude of "I'm not getting what I deserve," on Job's part. Job, in defending himself against the false accusations of his so-called friends, had fallen from an attitude of grace into thinking he deserved better treatment from God. He had fallen from an attitude of "The LORD gave and the LORD has taken away; may the name of the LORD be praised," into an attitude of "It profits a man nothing when he tries to please God" (Job 1:21; 34:9).

Job had, over the time of his suffering, shifted from the position of an eleventh-hour worker to one who felt he had indeed "borne the burden of the work and the heat of the day" (Matthew 20:12). And God directly addressed Job's attitude. If God were to deal with us today as He did with Job, I wonder how many of us would receive a similar rebuke?

Through the inspired pen of the apostle Paul, the Holy Spirit again asserts His freedom from obligation to anyone when He says, "Who has ever given to God that God should repay him?" (Romans 11:35). This assertion was not made in a vacuum. Paul had been dealing with the difficult question of the

Jews' future in the face of God's apparent spurning of them in favor of the Gentiles. Regardless of how we understand Paul's teaching about the Jews in Romans 9–11 (an issue on which many Christians disagree), the principle stated by the Holy Spirit through Paul is crystal clear: God does not owe anyone anything.

There is a very high sense of entitlement within modern society. Older people feel *entitled* to certain benefits from the government. Middle-aged people feel *entitled* to generous health and retirement benefits from their employers. Younger adults feel *entitled* to immediately enjoy the same standard of living their parents took years to achieve. And young people feel *entitled* to whatever material luxuries they desire.

Many observers of our culture are quite concerned about this pervasive sense of "rights" and expectations within our society as a whole. But for Christians, such a high sense of entitlement is especially detrimental to our spiritual lives. For one thing, God is the ultimate supplier of all our needs and desires. Every good gift is from Him, regardless of the intermediate means through which that gift is supplied. As James said, "Every good and perfect gift is from above, coming down from the Father of the heavenly lights, who does not change like shifting shadows" (James 1:17). However, God, through His providential workings, almost always uses some person or institution or other human instrumentality to meet our needs. Ultimately, though, He is the One who provides or withholds what we desire or think we need.

Therefore, a high sense of entitlement and expectations, though seemingly directed toward some person or institution, is actually directed toward God and His providential dealings in our lives. If we do not receive what we think we have a right to expect, it is ultimately God who has withheld.

More importantly, our sense of entitlement, which may be originally directed toward other people or institutions, is almost invariably transferred directly to God. We begin to be as demanding of our "rights" before God as we are toward people. It is bad enough, and certainly not very Christian, to have the attitude "The world owes me something just because I am," but to have the attitude that *God* owes me something is exceedingly dangerous to spiritual health. It will ruin our relationship with God, nullify our effectiveness in ministry, and perhaps turn us bitter or resentful. Unlike our government, or school, or family, or employer, God will not "give in" to our sense of rights or respond to pressure tactics. We never win the battle of "rights" with God. He cares too much about our spiritual growth to let that happen.

## GIVING TO GOD

We actually cannot give God anything that He has not first given to us. David recognized this fact when the leaders of Israel gave so generously for the building of the Temple. In his prayer of praise to God he said,

> But who am I, and who are my people, that we should be able to give as generously as this? Everything comes from you, and we have given you only what comes from your hand. . . . O LORD our God, as for all this abundance that we have provided for building you a temple for your Holy Name, it comes from your hand, and all of it belongs to you. (1 Chronicles 29:14,16)

David knew he and his people had not given anything to God that wasn't His already. Even our service to God comes from His hand. As the prophet Isaiah said, "LORD, . . . all that we have accomplished you have done for us" (Isaiah 26:12). Paul summed up the whole question of what we have given to God rather conclusively when he said, "And he is not served by human hands, as if he needed anything, because he himself gives all men life and breath and everything else" (Acts 17:25).

Notes and Observations

When every breath we breathe is a gift from God, there really is nothing left to give that hasn't been first given to us.

So where does all this emphasis on the fact that God doesn't owe us anything leave us? It leaves us in the blessed position of being eleventh-hour workers in God's kingdom. It leaves us going home at the end of the day from God's vineyard profoundly grateful, knowing that the gracious landowner has been generous beyond all measure. In a word it leaves us *content*, and "godliness with contentment is great gain" (1 Timothy 6:6).

Contentment with what we have — whether it is possessions, or station in life, or mental or physical abilities — is worth far, far more than all the things we don't have. A multimillionaire reportedly was once asked how much money was enough, to which he replied, "One dollar more."

The person who is living on the basis of merit is like the multimillionaire. He is never content. One day he thinks he is not being rewarded fairly by God; the next day he is afraid he has forfeited all hope for any reward. Far better to adopt the biblical attitude that grace does not depend on merit at all, but on the infinite goodness and sovereign purpose of God. I would much rather entrust my expectations of blessings and answers to prayer to the infinite goodness of God and His sovereign purpose for my life (a purpose He has already declared to be for my good) than rely on all the merit points I could ever possibly accumulate. We need to remember that God has already been shown to be the exceedingly gracious and generous landowner. To realize that grace, all we must do is acknowledge we are no more than eleventh-hour workers.

With this emphasis on contentment, I'm not suggesting we should always be satisfied with the status quo in every area of our lives and not pray for or seek improvement. Remember, God by His nature is graciously disposed to give us all good things (see Romans 8:32). But for all of us, there are certain things that simply are not going to change. In those areas, we must learn to be content, always accepting the fact that God does not owe us something different.

Frankly, I have had to struggle to learn this myself. God has given me a physical body that, in a number of ways, is less than average. He has given me spiritual gifts that lie largely outside the mainstream ministry of the organization He called me to serve with. Neither of these circumstances is going to change, so I have had to learn to be content with what God has given me. I have learned this by focusing on two facts: He doesn't owe me *anything*, and what He *has given* me was given by His grace alone.

## THE PERIL OF COMPARING

There is still another valuable lesson to be learned from the parable of the generous landowner. God is not only generous, He is also sovereign. That is, God has the right to dispense His blessings as He chooses. Jesus asserts this prerogative of God very clearly with the landowner's question: "Don't I have the right to do what I want with my own money?" (Matthew 20:15).

We constantly see believers around us who seem more blessed of God than we are. Some are more gifted in spiritual abilities, others always succeed with little effort, still others seem to have few problems or concerns, and on and on. Probably none of us is exempt from the temptation to envy someone else's blessings and to secretly grumble at God, or even to charge Him with rank injustice, for giving that person more in some way than He has given us.

Yet God in His sovereignty has the right to bless each of us as He chooses. Consider these words from the apostle Paul:

But who are you, O man, to talk back to God? "Shall what is formed say to him who formed it, 'Why did you make me like this?'" Does not the potter have the right to make out of the same lump of clay some pottery for noble purposes and some for common use? (Romans 9:20-21)

Regardless of how we understand the particular application of Paul's teaching, we cannot escape the basic principle in the passage: God is sovereign. And He is sovereign in every area of life. God as our Creator has the right to endow each of us at birth with different physical and mental abilities, with different temperament characteristics, and with different natural talents. He also has the right to give each of us different spiritual gifts. Not only does God have the right, it is obvious He exercises it. We are not created equal, nor are we given equal opportunities throughout life. Each of us has his or her own unique set of circumstances; those of some people being much more favorable than others. Since God is under no obligation to any of us, He is free to bless some more than others as He chooses. He has the right to do what He wants with His blessings.

Not only does God sovereignly determine how and to what extent He will bless us, He often blesses those who, in our opinion, seem most unworthy. We see this demonstrated rather forcefully in Jesus' recounting of two Old Testament incidents as recorded in Luke 4:25-27:

> I assure you that there were many widows in Israel in Elijah's time, when the sky was shut for three and a half years and there was a severe famine throughout the land. Yet Elijah was not sent to any of them, but to a widow in Zarephath in the region of Sidon. And there were many in Israel with leprosy in the time of Elisha the prophet, yet not one of them was cleansed — only Naaman the Syrian.

Luke recorded that "all the people in the synagogue were furious when they heard this." Why were these Jews who heard Jesus so enraged that, as verse 29 tells us, they wanted to kill Him? It was because the widow and Naaman were despised Gentiles. In the opinion of the Jews, these people were *most* unworthy. The reaction was, "How could God bless those

Gentile dogs instead of more deserving Jews?"

The fact is God *did* bless those two Gentiles while passing right by His own chosen people. Were the widow of Zarephath and Naaman the Syrian more "deserving" than anyone in Israel? Not at all. The Old Testament record of his healing indicates that Naaman, by his anger and haughtiness, was very *un*deserving. God often does bless people who seem to us to be quite unworthy. But that is what grace is all about, because we are all unworthy.

We rejoice in the generosity of God's grace as long as it is directed toward us, or toward our family or friends. But how do we feel when someone whom we think does not deserve it is blessed by God? Are we envious because of the generosity of God toward that person? Do we feel, as did the workers in the parable, that we "have borne the burden of the work and the heat of the day" and yet that other person has been blessed more than we have?

The workers who labored all day did not grumble because they received too little pay, but because less deserving workers received the same as they. The A students in the modem version of the parable were not outraged because they received only an A, but because some obviously undeserving students received the same grade.

The reality of the Christian life, though, is that there are no A students in God's kingdom. Some are more obedient than others, some have labored more and sacrificed more than others, but none of us measures up to an A. None of us wants to get what we actually deserve. We all want grace, but we cannot enjoy grace when there is an attitude of comparing.

William Arnot (1808–1875) has some helpful words on the perils of comparing. He wrote,

> See the two groups of labourers as they severally wend their way home that evening. As to amount of money in their pockets, they are all equal: but as to amount of content in their spirits there is a great difference.

The last go home each with a penny [a denarius] in his pocket, and astonished glad gratitude in his heart: their reward accordingly is a penny, and *more*. The first, on the contrary, go home, each with a penny in his pocket, and corroding discontent in his soul: their reward accordingly is *less* than a penny.[1]

Arnot believed it was in this sense that "the last will be first, and the first will be last" (Matthew 20:16). That is, the last workers hired ended up "first" because they had a day's wages plus contentment, whereas the first workers hired ended up "last" because of their discontentment.

While that is certainly a helpful observation about life, I understand Jesus' two statements in Matthew 19:30 and 20:16 somewhat differently than Arnot does. I believe Jesus is asserting the sovereign prerogative of God to dispense His favors as He pleases. I don't think His statement, "So the last will be first, and the first will be last," is to be taken in an absolute sense as if this would always be the case; rather, there is often no apparent correlation between what one seemingly "deserves" and what he or she receives. Remember, the whole point of the parable is to respond to Peter's attitude as expressed in the words of R. C. H. Lenski: "The more *we* do, the more *we* earn, and the more *God* owes us."[2]

If we are to succeed in living by grace, we must come to terms with the fact that God is sovereign in dispensing His gracious favors, and He owes us no explanation when His actions do not correspond with our system of merits. Indeed, as Paul said,

> How unsearchable His decisions,
>  and how mysterious His methods!
> For who has ever understood the thoughts of
>  the Lord,
>  or has ever been His advisor?
>  (Romans 11:33-34, WMS)

We are left without any grounds for grumbling about the treatment we receive from God. God never becomes obligated to us, so He can always say to us, "Friend, I am not being unfair to you" (Matthew 20:13). At the same time God reserves the right to treat each of us differently, bestowing blessings as He sovereignly chooses. In the words of the landowner, God says to us, "Don't I have the right to do what I want with my own money? Or are you envious because I am generous?" (verse 15).

## THE PROMISES OF GOD

The fact is, of course, God is gracious and generous to all who are His children. The parable doesn't teach us only about the sovereignty of God in dispensing His grace; it teaches us even more about His gracious generosity. The Bible is full of God's promises to provide for us spiritually and materially, to never forsake us, to give us peace in times of difficult circumstances, to cause all circumstances to work together for our good, and finally to bring us safely home to glory. *Not one of those promises is dependent upon our performance.* They are all dependent on the grace of God given to us through Jesus Christ.

The apostle Paul wrote, "For no matter how many promises God has made, they are 'Yes' in Christ. And so through him the 'Amen' is spoken by us to the glory of God" (2 Corinthians 1:20). What did Paul mean when he said all God's promises are "Yes" in Christ?

First of all, Christ in His Messianic mission is the personal fulfillment of all the promises in the Old Testament regarding a Savior and coming King. As Philip Hughes wrote,

In Christ is the yes, the grand consummating affirmative, to all God's promises. He is the horn of salvation raised up for us by God, "as He spake by the mouth of His holy prophets which have been since the world began" (Lk. 1:69f.). In Him all things "which are written in the law of Moses, and the prophets, and the psalms" achieve their fulfillment (Lk. 24:44). The covenant promises addressed to Abraham and his seed are realized in His single person (Gal. 3:16).[3]

Beyond the actual fulfillment of all the promises made about Him, Christ is also the meritorious basis upon which all of God's other promises depend. John Calvin wrote in his comments on 2 Corinthians 1:20,

> All God's promises depend upon Christ alone. This is a notable assertion and one of the main articles of our faith. It depends in turn upon another principle — that it is only in Christ that God the Father is graciously inclined towards us. His promises are the testimonies of His fatherly goodwill towards us. Thus it follows that they are fulfilled only in Christ. . . . Secondly, we are incapable of possessing God's promises till we have received the remission of our sins and that comes to us through Christ.[4]

Think just now of what you feel your greatest needs are, both spiritually and temporally. As you bring those needs to God in prayer, which would you rather present to Him as a consideration for meeting those needs: your spiritual disciplines, your obedience, and your sacrifice, imperfect as they are; or the infinite and perfect merit of Jesus? To ask the question is to answer it, is it not?

I don't mean to disparage any spiritual discipline, commitment, or sacrifice. These all have their place in the realm of grace. But they are never to be relied on as a meritorious cause for expecting God's blessing or answer to prayer. Martin Luther, in his exposition of Deuteronomy 8:17-18, spoke of "blessings that at times come to us through our labors and at times without our labors, *but never because of our labors*; for God always gives them because of His undeserved mercy" (emphasis added).[5]

If only we will learn to rest our entire case on the merits of Jesus Christ, instead of our own, we will learn the joy of living by grace and not by sweat.

# Does God Have a Right?

## (Chapter 5)

## STUDY QUESTIONS

### CENTRAL IDEA

God does not owe us anything. All we have comes graciously from His hand, therefore we should be content and grateful for the lot in life He has given us. In Christ we are blessed with all spiritual riches, and in Christ all of God's promises are fulfilled.

### WARM-UP

Imagine for a moment that you have worked hard for several years to save enough money to buy a car and that a close friend's parents simply hand him money for a new car.

- How do you feel toward your friend? How do you feel about your own circumstances?
- How do you think you should feel?

### EXPLORING GRACE

1.  Matthew 20:1-16 is the story of a generous landowner. Read this story and then answer these questions.

    a.  Assuming the landowner represents God, what do we learn about the character of God from this story?

b.  What can you observe about human nature and how people tend to respond to the good fortune of others?

c.  With which worker do you identify?

d.  Why do people tend to think of the landowner as unfair instead of generous?

e.  What does this story tell us about what God's grace means?

2.  Luke 7:1-10 is another helpful story. Read this story and then answer the following questions.

a.  On what basis did the Jewish elders appeal to Jesus to heal the centurion's servant? (See verses 4-5.)

b.  What was the centurion's perspective on what he deserved? (See verses 6-7.)

    c.    Do you tend to operate like the elders or the centurion? Explain.

3.   a.    According to Luke 17:10, what sort of attitude are we to have about the things we do for the Lord?

    b.    How easy is it for you to feel that way?

4.   We are told in 1 Timothy 6:6 that if we stop expecting or demanding certain things, we will enjoy contentment.

    a.    Are you failing to experience contentment in some areas of your life? If so, name some areas in which you struggle.

    b.    In which of these areas do you need to take some action?

    c.    In which areas do you need a change of attitude?

5. We are not created equal, nor are we given equal opportunities throughout life. Each of us has our own unique set of circumstances. Those of some people are much more favorable than others. How do you think God wants us to respond to this fact?

6. Read 2 Corinthians 1:20.

   a. What does this verse tell you about God's promises and how they are filled?

   b. How does this verse help you let go of your expectations and focus on what God has already done?

## CLOSING PRAYER

Search your heart. Do you base your hope for improved circumstances in your life on trust in God's love and contentment with whatever He decides, or do you focus on what you think you deserve? Do you think your attitude expresses more humble trust or resentful demanding? On your own, take a few minutes to write out a prayer expressing your thoughts and feelings to the Lord. Those who want can pray their prayers as you pray for the needs shared during your discussion.

GOING DEEPER (Extra questions for further study)

1.  What do the following verses say about our right to demand anything from God?

    • Job 41:11

    • Romans 11:35

2.  Today in our society we tend to have high expectations and a strong sense of our rights. Give some examples of these attitudes.

3.  What do the following verses tell us about the source of all that we have?

    • 1 Chronicles 29:14,16

    • Isaiah 26:12

    • Acts 17:25

    • James 1:17

4.  The world is set up on a system of rewards for achievement at school and in the workplace. Why doesn't God use the same system when it comes to our relationship with Him?

### Pondering Grace (For personal reflection)

*See the two groups of laborers as they wend their way home that evening. As to amount of money in their pockets, they are all equal; but as to amount of content in their spirits there is a great difference. The last go home each with a penny in his pocket, and astonished gratitude in his heart; their reward accordingly is a penny, and more. The first, on the contrary, go home each with a penny in his pocket, and corroding discontent in his soul; their reward accordingly is less than a penny.*

William Arnot, *Parables of Our Lord*

*Blessings at times come to us through our labors and at times without our labors, but never because of our labors; for God always gives them because of His undeserved mercy.*

Martin Luther

*Grace is not sought nor bought nor wrought. It is a free gift of Almighty God to needy mankind.*

Billy Graham

# Compelled by Love

Read the following portion of *Transforming Grace*. In the margins, record observations, illustrations, or questions that come to mind as you read. Then answer the study questions that follow the reading.

---

## Chapter Six: Compelled by Love

*For Christ's love compels us, because we are convinced*
*that one died for all, and therefore all died. And he died*
*for all, that those who live should no longer live for themselves*
*but for him who died for them and was raised again.*
2 CORINTHIANS 5:14-15

L iving by grace instead of by works means you are free from the performance treadmill. It means God has already given you an A when you deserved an F; He has already given you a full day's pay even though you may have worked only one hour. It means you don't have to perform certain spiritual disciplines to earn God's approval. Jesus Christ has already done that for you.

You are loved and accepted by God through the merit of Jesus, and you are blessed by God through the merit of Jesus. Nothing you ever do will cause Him to love you any more or any less. He loves you strictly by His grace given to you through Jesus.

How does this emphasis on God's free and sovereign grace make you feel? Does it make you a little nervous? Does it seem a bit scary to hear that nothing you do will ever make God love you any more or bless you any more? Do you think, *Well, if you take the pressure off like that and tell me all of my effort will never earn me one blessing, then I'm afraid I'll slack off and stop doing the things I need to do to live a disciplined Christian life?*

The Bible recognizes the possibility that the grace of God

can be misunderstood and even abused. It speaks of "godless men, who change the grace of our God into a license for immorality" (Jude 4). Anticipating the question, "Shall we go on sinning so that grace may increase?" (Romans 6:1), it warns us not to use our freedom to indulge the sinful nature (see Galatians 5:13). All of these passages recognize the possibility that the Bible's teaching that grace alone is the basis for God's blessing can be misconstrued as an excuse for indulgent, slothful living.

The apostle Paul wrote the entire sixth chapter of Romans to answer the question, "Shall we go on sinning so that grace may increase?" Why did he have to deal with such a question? What had he said to even raise the issue? His whole teaching to that point in Romans was that justification is by faith in Jesus Christ alone, culminating in his sweeping statement in Romans 5:20: "But where sin increased, grace increased all the more."

Paul realized his unqualified presentation of the grace of God left him open to being misunderstood. Paul himself knew that his insistence on the pure grace of God without any admixture of commitment or discipline or obedience on our part could cause us to misunderstand him. He knew his readers could respond with this attitude: "Well, if that's true, let's go out and sin all we want. The more we sin, the more we cause God's grace to abound."

This type of response is always a possibility. In fact, if our concept of grace does not expose us to that possible misunderstanding, then we do not thoroughly understand grace. I believe it is because we are afraid of this attitude that we often change the doctrine of grace into a doctrine of works.

"Shall we go on sinning so that grace may increase?" The late Dr. Martyn Lloyd-Jones of England, one of the ablest and most respected Bible expositors of the twentieth century, said this in response to that question:

The true preaching of the gospel of salvation by grace alone always leads to the possibility of this charge being brought against it. There is no better test as to whether a man is really preaching the New Testament gospel of salvation than this, that some people might misunderstand it and misinterpret it to mean that it really amounts to this, that because you are saved by grace alone it does not matter at all what you do; you can go on sinning as much as you like because it will redound all the more to the glory of grace.[1]

Obviously Dr. Lloyd-Jones was not saying that we should try to confuse people with our presentation of the gospel. He was simply saying that the presentation of salvation by grace alone, apart from any preconditions on the part of our hearers, leaves us open to the *possibility* that people may charge us with saying, "It does not matter what you do; sin as much as you like." That charge was brought against Martin Luther and all the other great preachers of the Reformation when they preached salvation by grace alone through faith in Christ. The charge was brought against the apostle Paul himself: "Why not say — as we are being slanderously reported as saying and as some claim that we say — 'Let us do evil that good may result'? Their condemnation is deserved" (Romans 3:8).

The grace of salvation is the same grace by which we live the Christian life. Paul said in Romans 5:2, "We have gained access by faith into *this grace in which we now stand*" (emphasis added). We are not only justified by grace through faith, we stand every day in this same grace. And just as the preaching of justification by grace is open to misunderstanding, so is the teaching of living by grace.

The solution to this problem is not to add legalism to grace. Rather, the solution is to be so gripped by the magnificence and boundless generosity of God's grace that we respond out of gratitude rather than out of a sense of duty. As Steven Brown, pastor of Key Biscayne Presbyterian Church in Miami, Florida, said, "The problem [isn't] that we made the gospel too good.

The problem is that we didn't make it good enough."[2]

We have loaded down the gospel of the grace of God in Christ with a lot of "oughts." "I ought to do this" and "I ought to do that." "I ought to be more committed, more disciplined, more obedient." When we think or teach this way, we are substituting duty and obligation for a loving response to God's grace.

Let me be very clear at this point. I firmly believe in and seek to practice commitment, discipline, and obedience. I am thoroughly committed to submission to the lordship of Jesus Christ in every area of my life. And I believe in and seek to practice other commitments that flow out of that basic commitment. I am committed to my wife "until death do us part." I am committed to integrity and fairness in business relationships. I am committed to seek to act in love toward everyone. But I am committed in these areas out of a grateful response to God's grace, not to try to earn God's blessings.

Most of my understanding of scriptural truths has come gradually through my personal study and the teaching of pastors and other capable teachers. On a few rare occasions the Lord has been pleased to enlighten my understanding of some aspect of His truth in a rather sudden fashion, like someone turning on a light in a dark room. I didn't suddenly learn a new spiritual fact, rather I understood some truth in a new and more scriptural way.

This was the case in my understanding of the sovereign grace of God. I had been a confirmed legalist, and I dutifully sought to live the Christian life that way. I was sometimes overwhelmed with what I thought were the "oughts" of the Christian life. But suddenly one day, I understood God's grace in an entirely new way. I am now convinced, after many years, that it is a more biblical understanding.

So what was my reaction to a new and better understanding of the grace of God? Did I abandon my commitment and give up my spiritual disciplines? Not at all. I remember well what I did. I was spending a half day with God, seated in a basement room with a cold, hard tile floor. As my understanding of God's grace was enlightened, Romans 12:1 came to mind:

> Therefore, I urge you, brothers, in view of God's mercy, to offer your bodies as living sacrifices, holy and pleasing to God — this is your spiritual act of worship.

I fell on my knees on that cold, hard floor and said something like this to God: "Lord, I have presented my body to You as a living sacrifice before, but I've never understood as I do now Your mercy and Your grace. And in view of my deeper understanding of Your grace, I now present myself to You in a new and deeper way. I give myself wholly to You without any reservation."

Now, more than thirty years later, I still build on the commitment I made in the basement room that morning. But more than that, I still seek to grow in my understanding of God's grace, because I know that only my growing understanding of His grace will make the commitment stick "through thick and thin."

Steve Brown was right. We often don't make the gospel "good enough." We preach grace to the non-Christian and duty to the Christian. As Richard Gilbert has written, "It sometimes seems that there is plenty of grace for you if you are not a Christian, but when you become a Christian then there are all sorts of laws you must obey and you feel like you were better off before you were converted."[3]

Even our terminology betrays the way we dichotomize the Christian life into "grace" and "works" compartments. We speak of the *gift of salvation* and the *cost of discipleship*. The "cost of discipleship" is not necessarily an unbiblical expression, but the connotation we build into it is. We often convey the idea that God's grace barely gets us inside the door of the kingdom, and after that, it's all our own blood, sweat, and tears.

How did the apostle Paul approach the subject of commitment and discipline? Let's look again at Romans 12:1. Paul's letter to the Romans is the foundation for the Bible's teaching on salvation. In that letter the teaching of justification by faith in Jesus Christ alone is set forth most cogently and completely. However, Paul wrote the letter to people who were already believers. He referred to them as those "who are loved by God and called to be saints." He thanked God that their "faith is being reported all over the world," and longed that they and he "may be mutually encouraged by each other's faith" (Romans 1:7-8,12). Clearly he was writing to believers.

Paul wrote this letter to help them understand more fully the salvation they already possessed. He spent eleven chapters going through the gospel, showing that salvation is entirely by God's grace through faith in Jesus Christ and then dealing with various questions his teaching on the grace of God would raise.

Not until Paul had spent eleven chapters teaching the gospel of the grace of God *to people who were already believers* did he ask for a response from them: a total commitment of themselves to God. He urged them, "Offer your bodies as living sacrifices, holy and pleasing to God" (12:1).

Paul made a strong appeal. Charles B. Williams' translation of the New Testament interprets the phrase "offer your bodies" as "make a decisive [footnote: once for all offer] dedication of your bodies." The phrase "living sacrifices," though, connotes the idea of a "perpetual sacrifice never to be neglected or recalled"[4] and a "constant dedication."[5] So Paul called for a decisive, once for all dedication that is to be constantly reaffirmed and kindled afresh. You cannot ask for any higher level of commitment than that.

What consideration did Paul bring forward as the basis or motivation for making such a total commitment? He did not appeal to a sense of duty but to the mercy of God ("in view of God's mercy"). He asked for a response based not on obligation but on heartfelt gratitude.

Now, the fact is we *do* have a duty and obligation to God. He is the Sovereign Ruler of this world, and in that capacity, He has "laid down precepts that are to be fully obeyed" (Psalm 119:4). But He motivates us to obedience, not on the basis of His sovereign rule, but on the basis of His mercy to us in Jesus Christ.

Martin Luther wrote on Romans 12:1, "A lawdriver insists with threats and penalties; a preacher of grace lures and incites with divine goodness and compassion shown to us; for he wants no unwilling works and reluctant services, he wants joyful and delightful services of God."[6]

I was asked to speak on the "Lordship of Jesus Christ" at a conference. I knew the intended objective was to challenge the audience to submit to Christ's lordship in the affairs of their everyday lives. But I began the message by speaking on God's goodness. After I had spent fifteen or twenty minutes on the goodness of God, then I began to talk about the lordship of Christ in our lives.

Why did I develop the message in that fashion? Because submission to the lordship of Jesus Christ should be in response to the love and mercy of God. *In view of God's mercy*, Paul urged the Roman believers to offer their bodies as living sacrifices. We must respond with a similar motivation to His lordship in our lives today.

Our *motivation* for commitment, discipline, and obedience is as important to God, perhaps even more so, than our *performance*. As Ernest F. Kevan wrote, "The Law's demands are inward, touching motive and desire, and are not concerned solely with outward action."[7]

David said to Solomon, "And you, my son Solomon, acknowledge the God of your father, and serve him with whole-hearted devotion and with a willing mind, for the LORD searches every heart and understands every motive behind the thoughts" (1 Chronicles 28:9). The apostle Paul echoed the importance of motives when he wrote that, at the Lord's coming, "He . . . will expose the motives of men's hearts" (1 Corinthians 4:5).

God searches the heart and understands every motive. To be acceptable to Him, our motives must spring from a love for Him and a desire to glorify Him. Obedience to God performed from a legalistic motive — that is, a fear of the consequences or to gain favor with God — is not pleasing to God. Abraham Booth (1734–1806), an English pastor and author, wrote, "To constitute a work truly good, it must be done from a right principle, performed by a right rule, and intended for a right end."[8]

Mr. Booth defined a right principle as the love of God, that is, our love for God. He defined the right rule as God's revealed will as contained in Scripture. The right end — or as we would say today, the right goal — is the glory of God.

Thus, our good works are not truly good unless they are motivated by a love for God and a desire to glorify Him. But we cannot have such a God-ward motivation if we think we must earn God's favor by our obedience, or if we fear we may forfeit God's favor by our disobedience. Such a works-oriented motivation is essentially self-serving; it is prompted more by what we think we can gain or lose from God than by a grateful response to the grace He has already given us through Jesus Christ.

Living under the grace of God instead of under a sense of duty frees us from such a self-serving motivation. It frees us to obey God and serve Him as a loving and thankful response to Him for our salvation and for blessings already guaranteed to us by His grace. Consequently, a heartfelt grasp of God's grace — far from creating an indifferent or careless attitude in us — will actually provide us the only motivation that is pleasing to Him. Only when we are thoroughly convinced that the Christian life is entirely of grace are we able to serve Him out of a grateful and loving heart.

I knew a man who was a very strict tither. He gave exactly 10 percent of his income to God's work: never one penny less and, as far as I know, never one penny more. I asked him why he tithed so religiously. He replied, "I'd be afraid not to." I knew this man fairly well, and I suspect his motivation was mixed. He did *somewhat* enjoy giving his 10 percent; but his basic motivation was a fear of the consequences if he did not tithe. He was not motivated to tithe from a joyful and grateful heart.

By contrast, the apostle Paul appealed to Christ's grace as a motivation to give. He said, "For you know the grace of our Lord Jesus Christ, that though he was rich, yet for your sakes he became poor, so that you through his poverty might become rich" (2 Corinthians 8:9). Paul was not "laying a guilt trip," as we say today, on the Corinthian believers. Rather, he wanted them not only to give generously, but to give from a sense of gratitude for God's grace. He wanted people to give, not from a sense of duty and compulsion, but cheerfully as a loving response to what God had already given them in Christ.

Many of us are often like the tither. We are motivated more by a fear that God will either punish us or withhold some blessing from us than we are from love of God. We get up early in the morning to have a quiet time, not because we truly desire fellowship with God, but because we're afraid we will forfeit God's blessing that day if we don't.

Once I was on my way to a weekend conference to speak on the pursuit of holiness. As I boarded the plane, I was confronted with an extremely alluring temptation to indulge in lustful glances at a young woman. Immediately the thought came to me, *You can't do that! You're on your way to speak about holiness.* In saying that to myself, I wasn't concerned about being truly holy in the way I would challenge others to be. Rather, I was afraid I might forfeit God's blessing on my messages.

As I realized my wrong motive, I bowed my head and said, "God, even if I never open my mouth to speak for You again, You are still worthy of my saying 'No' to temptation." I changed my motive for obedience from a self-centered to a God-centered motive.

Let me clarify one thing, lest I be misunderstood. When I stress a God-ward motivation for our discipline and obedi-

TRANSFORMING GRACE SMALL-GROUP CURRICULUM

ence, I am not talking about inclination or feeling. We are not to wait until we "feel like" having a quiet time to have one. And we certainly are not to wait until we are so inclined to obey God's commands. Motive has nothing to do with feelings or inclination; rather, it refers to the *reason* why we do, or don't do, something. For the person living by grace, that reason should be a loving response to the abundant grace of God already manifested in Christ.

## COMPELLED BY LOVE

In 2 Corinthians 5:14-15, Paul said,

> For Christ's love compels us, because we are convinced that one died for all, and therefore all died. And he died for all, that those who live should no longer live for themselves but for him who died for them and was raised again.

While there is a lot of spiritual truth in this passage, the essential teaching is that Christ's love compels us to live no longer for ourselves but for Him who died for us and was raised again.

The main subject is once again commitment to the lordship of Jesus Christ in every area of our lives. We are to live no longer for ourselves but for Him. We are to make His will the rule of our lives and His glory the goal for which we live. But what is the wellspring of this commitment? What motivating principle will cause a person to live no longer for himself but for God?

Paul said the love of Christ compels us to make this kind of commitment and to carry it out day by day. *Compel* is a strong word and often has a negative association with force or coercion. But here its meaning is positive. Charles Hodge wrote that the love of Christ "coerces, or presses, and therefore impels. It is the governing influence which controls the life."[9] It is not a fear of consequences or expectation of reward that motivates Paul. Rather, the love of Christ manifested in dying for him is the driving force of his life.

The *Williams' New Testament* is well regarded for its careful rendering of the tenses of the Greek verbs, and it is particularly helpful here. Williams translated the first phrase of 2 Corinthians 5:14 in this manner: "For the love of Christ continuously constrains me." Note the use of the word *continuously*, indicating that Christ's love is the constant wellspring of Paul's motivation every day. Paul never lost sight of, never forgot, never took for granted the death of Christ for him. And as he reflected on this infinite love manifested in Christ's death, he was motivated, no, he was compelled and impelled to live for the One who died for him and rose again.

Sometimes when I talk about living by grace instead of by works, I see people begin to get nervous. Some have warned me against "going too far," by telling me stories of people who, after hearing a message on God's grace, have committed some grossly sinful act. I grant the possibility that grace can be so misunderstood.

But I believe that, in most instances where people apparently abuse grace, they have not heard a message on grace but on freedom from the law. Freedom from the law is a result of grace and is an important application of the truth of grace, but it is not the same as grace. To teach freedom from the law without first teaching grace is like trying to build a house without laying the foundation. That approach can indeed lead to abuse. But when a person truly understands the grace of God in Christ, he or she will not abuse that grace.

Jude did speak of "godless men, who change the grace of our God into a license for immorality and deny Jesus Christ our only Sovereign and Lord" (Jude 4). Obviously, Jude was referring to unbelievers — people who are "godless" and who "deny Jesus Christ" — so that passage is not applicable to Christians.

People who truly understand the grace of God, not just

intellectually but in the very core of their being, will not abuse grace by living irresponsibly. During the couple of weeks I was working on this particular chapter, I happened to be reading through Romans in my daily Bible reading. One morning I came to Romans 4 and read these words in verses 7 and 8:

> Blessed are they
> > whose transgressions are forgiven,
> > whose sins are covered.
> Blessed is the man
> > whose sin the Lord will never count
> > against him.

When I read, "Blessed is the man whose sin the Lord will *never* count against him" (emphasis added), I wept with joy and gratitude. What a fantastic encouragement that God will *never* judge me for *any* of my sins. I know I have as wicked a sinful nature as anyone else, and apart from the sanctifying influence of the Holy Spirit in my life, I am fully capable of the so-called gross sins of immorality, drunkenness, stealing, and the like. But those are not the sins that trouble me at this time. Rather, I struggle with what I call "refined" sins: selfishness, pride, impatience, a critical attitude, and a judgmental spirit.

Despite my calling those areas "refined" sins, they are nevertheless very real sins. They are sins for which I would not want to give account at the judgment bar of God. They are sins that, apart from the atoning death of Christ for me, would send me to eternal hell. And, if God operated on the basis of merit instead of grace in this life, they are sins that would forfeit all blessing from Him. In short those "refined" sins are very troublesome.

So when I read that God will never count against me my selfishness, my pride, my impatience, and so on, I wept for joy. I stopped reading and uttered a prayer of deep, heartfelt thanksgiving to God for His gracious forgiveness. Then what did I do? Did I say to myself, *Well, if God is not going to count these sins against me, it really doesn't matter whether or not I deal with them?* Did I think, *Since God is not going to count them against me anyway, I might as well not bother with all the spiritual pain of putting to death those ungodly traits?*

Of course I did not think like that. Instead I asked God to purge those sinful traits from my character. I asked Him to enable me to become more and more aware of specific instances when I was committing those sins so that I could, by His Spirit, put them to death as Paul tells us to do in Romans 8:13. I was compelled by His love to seek to put away those sins.

## REVERENCE FOR GOD

Along with a sense of profound gratitude to God for His grace, I also find myself motivated to obedience by a deep sense of reverence for Him. When Joseph was tempted to immorality by Potiphar's wife, his response was, "How then could I do such a wicked thing and sin against God?" (Genesis 39:9). He did not calculate the possible wrath of Potiphar or the forfeiture of God's blessing. He was motivated by reverence for God. He was concerned about disobedience to a sovereign, holy God, even though that God had allowed him to be sold into slavery by his own brothers.

The apostle Paul combined these two elements of a Godward motivation — gratitude and reverence — when he wrote to the Corinthian believers, "Since we have these promises, dear friends, let us purify ourselves from everything that contaminates body and spirit, perfecting holiness out of reverence for God" (2 Corinthians 7:1).

Paul referred to the promises that God would be our God and Father and would make us His sons and daughters. Philip Hughes commented on this passage, "The logical consequence of possessing such promises is that Christ's followers should make a complete break with every form of unhealthy compromise."[10] Here again we see that promises come before duty and that duty flows out of a heartfelt response to the promises of God.

But Paul went on to say, "out of reverence for God." *Reverence* is a sense of profound awe, respect, and devotion. It is a recognition of God's intrinsic worthiness, the infinite majesty of His being, and the infinite perfection of His character. Because of who He is and what He is, God is infinitely worthy of my most diligent and loving obedience, even if I never receive a single blessing from His hand. The fact is, of course, I have received innumerable blessings from Him. But His worthiness is intrinsic within Himself; it is not conditioned on the number of blessings you or I receive from Him.

In the apostle John's vision of God's throne, the twenty-four elders never cease saying,

> You are worthy, our Lord and God,
>     to receive glory and honor and power,
> for you created all things,
>     and by your will they were created
>     and have their being. (Revelation 4:11)

God is worthy of my loving obedience because of who He is, not because of what He does.

In Romans 12:1, Paul urges us, in view of God's mercy, to offer our bodies as living sacrifices to Him. Is He worthy of such sacrifice? Of course He is! He is infinitely worthy. But our motivation to obey and serve God cannot rise to such heights until we learn to live daily by grace and to experience freedom each day from the bondage of the performance treadmill.

I believe a genuine heart response to the worthiness of God is the highest possible motivation for obedience and service to God. But we cannot "break through" to that level of motivation until we are first motivated by His grace, mercy, and love. We cannot be free to think about God's worthiness and God's glory as long as we are struggling to earn our own acceptance with Him.

## GROWING IN GRACE

The term *growing in grace* is most often used to indicate growth in Christian character. While I think that usage has merit, a more accurate meaning is to continually grow in our understanding of God's grace, especially as it applies to us personally, to become progressively more aware of our own continued spiritual bankruptcy and the unmerited, unearned, and undeserved favor of God. May we all grow in grace in this sense.

As we grow in grace this way, we will grow in our motivation to obey God out of a sense of gratitude and reverence to Him. Our obedience will always be imperfect in performance in this life. We will never perfectly obey Him until we are made perfect by Him. In the same way, our motives will never be consistently pure; there will frequently be some "merit points" mentality mixed in with our genuine love and reverence for God.

So don't be discouraged if you realize your motives have been largely merit-oriented. Just begin now to move toward grace motives. Begin to think daily about the implications of the grace of God in your life. Memorize and meditate frequently on such Scripture passages as Romans 12:1 and 2 Corinthians 5:14-15. Pray about the aspects of truth in those passages and ask God to motivate you by His mercy and love. When you recognize merit-oriented motives at work in you, renounce them and cast yourself completely on the grace of God and the merit of Jesus Christ. As you grow in grace in this way, you will indeed discover that His love compels you to live, not for yourself, but for Him who died for you and was raised again.

# Compelled by Love

## (Chapter 6)

## STUDY QUESTIONS

### CENTRAL IDEA

When we understand God's magnificent and boundless grace, we become motivated by gratitude and love to respond with a life devoted to Him.

### WARM-UP

Think about some of the people you come in contact with regularly (neighbors, coworkers, family, friends, acquaintances). What appear to be the basic motives behind why they live the way they live and why they make the decisions they make? (There is no need to be overly personal or specific about exactly whose life you are drawing conclusions from.)

### EXPLORING GRACE

1.   a.   Read 1 Chronicles 28:9, Proverbs 16:2, and 1 Corinthians 4:5. Why do you think our motives are so important to God?

     b.   Do you believe that the people you come in contact with think much about the motives behind their actions? Explain.

2.  How does an understanding of God's grace help give us the right motives for the way we live?

3.  a.  How do our motives affect the outcome of what we do?

    b.  Give an example of how the wrong motives can completely undermine a good action.

4.  a.  Read the following verses and list some of the wrong motives people can have for trying to live a "good" life.

    •   John 12:42-43

    •   Galatians 6:12-13

    •   Ephesians 2:8-9

    •   Colossians 2:16-23

b. What other wrong motives can drive people's actions?

5. a. Look at the following verses and list some of the pure or godly motives that *should* be behind our actions.

- Romans 12:1

- 2 Corinthians 5:14-15

- 2 Corinthians 7:1

- Colossians 3:12-14,23-24

- Revelation 4:11

b. What other good motives can people have?

6.  Do you think it is possible to keep your motives pure at all times? Explain.

7.  Examine for a moment the motivations behind some of your actions. For each of the following areas of your life, determine how often you think you are motivated by impure motives instead of pure or godly motives. Rate your motives on a scale of 1 to 5 (1 = impure motives, 5 = godly motives). Do this individually. Then a few people can share their thoughts after doing this exercise.

    _____ Time spent in prayer
    _____ Time spent in praise and worship
    _____ Bible study
    _____ Bible reading
    _____ Memorizing Scripture
    _____ Building relationships with non-Christians
    _____ Helping young Christians grow
    _____ Fellowship with other believers
    _____ Serving others
    _____ Giving financially to God

8.  In the previous question you may have become aware of some less-than-pure motives in your life. What do you think a person can do to help purify his or her motives in an area?

9.  Take a minute to choose one of the following ways to work on having the right motives this week, or to come up with your own plan.

    a.  Write in a journal every day for a week. Try to be especially aware of your motives, during the day. When you recognize poor motives, confess this to the Lord. Ask Him to help you sort out whether you need to change some of your actions or change the way you think about these activities.

    b.  Memorize one of the following verses. Remind yourself of the vastness of God's grace when you fall into doing things to try to earn His love.

        • Jeremiah 31:3
        • Romans 8:38-39 (For a bigger challenge, memorize a larger portion or all of Romans 8.)
        • Romans 12:1-2
        • 2 Corinthians 5:14-15
        • Ephesians 2:8-10

    c.  Spend an extra hour in prayer and meditation. Make a list of all the things you do on a weekly basis to serve God and to enhance your relationship with Him. Ask the Lord to help you evaluate your commitments and the motives behind them. Use the following questions to help you think through what He is doing in your life.

        • Are there "good" things you are doing that you do primarily to please other people? Is it possible that God may want you to give up any of these?
        • Have you failed to make commitments that you know the Lord has asked you to make?

## CLOSING PRAYER

Romans 12:1-2 gives us a beautiful picture of how we should respond to the grace of God. Read this passage and then write your thoughts in the form of a prayer. Let those who feel comfortable pray their prayers out loud.

## GOING DEEPER (Extra questions for further study)

1.  a.  Share a time when you felt pressured by a sense of duty and obligation in your Christian life instead of a sense of joy, peace, and love.

    b.  What was the source of this sense of drudgery in your life?

    c.  What helped you put things back in the right perspective?

2.  a.  If a person does something even though he doesn't feel like doing it, does that mean his motives are wrong? Explain.

    b.  How are our feelings and motivations related?

### Pondering Grace (For personal reflection)

The biggest gap in the world is the gap between the justice of a cause and the motives of the people pushing it.

John P. Grier

A lawdriver insists with threats and penalties; a preacher of grace lures and incites with divine goodness and compassion shown to us, for he wants no unwilling works and reluctant services; he wants joyful and delightful services of God.

Martin Luther

The Law's demands are inward, touching motive and desire, and are not concerned solely with outward action.

Ernest F. Kevan, The Grace of Law

Our only business is to love God, and delight ourselves in Him. All kinds of disciplines, no matter how rugged, are quite useless if not motivated by love for God.

Brother Lawrence, The Practice of the Presence of God

# The Proof of Love

Read the following portion of *Transforming Grace*. In the margins, record observations, illustrations, or questions that come to mind as you read. Then answer the study questions that follow the reading.

---

## Chapter Seven: The Proof of Love

*This is love for God: to obey his commands.*
*And his commands are not burdensome.*
1 JOHN 5:3

Notes and Observations

In his book *Loving God*, Charles Colson told how he asked a number of more experienced Christians how they loved God. The answers he got ran the gamut of spiritual exercises — reading the Bible, prayer, attending church, tithing — along with giving up favorite sins, and a warm feeling in one's heart.[1]

Amazingly, one answer that was not given was Jesus' own response to the question of how to love God. In fact, few things in the Bible are more clear than Jesus' precise answer: obey His commands. In just the short space of nine verses, Jesus reiterates this thought three times: "If you love me, you will obey what I command"; "Whoever has my commands and obeys them, he is the one who loves me"; and "If anyone loves me, he will obey my teaching" (John 14:15,21,23).

One issue believers frequently struggle with is the relationship between living by grace and obedience to God's commands. For example, I stated in session 4 that nothing you ever do or don't do will make God love you any more or any less. Rather, He accepts you strictly by His grace through the merit of Jesus Christ alone. Such an unqualified statement about the love of God sounds exceedingly dangerous, leaving me open to the charge of saying in effect that God doesn't care whether you sin or not.

But consider the alternative: "God loves you if you are obedient and doesn't love you if you are disobedient. Since God's love is conditioned on obedience and you are never perfectly obedient, God never loves you perfectly or accepts you completely." Such a bald description of the all-too-common works/merit way of thinking about our relationship with God puts the issue into focus. We are accepted by God, not only in salvation but also in our present relationship with Him, either on the merit of Jesus Christ or on the basis of our own performance.

Are we to conclude, then, that since we are saved by grace and accepted by God continuously by grace, He does not care whether we sin or not? To use Paul's strong exclamation in Romans 6:2, "By no means!" Such a conclusion flies in the face of all the ethical commands of the New Testament. (I will address the Old Testament commands later in this chapter.) Such a conclusion also ignores the very clear relationship that Jesus insisted on between love for Him and obedience to His commands.

Our love for God, expressed through obedience to Him, is to be a response to His love, not a means of trying to earn it. The apostle John said, "We love because he first loved us" (1 John 4:19). It is not clear whether John was saying that we love God because He first loved us, or that we love *one another* because God first loved us. It really doesn't make any difference in this discussion because both are true. Jesus said that love for God and for one another essentially sum up all His commands (see Matthew 22:36-40).

So one clear evidence that we are living by grace is a loving obedience to the commands of God. Anyone who thinks, *Since God's love is not conditioned on my obedience, I am free to live as I please,* is not living by grace, nor does he understand grace. What he perceives as grace is really a caricature of grace.

Jesus said that if we love Him, we will obey His commands. Now a command suggests two things. First, it gives clear direction. We are told what to do or not to do. We are not left in doubt as to how we are to live. The commands in the Bible provide a clear set of moral standards.

One very popular philosophy today is "situation ethics," in which actions are morally evaluated in terms of a "loving" response to the situation at hand rather than by application of moral absolutes. Situation ethics knows no external, objective standard of behavior. Rather, it responds to what "seems right at the moment." The problem with this philosophy is, as Scripture says, "The heart is deceitful above all things and beyond cure" (Jeremiah 17:9). Therefore, anything can be made to "seem right." And because of the sinful nature still at work in us, this description of the heart is true to varying degrees even among believers.

Through "Christianized" situation ethics, all kinds of sinful actions have been committed in the name of "love." Christians have engaged in adultery — illicit sexual intimacy — on the pretense that they were acting in love toward a "lonely" or "hurting" person. Recently I heard of a man who allegedly conspired to have his incurably ill wife murdered because "she would be happier with Jesus."

This is the type of trap even Christians fall into when we do not let the commands of God give definition to love. An objective standard of love such as, "love does not commit adultery," or "love does not murder," should at least give people pause and certainly leaves them without excuse. God's commands provide us this objective standard and, when obeyed, keep us from falling into situation ethics.

For this reason, the apostle Paul told us, "Do not be foolish, but understand what the Lord's will is" (Ephesians 5:17). His will as used here is not His particular will for us in some issue of personal guidance; rather, it is His moral will as used, for example, in 1 Thessalonians 4:3: "It is God's will that you should be sanctified: that you should avoid sexual immorality."

A few verses before Ephesians 5:17, Paul said to "find out what pleases the Lord" (verse 10). To understand what the

Lord's will is and to find out what pleases the Lord are essentially the same; both expressions refer to the specific directions given in the ethical commands of Scripture. But these verses are themselves commands. That is, we are commanded to know and understand the commands contained in Scripture. And quite obviously, we are to seek to know God's will in order to *obey* it. As my first Bible study leader said many years ago, "The Bible was not given just to increase your knowledge, but to guide your conduct."

A command, however, is more than a set of directions. We've all heard the humorous statement, "When everything else fails, read the directions." Such a statement suggests that directions are optional, that sometimes we can "muddle through," sort of figuring out things on our own without bothering to read the directions. Some Christians seem to think the commands of Christ are nothing more than a set of directions.

If we follow them, they will help us get through life without falling on our face and getting hurt too many times.

But the word *command* carries the idea of authority. The most basic meaning of the word is "to direct with authority." A command does not just give guidance that one may accept or reject; a command implies that the one giving it has the authority to require obedience and the intention of doing so. This is true of the commands of God. As the Sovereign God of the universe, He has the authority to require obedience and He does insist that we obey Him.

## LAW AND GRACE

This brings us to a core issue in understanding the relationship of the law of God to the grace of God. (*Law* is used here as a summation of God's moral commands.) Under the reign of grace, is the moral will of God, considered as a whole, a request or a command? This question is not a theoretical exercise in semantics. The word *request* connotes desire; whereas the word *command* connotes authority to require. Response to a desire is optional; response to a command is not.

So when Jesus said we love Him by obeying His commands, was He using the word *command* as we ordinarily understand it, or was He using it as an expression of God's desire? In the realm of grace, does the moral will of God express the *desire* of God as to how He would *like* us to live, or does it express the requirement of God as to how we are to live?

Some people believe that, under grace, God's law no longer has the meaning of requirement but is an expression of His desire. They would readily say God *desires* that we be holy, but God does not *require* that we be holy. They maintain that we have been freed, not only from the curse and condemnation resulting from breaking the law, but also from the requirements of the law as a rule of life. They believe that to insist on obedience as a requirement for a Christian is to teach legalism instead of grace. In other words, to assign the concept of requirement to the will of God is legalism, but to assign the concept of desire to it is grace.

I believe such a view is a misunderstanding of grace. God's grace does not change the fundamental character of God's moral law. Rather, the grace of God provides for the forgiveness and acceptance of those who have broken the law. The good news of the gospel is that God has removed the guilt we incur by breaking His law and has bestowed on us the righteousness of Christ, who perfectly kept His law. Legalism does not consist in yielding obedience to the law. Rather, it is to seek justification and good standing with God through the merit of works done in obedience to the law — instead of by faith in Christ.

We need to always keep in mind that God is not only our Savior and heavenly Father through Christ, but He is also still God, the supreme Ruler and moral Governor of His creation. The sons and daughters of a king are still under obligation to obey the laws their father has decreed for his realm, even though they are his children. They are no more exempt from the laws than any other citizen.

Even when the children of the king freely and willingly obey the laws, because they love their father and understand and agree with the laws he has pronounced, they are still subject to the laws of the realm. So we as God's children are subject to the laws of His realm. Out of a response to His grace, we should obey in a loving and grateful way. And, as we'll see in chapter 8, because God has written His law on our hearts, we will, as a rule, be in agreement with His law written in His Word. But we are still to regard God's law as commands to be obeyed, not merely as expressions of His desires.

Along the highways in the United States we have white speed limit signs and yellow speed advisory signs. The speed limit signs declare the law of the state. The speed advisory signs caution you to slow down, perhaps because an upcoming curve is too tight to be rounded at the legal speed limit. You can be fined for exceeding the posted speed limit because you have broken the law of the state. You will not be fined for exceeding the advisory speed because you have not broken any law.

The law of God is like the white speed limit sign. It is the declared law of the realm. We have broken that law many times, but Christ has paid our "fine" (which is death) for us. But His paying our "fine" did not abolish the law. Christ's death did not, so to speak, change a speed limit sign to a speed advisory sign. God's law has not become optional because of His grace, merely advisory to keep us from getting hurt as we go through life.

So the fundamental character of God's law has not changed. What has changed is our *reason* for obedience, our *motive* as we discussed in session 4. Under a sense of legalism, obedience is done with a view to meriting salvation or God's blessing on our lives. Under grace, obedience is a loving response to salvation already provided in Christ, and the assurance that, having provided salvation, God will also through Christ provide all else that we need.

There is no question that obedience to God's commands prompted by fear or merit-seeking is not true obedience. The only obedience acceptable to God is constrained and impelled by love, because "love is the fulfillment of the law" (Romans 13:10). God's law as revealed in His Word prescribes our duty, but love provides the correct motive for obedience. We obey God's law, not to be loved, but because we are loved in Christ.

I readily acknowledge that it is indeed difficult to keep in our minds and hearts the commandment nature of God's will without falling into the trap of legalism. Samuel Bolton recognized this difficulty when he wrote,

> It is a hard lesson to live above the law, and yet to walk according to the law. But this is the lesson a Christian has to learn, to walk in the law in respect of duty, but to live above it in respect of comfort, neither expecting favour from the law in respect of his obedience nor fearing harsh treatment from the law in respect of his failing.[2]

Ironically, the law of God, viewed as commands to be obeyed, should actually promote living by grace. When we view God's commands as optional — or think that as God's children we are no longer under the law as a moral requirement — we subtly slip into a works mentality. If obedience to God's law is optional, then in our minds we begin to accumulate merit or extra points. "After all, we didn't *have* to obey, so we must gain some merit by voluntary obedience."

But the person who knows that he is required to obey God's commands, even as a child of God, will see more and more how far short he comes in obedience. And if that person understands the biblical concept of grace, he will be driven more and more into the arms of the Savior and His merit alone.

Evangelist D. L. Moody is reported to have said something to this effect: "You've got to get people lost before you can get them saved." He was saying that only those who recognize they are lost will turn to the Savior. The Lord Jesus stated the same principle: "For I have not come to call the righteous, but sinners" (Matthew 9:13).

This principle applies to us even as believers living under grace. We don't have to get "lost" time and again, but we certainly need to be reminded that we are still sinners. The best way to do this is to take seriously the commands of God as a required rule of life. As we do, we will be continually reminded that we really are spiritually bankrupt—even as believers. And as redeemed sinners in a perpetual state of bankruptcy, we will come to appreciate more each day the superabounding grace of God.

So, then, God's law, as a rule of life, is not opposed to grace. Rather, used in the right sense, it is the handmaid of grace. Or, to use an analogy, it is like a sheepdog that keeps driving us back into the fold of grace, when we stray out into the wilderness of works.

## LAW AND LOVE

Some people maintain that the "law of love" has replaced even the moral commands of Jesus, and that our only rule is to "love our neighbor as ourself." They quote the apostle Paul, who said,

> He who loves his fellowman has fulfilled the law. The commandments, "Do not commit adultery," "Do not murder," "Do not steal," "Do not covet," and whatever other commandment there may be, are summed up in this one rule: "Love your neighbor as yourself." Love does no harm to its neighbor. Therefore love is the fulfillment of the law. (Romans 13:8-10)

Some people understand Paul to say that the New Testament principle of love has replaced the Old Testament principle of law. That is, whereas the Jewish nation in the Old Testament lived under a number of specific moral laws, the church in the New Testament has "come of age" and now lives by the higher principle of love. Since love must be voluntary and cannot be compelled, so the thinking goes, love and law are mutually exclusive.

But if we realize the moral law is a transcript — a written reproduction — of the moral character of God and that "God is love" (1 John 4:8), we see that we cannot distinguish between law and love. Both express the character of God. They are, to use a figure of speech, two sides of the same coin. In our case, love provides the motive for obeying the commands of the law, but the law provides specific direction for exercising love.

For example, Paul said in Romans 13:10, "Love does no harm to its neighbor." But suppose that were all we knew about love. Suppose we didn't have the Ten Commandments, from which Paul quoted in verse 9: "'Do not commit adultery,' 'Do not murder,' 'Do not steal,' 'Do not covet.'" If we didn't have those specific directions, how would we know what it means to harm one's neighbor?

Most of us are familiar to some degree with the classic description of love given by Paul in 1 Corinthians 13:4-7:

Love is patient, love is kind. It does not envy, it does not boast, it is not proud. It is not rude, it is not self-seeking, it is not easily angered, it keeps no record of wrongs. Love does not delight in evil but rejoices with the truth. It always protects, always trusts, always hopes, always perseveres.

Paul did not give a dictionary definition of love; instead, he described it in terms of specific attitudes and actions toward one another. What are these attitudes and actions? They are nothing more than various expressions of the moral law of God.

Leviticus 19 is basically an amplification of the Ten Commandments as originally set forth in Exodus 20. Let's consider verses 11-18 of Leviticus 19:

Do not steal.
Do not lie.

Do not deceive one another.

Do not swear falsely by my name and so profane the name of your God. I am the LORD.

Do not defraud your neighbor or rob him.

Do not hold back the wages of a hired man overnight.

Do not curse the deaf or put a stumbling block in front of the blind, but fear your God. I am the LORD.

Do not pervert justice; do not show partiality to the poor or favoritism to the great, but judge your neighbor fairly.

Do not go about spreading slander among your people.

Do not do anything that endangers your neighbor's life. I am the LORD.

Do not hate your brother in your heart. Rebuke your neighbor frankly so you will not share in his guilt.

Do not seek revenge or bear a grudge against one of your people, but love your neighbor as yourself. I am the LORD.

Now, let's paraphrase those verses using the format "Love does not," which Paul used in 1 Corinthians 13. When we do this, the passage from Leviticus 19 reads as follows:

Love does not steal, it does not lie, it does not deceive. Love does not profane God's name. It does not defraud nor rob its neighbor. It does not hold the wages of a hired man overnight. Love does not curse the deaf, nor put a stumbling block in front of the blind.

Love does not pervert justice, nor show partiality to the poor or favoritism to the great. Instead, it judges its neighbor fairly. Love does not slander another, nor do anything that endangers his life.

Love does not hate its brother, nor seek revenge, nor bear a grudge, but rather treats its neighbor as itself.

We can see from this paraphrase that the various expressions of God's moral law, wherever they occur in Scripture, are simply a description of love in action.

Leviticus 19 also helps us understand who our neighbor is. He is the hired man, the deaf, the blind, the poor, the great, the person whom we are tempted to lie to or steal from or slander. He is the person who has wronged us and against whom we are tempted to hold a grudge. Our neighbor is even the person whose life we might endanger by reckless behavior. We can easily say our neighbor is anyone with whom we come in contact. But because of our human frailty and our tendency to have moral "blind spots," it is helpful to think in terms of specific situations.

The principle of love is not a "higher principle" over God's moral law. Rather, it provides the motive and the motivation for obedience, while the law provides the direction for the biblical expressions of love. The actions prescribed by God's law would be hollow indeed if they were not motivated by love for both God and our neighbor. I would much rather do business with someone who wanted to treat me fairly because he loved me than someone who deals fairly only because "it's good for business." I would also want his love to be guided by the moral and ethical principles of the Bible.

## OLD TESTAMENT LAW

Earlier in this chapter, I promised to address the issue of the moral commands of the Old Testament as they relate to us as believers today. Gordon Wenham was especially helpful in this area when he wrote,

> As far as basic principles of behavior are concerned the OT [Old Testament] and the NT [New Testament] are in broad agreement. "You shall love the Lord your God with all your heart, and with all your soul, and with all your mind, and with all your strength. You

shall love your neighbor as yourself" (Mark 12:20-31; Deut. 6:5; Lev. 19:18). With this double quotation from Deuteronomy and Leviticus Jesus drew out the quintessence of OT law and gave it his own seal of approval. The ten commandments are often quoted by the NT. Peter quotes the Levitical injunction to holiness (1 Pet. 1:16). The examples could be multiplied to show that the NT advocates the same standard of personal morality as the OT. This is to be expected, since the God of the OT is the God of the NT. The people of God are supposed to imitate God. If Leviticus summons men to "be holy, for I am holy," our Lord urges us: "You, therefore, must be perfect as your heavenly Father is perfect" (Matt. 5:48). It is evident that the personal ethics of both testaments are similar. . . .

The principles underlying the OT are valid and authoritative for the Christian, but the particular applications found in the OT may not be. The moral principles are the same today, but insofar as our situation often differs from the OT setting, the application of the principles in our society may well be different too.[3]

One of the examples Wenham cited is Deuteronomy 22:8: "When you build a new house, make a parapet around your roof so that you may not bring the guilt of bloodshed on your house if someone falls from the roof." A parapet is a low, protective wall or rail along the edge of a roof. In an area where flat roofed houses were common, it was obviously intended to keep people from falling off the roof. The underlying principle shows that safety measures are more than just a good idea, they are the will of God. This should help us respond in a Christian way to the proliferation of occupational safety and product liability laws. While some aspects of those laws seem to go too far in addressing safety problems, they are — although unintentional on the part of their authors — applications of the safety principle God set forth in Deuteronomy 22:8. Therefore, out of love to God and to our neighbor, we should make our workplaces and our products as safe as possible.

The apostle Paul used this method of applying principles from Old Testament law in 1 Corinthians 9:9-10:

> For it is written in the Law of Moses: "Do not muzzle an ox while it is treading out the grain." Is it about oxen that God is concerned? Surely he says this for us, doesn't he? Yes, this was written for us, because when the plowman plows and the thresher threshes, they ought to do so in the hope of sharing in the harvest.

The specific application Paul made to ministers of the gospel was far removed from the Old Testament agricultural economy. Yet, it is as applicable today as it was in Paul's day, not only to the ministry but to all employment situations. In this sense, then, the law of God as expressed in the Old Testament has not been abolished.

## THE FREEDOM OF THE GOSPEL

"But," some say, "didn't Paul say in Ephesians 2:15 that Christ '[abolished]' in his flesh the law with its commandments and regulations'? Didn't he say that Christ has set us free from the law, and didn't he *urge* us to stand firm in that freedom?" (see Galatians 5:1). We must honestly address these questions if we are to correctly understand the relationship of God's law to grace.

In answer to the first question, Paul surely cannot mean that Christ abolished the moral will of God. Such a meaning would contradict what he wrote so abundantly elsewhere. In fact, Paul himself referred explicitly to the Ten Commandments later in the same letter: "Children, obey your parents in the Lord, for this is right. 'Honor your father and mother' — which is the first commandment with a promise" (Ephesians 6:1-2).

So Paul cannot mean that Christ abolished the law of God as an expression of God's moral will. Neither can he mean that the requirements of the law have now been changed to the *desire* of God. The word *abolished* would not sustain such a meaning. Paul, then, surely meant that Christ abolished the curse of the law and the condemnation of the law for those who have faith in Him.

In Galatians 3:10, Paul wrote, "All who rely on observing the law are under a curse, for it is written: 'Cursed is everyone who does not continue to do everything written in the Book of the Law.'" This passage gives us a clue as to what Paul meant in Ephesians when he said Christ abolished the law. It is the law viewed as that which condemns and curses for disobedience that is abolished. Christ abolished the law in this sense by bearing its curse for us. Paul went on to say in Galatians 3:13, "Christ redeemed us from the curse of the law by becoming a curse for us, for it is written: 'Cursed is everyone who is hung on a tree.'" This verse also helps us understand the sense in which Paul said we were called to be free (see Galatians 5:1).

The issue in the Galatian church was not obedience to the moral law of God; rather, it was a *reliance* on the moral law and the Mosaic ceremonial law for salvation. Some Jewish teachers were saying, "The Gentiles must be circumcised and required to obey the law of Moses" (Acts 15:5). Christ has freed us from this Jewish insistence on observance of the Mosaic law. We are freed from the curse on those who rely on the law as a means of salvation.

It is difficult for us today to appreciate the struggle the newly emerging Gentile churches had with the Jewish "law-keepers" in Paul's day. We must seek to understand what Paul meant by freedom in the context of the issue he was contending against. Otherwise, we may interpret Paul as saying more than he actually said.

In the history of the United States, a famous patriot cried out, "Give me liberty, or give me death!" Because we know he uttered this in the context of the American Revolution, we

Notes and Observations

readily understand he was speaking specifically of liberty from the rule of the British monarch. He was not crying out for liberty from all civil law, but from what he considered the tyranny of unjust laws.

In the same manner, Paul did not call for freedom in an absolute sense, but freedom from the bondage of the Jewish law system, which was abolished by Christ in His death. When we stop to think about it, there is no such thing as unqualified freedom. Such "freedom" would not be freedom, it would be anarchy. It would be everyone doing what is right in his own eyes; and given our sinful nature, it would be total chaos.

In the United States, we say we live in a "free country." We understand that freedom to be political freedom: the right to have a say in our government. But we all recognize we are not free to disobey the laws of our state or nation. We are not free, for example, to drive on the left side of the highway.

My son observed a humorous example of "freedom" when he visited a country in which automobile drivers are undisciplined and "free spirited." He saw cars stopped at a railroad crossing for a passing train. Instead of lining up behind one another to cross in their proper turn, several cars lined up at the crossing guard across the entire road. Each driver wanted to be first to cross when the guard was raised. But when the train had passed, lo and behold, cars were lined up completely across the road on the other side of the tracks. "Freedom" quickly turned to chaos! That kind of thing happens in a much more serious way when we insist on unqualified freedom from the law of God.

We have indeed been set free from the bondage and curse that results from breaking the law. And we have been called to freedom from works as a means of obtaining any merit with God. But we have not been called to freedom from the law as an expression of God's will for our daily living.

Paul said, "For in my inner being I delight in God's laws," and "I myself in my mind am a slave to God's law" (Romans 7:22,25). A few verses before he had characterized God's law as "holy, righteous and good" (verse 12). It seems inconceivable that Paul would want to be free, or urge others to be free, from what was holy, righteous, and good — that in which he himself delighted.

So, then, God's law is not opposed to grace, nor is it an enemy of grace. Neither is the law of God opposed to us as we seek to live by grace. To live by grace means we understand that God's blessing on our lives is not conditioned by our obedience or disobedience but by the perfect obedience of Christ. It means that out of a grateful response to the grace of God, we seek to understand His will and to obey Him, not to be blessed, but because we have been blessed.

---

## Chapter Eight: Holiness: A Gift of God's Grace

*Then he said, "Here I am, I have come to do your will." . . .*
*And by that will, we have been made holy through the*
*sacrifice of the body of Jesus Christ once for all.*
HEBREWS 10:9-10

"The great mistake made by most of the Lord's people is in hoping to discover *in themselves* that which is to be found in Christ alone."[4] These words of Arthur W. Pink focus on a key issue in living by grace. Most of us have the tendency that Arthur Pink identified: to seek within ourselves what is to be found in Christ alone.

To live by grace is to live solely by the merit of Jesus Christ. To live by grace is to base my entire relationship with God, including my acceptance and standing with Him, on my union with Christ. It is to recognize that in myself I bring nothing of worth to my relationship with God, because even my righteous acts are like filthy rags in His sight (Isaiah 64:6). Even my best works are stained with mixed motives and imperfect performance. I never truly love God with *all* my heart, and I never truly love my neighbor with the degree or consistency with which I love myself.

Yet God requires perfection. Jesus said, "Be perfect, there-fore, as your heavenly Father is perfect" (Matthew 5:48). When we take Jesus' words seriously, we are forced to say with the psalmist, "Your commandment is exceedingly broad" (Psalm 119:96, NASB).

What is the answer to our dilemma? All Christians recog-nize that we are justified — that is, declared righteous — solely on the basis of the righteousness of Christ imputed to us by God through faith (see Romans 3:21-25). But few of us fully recognize that we are also sanctified through faith in Christ.

Sanctification, or holiness (the two words are virtually interchangeable), is essentially conformity to the moral charac-ter of God. We normally think of sanctification as progressive, as an inner change of our character whereby we are conformed more and more to the likeness of Christ. That is certainly a major part of sanctification, but that is not all of it.

Scripture speaks of both a holiness we already possess in Christ before God and a holiness in which we are to grow more and more. The first is the result of the work of Christ *for* us; the second is the result of the work of the Holy Spirit *in* us. The first is perfect and complete and is ours the moment we trust Christ; the second is progressive and incomplete as long as we are in this life.

The objective holiness we have in Christ and the subjective holiness produced by the Holy Spirit are both gifts of God's grace and are both appropriated by faith. However, the perfect holiness we have in Christ is the answer to our dilemma of how we can appear daily before a perfectly holy God, when even our best deeds are stained and polluted. Our lack of understanding of the distinction between the holiness we *do* have in Christ and the holiness we *want* to find in ourselves caused Mr. Pink to say that we mistakenly hope to find in ourselves something that can be found in Christ alone.

Notes and Observations

135

## CHRIST OUR HOLINESS

The apostle Paul wrote, "It is because of him [God] that you are in Christ Jesus, who has become for us wisdom from God — that is, our righteousness, holiness and redemption" (1 Corinthians 1:30). In other words, it is God Himself who chose us to be in Christ.

But the truth I want to call attention to in the passage is that Christ Jesus has become our righteousness, holiness, and redemption. That Christ is our righteousness is an accepted and well-understood truth and the basis for our justification. But Christ is also our *holiness*. This fact is not as well understood. All Christians look to Christ alone for their justification, but not nearly as many also look to Him for their perfect holiness before God. The blessed truth, though, is that all believers are sanctified in Christ, even as we are justified in Christ.

In ourselves, apart from Christ, we are both guilty and filthy. We are guilty of breaking God's law, and we are filthy in God's sight because of the vile, polluting effect of sin. We need both forgiveness from our guilt and cleansing from our filth. Through justification we are forgiven and are declared righteous in the courtroom of God's justice. Through the perfect holiness we have in Christ, our moral filth is removed, and we become fit to enter into the very presence of an infinitely holy God and enjoy fellowship with Him.

Hebrews 10:10,14 help us see this objective aspect of sanctification — the holiness we have in Christ alone. Verse 10 says, "And by that will [of God], we have been made holy through the sacrifice of the body of Jesus Christ once for all." Note that *we have been made* holy. This speaks of a completed work. The emphasis here is on the holiness we have in Christ through His once-for-all sacrifice.

Verse 14, on the other hand, says, "By one sacrifice he [Christ] has made perfect forever those who are being made holy." This verse mentions *being made holy* — the work of the Holy Spirit in progressive sanctification. But this verse also refers to our completed, objective sanctification in Christ when it speaks of those He *has made perfect forever*. So, in one aspect of sanctification you are already holy because Christ's holiness is imputed to you. You have been made perfect forever. In another aspect, you are being made holy day by day through the work of the Holy Spirit imparting Christ's life to you.

Holiness should be an objective for your daily life. But to live by grace, you must never, never look to the work of the Holy Spirit in you as the basis for your relationship with God. You must always look outside of yourself to Christ. You will never be holy enough through your own efforts to come before God. You are holy only through Christ.

Two parallel passages in Paul's letters to the Ephesians and Colossians should encourage all of us:

> For he chose us in him before the creation of the world
> to be holy and blameless in his sight. (Ephesians 1:4)

> But now he has reconciled you by Christ's physical body
> through death to present you holy in his sight, without
> blemish and free from accusation. (Colossians 1:22)

The common teaching in both verses is that we are holy and blameless in God's sight. It seems like a paradox to state that we are holy in God's sight. How can we who are not only guilty but morally filthy possibly be holy in the sight of One whose gaze penetrates our very hearts, who knows our every motive and thought as well as our words and actions? The answer is that because of our union with Christ, God sees *His* holiness as *our* holiness. Arthur Pink said, "In the person of Christ God beholds a holiness which abides His closest scrutiny, yea, which rejoices and satisfies His heart; and whatever Christ is before God, He is for His people."[5]

Many Christians grew up in homes where parental acceptance was based, to a large degree, on academic, athletic, musical, or perhaps some other standard of achievement. Often, in that kind of performance environment, they never quite felt as if they measured up to expectations, regardless of how successful they were. Then they transfer that sense of inadequacy to their relationship with God. They continually wonder, *Is God pleased with me? Is He smiling on me with Fatherly favor?*

The answer to that question is an unqualified *yes*. God is smiling on you with Fatherly favor. He is pleased with you because He sees you as holy and without blemish in Christ. Do you want to talk about performance? Then consider that Jesus could say matter-of-factly and without any pretentiousness, "I *always* do what pleases him [the Father]" (John 8:29, emphasis added). When our Father looks at us, He does not see our miserable performance. Instead, He sees the perfect performance of Jesus. And because of the perfect holiness of Jesus, He sees us as holy and without blemish.

I like the translation of Ephesians 1:6 in the King James Version: "To the praise of the glory of his grace, wherein he hath made us *accepted in the beloved*" (emphasis added). Or to be more direct, God has made us acceptable to Himself through our union with Christ. You will never be accepted in yourself. You can never, to use a figure of speech, "scrub yourself clean."

I teach a lot at various conferences and retreats. I always seek the Lord's enabling and anointing on my messages, and I want my motive to be *strictly* to glorify God and build up His people. But I know it never is, because deep down inside, I also want to succeed as a teacher. As hard as I try to dismiss that base motive, I know full well I never will completely. I can never "scrub clean" that motive.

That is only one of many illustrations I could give from my own life to show that we never reach the point where we can look inside ourselves to find the holiness we need to stand before a holy God. But God in His grace has provided a perfect holiness

in the person of His Son. Through our union with Him we have
been made holy.

## EXPERIENTIAL SANCTIFICATION

God's ultimate goal for us, however, is that we be truly conformed to the likeness of His Son in our person as well as in our
standing. This goal is expressed in Romans 8:29: "For those
God foreknew he also predestined to be conformed to the likeness of his Son, that he might be the firstborn among many
brothers."

All through the New Testament we see this ultimate end
in view as the writers speak of salvation. For example, Paul said
that Jesus "gave himself for us to redeem us from all wickedness
and to purify for himself a people that are his very own, eager
to do what is good" (Titus 2:14). Jesus did not die just to save
us from the penalty of sin, nor even just to make us holy in our
standing before God. He died to purify for Himself a people
eager to obey Him, a people eager to be transformed into His
likeness.

So holiness or sanctification is more than just our standing
before God in Christ. It is an actual conformity within us to the
likeness of Christ begun at the time of our salvation and completed when we are made perfect in His presence. This process
of gradually conforming us to the likeness of Christ begins at
the very moment of our salvation when the Holy Spirit comes to
dwell within us and to actually give us a new life in Christ. We
call this gradual process progressive sanctification, or growing
in holiness, because it truly is a growth process.

The holiness we have in Christ is purely objective, outside
of ourselves. It is the perfect holiness of Christ imputed to us
because of our union with Him, and it affects our standing
before God. God is pleased with us because He is pleased with
Christ. Progressive sanctification is subjective or experiential
and is the work of the Holy Spirit within us imparting to us the

life and power of Christ, enabling us to respond in obedience to Him. Both aspects of sanctification, however, are gifts of God's grace. We do not deserve our holy standing before God, and we do not deserve the Spirit's sanctifying work in our lives. Both come to us by His grace because of the merit of Jesus Christ.

Progressive sanctification begins in us with an instantaneous act of God at the time of our salvation. God always gives justification and this initial imparting of sanctification at the same time. The author of Hebrews described this truth in this way:

> "This is the covenant I will make with them
> after that time, says the Lord.
> I will put my laws in their hearts,
> and I will write them on their minds."

Then he adds,

> "Their sins and lawless acts
> I will remember no more."
> (Hebrews 10:16-17)

God promises to put His laws in our hearts and write them on our minds. That's sanctification in principle or, as I like to express it, sanctification begun. Then He promises to remember our sins no more. That's justification. Note that sanctification and justification are both gifts from God and expressions of His grace. Though they are each distinct aspects of salvation, they can never be separated. God never grants justification without also giving sanctification at the same time.

I think of justification and sanctification as being like the jacket and pants of a suit. They always come together. A friend once wanted to give me a suit. He took me to a clothing store, and I walked out with a jacket and matching pants — a complete suit. Neither the jacket nor the pants alone would have been sufficient. I needed both to have the suit that my friend wanted to give me.

Sometimes we think of salvation as more like a sports coat and a pair of slacks. We think God gives us the sports coat of justification by His grace, but we must "buy" the slacks of sanctification by our own efforts. But salvation is like a suit. It always comes with the jacket of justification and the pants of sanctification. God never gives one without the other because both are necessary to have the complete suit of salvation.

Sanctification in us begins as an instantaneous act of the Holy Spirit and is carried forward by His continued action in our lives. This instantaneous act is described in a number of ways in Scripture. It is called the "renewal by the Holy Spirit" (Titus 3:5), making us alive with Christ when we were dead in transgressions and sins (see Ephesians 2:1-5). It results in the new creation Paul referred to in 2 Corinthians 5:17: "Therefore, if anyone is in Christ, he is a new creation; the old has gone, the new has come!"

One of the best descriptions of this initial act of God in sanctification is found in Ezekiel 36:26-27 where God makes this gracious promise: "I will give you a new heart and put a new spirit in you; I will remove from you your heart of stone and give you a heart of flesh. And I will put my Spirit in you and move you to follow my decrees and be careful to keep my laws."

Note the changes God brings about in our inner being when He saves us. He gives us a *new* heart and puts a *new* spirit within us — a spirit that loves righteousness and hates sin. He puts His own Spirit within us and *moves* us to follow His decrees and keep His law; that is, God gives us a growing desire to obey Him. We no longer have an aversion to the commands of God, even though we may not always obey them. Instead of being irksome to us, they have now become agreeable to us.

David said in Psalm 40:8, "I desire to do your will, O my God." Why did David have this desire? It was because, as the remainder of the verse says, "Your law is within my heart." David found a law written in his own heart corresponding to the law written in God's Word. There was an agreeableness between the spiritual nature within him and the objective law of God external to him.

It is that way with a person who is a new creation in Christ. There is a basic though imperfect correspondence between the law written in a believer's heart and the law written in Scripture. This does not mean we can discard the law written in Scripture, because the law written in the heart is not self-directing — that is, it does not tell us what to do. It only agrees with and responds to the law written in Scripture.

This instantaneous act of God by which He begins sanctification in us is just as much a gift of God's grace as is justification. God does not wait until we "surrender all," make a second commitment to Christ's lordship, or anything like that. God gives sanctification by His grace.

Immediately after Paul's declaration in 2 Corinthians 5:17, "If anyone is in Christ, he is a new creation," he said, "All this is from God" (verse 18). God has made us new creatures. God has given us the gift of sanctification, and He gives it by the same grace and at the same time as He gives us justification.

One reason we do not appreciate the grace of God more is that we either do not understand or do not appreciate the radical dimension of this instantaneous act of sanctification, which God gives at salvation. Perhaps because many of us had a moral lifestyle before conversion, we find it difficult to accept Paul's description of our attitude toward God: "The sinful mind is hostile to God. It does not submit to God's law, nor can it do so. Those controlled by the sinful nature cannot please God" (Romans 8:7-8). As we think back to our pre-conversion days, we don't think of our attitude as being hostile to God's law.

But human morality and submission to God's law are entirely different in principle, though they may appear to be similar in outward appearance. Human morality arises out of culture and family training and is based on what is proper and expected in the society we live in. It has nothing to do with God except to the extent that godly people have influenced that society. Submission to God's law arises out of a love for God and a grateful response to His grace and is based on a delight in His law as revealed in Scripture. When the societal standard of morality varies from the law of God written in Scripture, we then see the true nature of human morality. We discover that it is just as hostile to the law of God as is the attitude of the most hardened sinner.

Sanctification begun in our hearts by the Holy Spirit changes our attitude. Instead of being hostile to God's law, we begin to delight in it (see Romans 7:22). We find that "his commands are not burdensome" (1 John 5:3), but rather are "holy, righteous and good" (Romans 7:12). This radical and dramatic change in our attitude toward God's commands is a gift of His grace, brought about solely by the mighty working of His Holy Spirit within us. We play no more part in this initial act of sanctification than we do in our justification. As Paul said, "All this is from God."

## WE DIED TO THE LAW

One reason we have this new attitude toward sin and God's law is that we "died" to the law. Such a statement may sound strange after my insistence in chapter 7 on the importance of God's law as a moral rule in the believer's life. But though the law reveals God's moral will for us, the law in itself has no power to enable us to obey it.

Because the law commands obedience without providing any enabling power, it is in this sense a source of bondage. And because we were hostile to God's law prior to our salvation (see Romans 8:7), it was also a source of provocation to us. Instead of being a means of obedience to God, the law actually provoked us and incited us to sin (see 7:7-8).

But Paul said we died to the law. Here is how he put it:

So, my brothers, you also died to the law through the body of Christ, that you might belong to another, to him who was raised from the dead, in order that we

143

might bear fruit to God. For when we were controlled by the sinful nature, the sinful passions aroused by the law were at work in our bodies, so that we bore fruit for death. But now, by dying to what once bound us, we have been released from the law so that we serve in the new way of the Spirit, and not in the old way of the written code. (Romans 7:4-6)

In verse 4, Paul said we died to the law. In what sense did we die to it? Three passages of Scripture will help us understand what he meant:

Therefore no one will be declared righteous in his sight by observing the law; rather, through the law we become conscious of sin. (Romans 3:20)

For sin shall not be your master, because you are not under law, but under grace. (Romans 6:14)

All who rely on observing the law are under a curse, for it is written: "Cursed is everyone who does not continue to do everything written in the Book of the Law." (Galatians 3:10)

From these passages we understand that we died to the observance of the law as *a requirement for attaining righteousness before God*. We died to the *curse and condemnation* that resulted from our inability to perfectly keep the law. Then we see in Romans 6:14 that being under the law is the opposite of being under grace. Because of our sin against the law, being under law implies the wrath of God, whereas grace implies forgiveness and favor. Law implies a broken relationship with God, whereas grace implies a restored relationship with Him. So when Paul said we died to the law, he meant we died to that entire state of condemnation, curse, and alienation from God.

The most important thing for us to see in our death to the law, however, is the purpose of our death. We died to the law in order that we might live in the realm of grace. We died to the law that we might bear fruit to God. And, according to Romans 7:6, we died that we might "serve [God] in the new way of the Spirit, and not in the old way of the written code [the law]."

The new way of the Spirit is not a new and less rigorous ethic than the old way of the written code. The difference does not lie in the content of the moral will of God. Since that is a reflection of the holy character of God, it cannot change. Rather, the difference lies in the reason to obey and in the ability with which to obey.

Verse 6 gets right to the heart of what it means to live by grace. For serving in the new way of the Spirit is the same as living by grace instead of by works. Although it is clearly God's design that we serve in the new way of the Spirit, far too many Christians still serve in the old way of the law.

Consider the following contrasts between the old way of the law and the new way of the Spirit:

| Old Way of Law | New Way of Spirit |
| --- | --- |
| *External Code* | *Internal Desire* |
| 1. The moral precepts of God are only an external code of conduct. The law commands obedience but provides no inclination or desire to obey. | 1. The moral precepts of God are written on our hearts as well as being an external code. The Spirit inclines our hearts and gives us a desire to obey. |
| *Commanding* | *Enabling* |
| 2. The law commands but gives no enabling power for obedience. | 2. The Spirit enables us to obey the law's commands. |
| *Hostility* | *Delight* |
| 3. Because of our hostility to God's law before our conversion, the commands of the law actually provoked and incited us to sin. | 3. The Spirit, by removing our hostility and writing the law on our hearts, actually causes us to delight in God's law. |
| *Fear* | *Gratitude* |
| 4. The law produces a legalistic response to God. We try to obey because of a fear of punishment for | 4. The Spirit, by showing us God's grace, produces a response of love and gratitude. We obey, not out of fear or |

disobedience or in order to win favor with God.

*Working*

**5.** Under the law, we perform in order to be accepted by God. Since our performance is always imperfect, we never feel completely accepted by Him. Thus, in our Christian life, we always work from a position of weakness. We work to be accepted, but feel we never quite make it.

to earn favor, but out of gratitude for favor already given.

*Relying*

**5.** The Spirit bears witness with our spirit that we are accepted by God through the merit of Christ. By relying solely on His perfect righteousness, we feel accepted by Him. Thus, in our Christian life, we work from a position of strength, because we have been accepted through Jesus, and through Him, we have "made it."

Look back over the five contrasts I have listed, asking yourself, "Am I serving under the old way of a written code, or under the new way of the Spirit?" I'm not asking, "Are you a Christian?" I'm asking how you view God's law and God's grace. Are you seeking to build and maintain your relationship with Him on the basis of "keeping the law," that is, on the basis of your personal performance, or on the basis of the merit of Jesus Christ?

Do you view God's moral precepts as a source of bondage and condemnation for failure to obey them, or do you sense the Spirit producing within you an inclination and desire to obey out of gratitude and love? Do you try to obey by your own sheer will and determination, or do you rely on the Spirit daily for His power to enable you to obey?

Do you view God as an ogre who has set before you an impossible code of conduct you cannot keep, or do you view Him as your divine heavenly Father who has accepted you and loves you on the basis of the merit of Christ? In other words, in terms of your acceptance with God, are you willing to rely solely on the finished perfect work of Jesus, instead of your own pitifully imperfect performance?

There probably is no other passage of Scripture that suggests more starkly the contrast between living by grace and living by works than does Romans 7:6. Paul intended the contrast between serving in the new way of the Spirit and the old way of the written code to represent the contrast between the believer and the unbeliever.

All believers *have* died to the law, whether we recognize it or not. But the sad fact is, many believers do not recognize it or are unwilling to accept it because, to them, it seems too good to be true. All too often we who are believers living in the realm of grace, live out our daily lives as if we were still living under the bondage of the law. And to the extent we live that way, we are still serving in the old way of the written code and not in the new way of the Spirit.

I am convinced that the sinful nature still present within every believer tends toward a legalistic spirit as much as it tends toward sin. The sinful nature despises the righteousness that comes by faith in Jesus Christ as much as it despises the ethical righteousness that comes from obeying God's law. If we are going to serve in the newness of the Spirit, we must resist the legalistic spirit of trying to "live by the law" as vigorously and persistently as we do temptations to sin.

## GROWING IN CHRISTLIKENESS

In the last few pages, we have been focusing on the initial act of sanctification: the radical change God brings about in the heart of a person who trusts Jesus Christ as Savior. It is the passing from spiritual death to spiritual life. It is the beginning of a new creation in Christ and the writing of God's law in our hearts. It means a new relationship to the law of God and a new attitude toward it. And all this is from God. It is a gift of His grace just as surely as is the gift of justification.

God does not bring us into His Kingdom then leave us on our own to grow. He continues to work in our lives to conform us more and more to the likeness of His Son. As Paul said, "He who began a good work in you will carry it on to completion until the day of Christ Jesus" (Philippians 1:6). This continuing work of God is called "progressive sanctification." It differs

147

from initial sanctification in two respects.

Initial sanctification occurs instantly at the moment of salvation when we are delivered from the kingdom of darkness and brought into the kingdom of Christ (see Colossians 1:13). Progressive sanctification continues over time until we go to be with the Lord. Initial sanctification is entirely the work of God the Holy Spirit who imparts to us the very life of Christ. Progressive sanctification is also the work of the Holy Spirit, but it involves a response on our part so that we as believers are actively involved in the process.

The progressive nature of sanctification is implied throughout the New Testament epistles in all those instances where we are exhorted to grow, to change, to put off the deeds of the old man and put on Godlike character, and so on. It is also clearly implied in Paul's own testimony that he had not yet been made perfect and his statement that he had *learned* to be content in all circumstances (see Philippians 3:12-14; 4:11).

Romans 12:2 and 2 Corinthians 3:18 explicitly teach the progressive nature of sanctification:

> Do not conform any longer to the pattern of this world, but be transformed by the renewing of your mind. Then you will be able to test and approve what God's will is — his good, pleasing and perfect will. (Romans 12:2)

> And we, who with unveiled faces all reflect the Lord's glory, are being transformed into his likeness with ever-increasing glory, which comes from the Lord, who is the Spirit. (2 Corinthians 3:18)

The common word in both passages is *transformed*. In both instances the verb *transformed* is in the present tense, indicating that the action is continuous. William Hendriksen translated the phrase *be transformed* in Romans 12:2 as "continue to let yourselves be transformed."[6] And John Murray commented,

The term [transformed] used here implies that
we are to be constantly in the process of being
metamorphosed by renewal of that which is the seat of
thought and understanding. . . . Sanctification is a process of revolutionary change in that which is the centre
of consciousness. . . . It is the thought of progression
and strikes at the stagnation, complacency, pride of
achievement so often characterizing Christians.[7]

As to the nature of this process, 2 Corinthians 3:18 indicates
it is the work of the "Lord, who is the Spirit," while Romans
12:2 indicates it is through the renewing of our minds. In both
passages, however, the verb *transformed* is passive, indicating it is
a work done in us rather than by us. (Plenty of Scripture passages stress our part in the work of progressive sanctification.
And I have examined our responsibility in detail in an earlier
book, *The Pursuit of Holiness*.[8]) Since in this book we are studying
God's grace, I want to focus primarily on the work of God in
our sanctification. And the passive voice of the verb *be* (or being)
*transformed* indicates that the transforming work of progressive
sanctification is the work of God's Spirit. He is the One who
changes us more and more into the likeness of Jesus Christ.

This transformation is much more than merely a change
of outward conduct. It is a renovation of our inner being, or as
someone has said, it is a transformation of the essential man. It
means our motives as well as our motivations are being constantly
changed, so that we can say with the psalmist, "Oh, how I love
your law! I meditate on it all day long," and "I rejoice in following
your statutes as one rejoices in great riches" (Psalm 119:97,14).

However, although the verb *be transformed* is in the passive
voice, it is in the imperative mood; that is, it is a command to
*do* something. This indicates that we as believers are not passive
in this transforming process. We are not like blocks of marble
being transformed into a beautiful sculpture by a master
sculptor. God has given us a mind and heart with which to

Notes and Observations

respond to and cooperate with the Spirit as He does His work in us. That thought leads naturally to the Scripture passage that is considered to be the classic statement of the working together of the believer with the Holy Spirit who is at work within him. The passage is Philippians 2:12-13:

> Therefore, my dear friends, as you have always obeyed — not only in my presence, but now much more in my absence — continue to work out your salvation with fear and trembling, for it is God who works in you to will and to act according to his good purpose.

In verse 12 Paul urged the Philippian believers to apply themselves diligently to working out their salvation. He urged them to display the evidences of salvation in their daily lives through their obedience to God's commands and through putting on the godly character traits that Paul elsewhere called the fruit of the Spirit. And, according to William Hendriksen, the tense of the verb *continue to work out* indicates "continuous, sustained, strenuous effort."[9] Here again we see that sanctification is a process, and a process in which we, as believers, are very actively involved.

But Paul's strong exhortation to the Philippians is based on the confidence that God's Spirit is working in them. He is working in them to enlighten their understanding of His will, to stimulate in their emotions a desire to do His will, and to turn their wills so they actually obey. Most of all, He gives them the enabling power so that they are *able* to do His will.

So progressive sanctification very much involves our activity. But it is an activity that must be carried out in dependence on the Holy Spirit. It is not a partnership with the Spirit in the sense that we each — the believer and the Holy Spirit — do our respective tasks. Rather, we work as He enables us to work. His work lies behind all our work and makes our work possible.

The Holy Spirit can and does work within us apart from

any conscious response on our part. We have seen this in the initial act of sanctification when He creates within us a new heart and gives us an entirely new disposition toward God and His will. He is not dependent on us to do His work.

But we are dependent on Him to do our work; we cannot do anything apart from Him. In the process of sanctification there are certain things only the Holy Spirit can do, and there are certain things He has given us to do. For example, only He can create in our hearts the *desire* to obey God, but He does not obey for us. We must do that, but we can do so only as He gives us the enabling power to obey.

So we must depend on the Holy Spirit to do within us what only He can do. And we must depend on Him just as much to enable us to do what He has given us to do. So whether it is His work or our work, in either case, we are dependent on Him.

We are not just dependent on Him; we are *desperately* dependent on Him. Because we so often equate Christlike character with ordinary morality, we fail to realize how impossible it is for us to attain any degree of conformity to Christ by ourselves. But if we take seriously the long lists of Christlike character traits we are to put on, we see how impossible it is to grow in Christlikeness apart from the sanctifying influence and power of the Spirit in our lives.

Consider, for example, the lists of Christlike character traits found in Galatians 5:22-23 and Colossians 3:12-15 (I have eliminated five duplications in the two lists):

| Galatians 5:22-23 | Colossians 3:12-15 |
|---|---|
| • Love | • Compassion |
| • Joy | • Kindness |
| • Peace | • Humility |
| • Patience | • Gentleness |
| • Goodness | • Forbearance |
| • Faithfulness | • Forgiveness |
| • Self-control | • Thankfulness |

Those are fourteen positive character traits we are to put on (and there are others in Scripture), in addition to the many negative traits — pride, envy, jealousy, lust, covetousness, selfish ambition — we are to put off. Surely we must say with Paul, "And who is equal to such a task?" (2 Corinthians 2:16).

We've all been to the circus or the carnival or the county fair and watched with amazement the juggler tossing and catching his four or five Indian clubs. Think what it would be like to juggle fourteen! Yet that is essentially what we are called to do when we are told to put on fourteen — or more — different character traits, as well as trying to put away some bad ones.

Only the Holy Spirit is equal to such a task. Only the Holy Spirit can orchestrate such a diverse and well-rounded development of Christian character. And yet we are told to clothe ourselves with these Christlike qualities. We are to do it; we are responsible. But in Galatians 5:22, Paul called the qualities the "fruit of the Spirit" — the result of the Spirit's work in our lives. Putting together those two thoughts leads to the conclusion that we are both *responsible* and *dependent*. We are responsible to clothe ourselves with Christlike character, but we are dependent on God's Spirit to produce within us His "fruit." We cannot make one inch of progress in sanctification apart from the powerful working of the Spirit in us. And He does this, not because we have earned it with our commitment and discipline, but because of His grace.

God has blessed us with every spiritual blessing — including the working of the Spirit in our lives — in Christ Jesus, that is, by His grace through the infinite merit of Christ. As we pray for the sanctifying influence and power of the Spirit in our lives, we can do so in confidence that God will answer our prayers because His answers are not dependent on us and our holiness, but on the merit of His Son.

We have seen, then, in this chapter a threefold view of sanctification or holiness. We have seen that our holiness is first of all an objective, perfect holiness, which is ours by virtue of our union with Him who is perfectly holy. Then we have seen that there is an initial act of sanctification in which a person's basic disposition toward God and His law is changed. This change is experienced by the believer, but is not dependent on the believer. It is solely a work of the Holy Spirit. Finally, we have seen that this initial act of sanctification is followed up by the continuous action of the Holy Spirit throughout our lives as He works in us "to will and to act according to his good purpose" (Philippians 2:13).

In every one of these views of sanctification we see the grace of God. God in His grace sees us as perfectly holy in Christ. God in His grace sends His Holy Spirit to create a new heart within us and to write His law on our hearts, thus changing our basic disposition. And God in His grace continues to work in us through His Spirit to transform us more and more into the likeness of His Son.

# The Proof of Love

## (Chapters 7 and 8)

## STUDY QUESTIONS

### CENTRAL IDEA

As followers of Jesus Christ we are set free to obey the moral laws of God out of love for Him. His ultimate purpose for us is that, through the enabling influence of the Holy Spirit, we will become more like Jesus.

### WARM-UP

- What did you observe in your life this week as you thought more about the motives behind your actions?
- What difference has observing your motives made to your thoughts or your actions?

### EXPLORING GRACE

1. Read John 14:15,21,23.

   a. Why do you think obedience is such an important way to express our love to God?

   b. What do you suppose often makes obedience so difficult?

c.  Share a time when you showed the Lord your love through an act of obedience.

2.  a.  Ephesians 5:17 tells us to "understand what the Lord's will is." God's will is revealed to us in the specific directions given in the ethical commands of Scripture. How does our attitude toward these commands change when we understand His grace and the purpose of the commands?

b.  What attitudes toward God's commands do the following writers express?

•  Psalm 19:7-11

•  Psalm 119:97

•  Romans 7:12

•  1 John 5:2-3

3.  Galatians 5:6 gives a good summary of what God wants from us: "The only thing that counts is faith expressing itself through love." In what ways is your faith expressing itself through love at present in your particular circumstances?

4.  a.  What is the ultimate goal of our obedience?

    •   Romans 8:29

    •   2 Corinthians 3:18

    •   Philippians 1:9-11

    b.  What difference does knowing this goal make to you?

5.  Read Romans 13:8-10. Describe the relationship between the laws given to Moses and the two greatest commandments that Jesus states in Matthew 22:37-40.

6. The laws of Moses that deal with moral issues are still an important standard because they are the natural outcome of love. Explain what you believe the right decision would be in each of the following situations. How do the Ten Commandments influence your decision, and how is this actually the decision of love?

   a. A man meets a woman he finds very attractive. She has the potential to be a close friend in a way his wife has not been. What should he do and not do in relating to this woman? What should he do in his relationship with his wife?

   b. A woman finds that she is pregnant with her fourth child. Her husband has just informed her that he is having an affair and will file for divorce. She has no way to support herself. Should she consider having an abortion? Why, or why not?

   c. A family is struggling to survive. They never have enough to eat and other necessities are scarce. The husband has an opportunity to make a lot of money on a business deal if he tells some lies in the process. What should he do?

7. Many excellent passages in the Bible spell out guidelines for living. The Holy Spirit uses these passages to show us what He wants to change in our lives. We are active participants in this process of sanctification. In dependence upon His help, we must respond in obedience. We must ask Him to change our inward disposition so that we want to obey, and then we must ask Him for the power to obey.

   Read all of Colossians 3 on your own. Ask God to show you what He wants to do in your life this week. Write down your thoughts. If you feel comfortable, share your thoughts with the group. Accountability to others is a great help when it comes to making difficult changes.

## CLOSING PRAYER

Reread Psalm 19:7-11 as a part of your prayer time. Express your gratitude to the Lord for His perfect commands. Ask Him for the grace to respond to His work in your life more fully this week.

## GOING DEEPER (Extra questions for further study)

1.  Read 1 Thessalonians 4:3. Do you think that growing in our faith is optional?

2.  Read Ephesians 4:22-24 and Philippians 2:12-13. Put into your own words the relationship between God's work in our lives and our own effort in the process of sanctification.

3.  Although we could never earn our salvation or any blessings we now enjoy as Christians, God cares about how we choose to live our lives. According to the following verses, how does God feel about the things we do?

    •   Ephesians 4:30

    •   Ephesians 5:8-10

- 1 Timothy 2:1-3

- 1 Timothy 5:4

## *Pondering Grace (For personal reflection)*

*Moral law is more than a test; it is for man's own good. Every law that God has given has been for man's benefit. If man breaks it, he is not only rebelling against God; he is hurting himself.*

Billy Graham

*The beginning and the end of the law is kindness.*

Jewish proverb

*If Jesus gave us a command He could not enable us to fulfill, He would be a liar; and if we make our inability a barrier to obedience, it means we are telling God there is something He has not taken into account. Every element of self-reliance must be slain by the power of God. Complete weakness and dependence will always be the occasion for the Spirit of God to manifest His power.*

Oswald Chambers, *My Utmost for His Highest*

*The great mistake made by most of the Lord's people is in hoping to discover in themselves that which is to be found in Christ alone.*

Arthur W. Pink, *The Doctrine of Sanctification*

*Joy is love exalted; peace is love in repose; long-suffering is love enduring; gentleness is love in society; goodness is love in action; faith is love on the battlefield; meekness is love in school; and temperance is love in training.*

Dwight L. Moody

# Called to Be Free

Read the following portion of *Transforming Grace*. In the margins, record observations, illustrations, or questions that come to mind as you read. Then answer the study questions that follow the reading.

---

### Chapter Nine: Called to Be Free

*It is for freedom that Christ has set us free. Stand firm, then, and do not let yourselves be burdened again by a yoke of slavery. . . . You, my brothers, were called to be free. But do not use your freedom to indulge the sinful nature; rather, serve one another in love.*
GALATIANS 5:1,13

Notes and Observations

I n the year 1215, English barons forced King John to sign a historic document, the Magna Carta, giving his assent to a charter of civil liberties for the English people. He did not do this freely and voluntarily, but actually under duress from the English nobles who had confronted him about his totalitarian and unjust rule.

The apostle Paul's letter to the Galatians has been called the great charter of religious freedom, the Christian Declaration of Independence, and the Magna Carta of the church. The freedom set forth in Galatians is not freedom from God, but from those who insist on some form of legalism in the life of a believer.

The legalism the Galatian believers were in danger of succumbing to was, as we saw in session 5 (chapter 7), the teaching that believers must be circumcised and keep the law of Moses in order to be saved. Paul wrote the letter to the Galatians to refute that heresy. Yes, it was heresy, and Paul felt so strongly about it he called down a divine curse on those who were teaching it:

161

"But even if we or an angel from heaven should preach a gospel other than the one we preached to you, let him be eternally condemned!" (1:8).

Paul took a strong stand for the cause of freedom against this form of legalism when he wrote, "It is for freedom that Christ has set us free. Stand firm, then, and do not let yourselves be burdened again by a yoke of slavery" (5:1). And he was calling them from this form of legalism when he said, "You, my brothers, were called to be free" (5:13).

We've gotten beyond the Galatian brand of legalism today. We haven't resurrected circumcision as a requirement for salvation, and we're clear that salvation is by grace through faith in Christ apart from keeping the law. Instead, we have developed another brand of legalism, a brand that is concerned, not with salvation, but with how we live the Christian life. I call this "evangelical legalism" (a contradiction in terms, I realize — nevertheless the phrase fits the problem). Here is how I describe our form of legalism.

Legalism is, first of all, anything we do or don't do in order to *earn* favor with God. It is concerned with rewards to be gained or penalties to be avoided. This is a legalism we force on ourselves.

Second, legalism insists on conformity to *manmade* religious rules and requirements, which are often unspoken but are nevertheless very real. To use a more common expression, it requires conformity to the "dos and don'ts" of our particular Christian circle. We force this legalism on others or allow others to force it on us. It is conformity to how other people think we should live instead of how the Bible tells us to live. More often than not, these rules have no valid biblical basis. Like the Pharisees of Jesus' time, we have tried to "help" God by adding our manmade rules to His commands. Jesus' charge against the Pharisees, recorded in Mark 7:6-8, is still valid today:

"These people honor me with their lips,
    but their hearts are far from me.
They worship me in vain;
    their teachings are but rules taught by men."

You have let go of the commands of God and are holding on to the traditions of men.

This may seem like a rather severe charge to bring against
contemporary Christianity, but it *is* true today. There are far too
many instances within Christendom where our traditions and
rules are, in practice, more important than God's commands.

These two descriptions of legalism are closely related. More
often than not, we try to earn favor with God in the area of
manmade rules, or we feel guilty because we have failed in
keeping them. We do or don't do a particular thing because
someone or some group or our cultural background tells us we
ought or ought not to do it. And these "oughts" or "ought nots"
are usually communicated by people in such a way that the favor
or frown of God is tied to our compliance.

I have been addressing the first type of legalism all through
this book up to now. I hope we at least *understand* that we can do
nothing to earn favor with God, that His favor is given solely by
His grace through Christ. I realize our practice may lag behind
our understanding, but we cannot begin to practice the truth
until we understand it.

In this chapter, I want to address the second type of legalism: the observance of manmade rules. Paul's call to stand firm
in our freedom in Christ and not let ourselves be burdened by
a yoke of slavery is just as valid today with our rules as it was in
the Galatians' day with the Mosaic law.

I noted in this chapter's opening paragraph that King John
was forced to sign the Magna Carta. But God *gave* us our spiritual Magna Carta. Through Paul, He called us to be free: "You,
my brothers, were called to be free." In fact, God doesn't just

call us to freedom, He actually exhorts us to stand firm in our freedom — to resist all efforts to abridge or destroy it.

Despite God's call to be free and His earnest admonition to resist all efforts to curtail it, there is very little emphasis in Christian circles today on the importance of Christian freedom. Just the opposite seems to be true. Instead of promoting freedom, we stress our rules of conformity. Instead of preaching living by grace, we preach living by performance. Instead of encouraging new believers to be conformed to Christ, we subtly insist that they be conformed to our particular style of Christian culture. We don't intend to do this and would earnestly deny we are. Yet that's the "bottom line" effect of most of our emphases in Christian circles today.

For example, many people would react negatively to my quoting only part of Galatians 5:12, "You, my brothers, were called to be free." Despite the fact that this statement is a complete sentence, they would say, "But that's not all of the verse. Go on to quote the remainder: 'But do not use your freedom to indulge the sinful nature; rather, serve one another in love.'" (We seem to forget that verse divisions were not inspired.)

The person who reacts that way has made my point. We are much more concerned about someone abusing his freedom than we are about his guarding it. We are more afraid of indulging the sinful nature than we are of falling into legalism. Yet legalism does indulge the sinful nature because it fosters self-righteousness and religious pride. It also diverts us from the real issues of the Christian life by focusing on external and sometimes trivial rules.

## FENCES

The legalism of manmade rules goes back at least to New Testament times, if not before, but it is still with us today. In his book *The Pharisees' Guide to Total Holiness*, William L. Coleman described the Pharisees' concept of moral fences. He said,

The Pharisees were desperately determined to not break the laws of God. Consequently they devised a system to keep them from even coming close to angering God. They contrived a "fence" of Pharisaic rules that, if man would keep them, would guarantee a safe distance between himself and the laws of God. . . .

The "fence" or "hedge" laws accumulated into hundreds over the years and were passed around orally. Soon it became apparent that they were far from optional. These laws became every inch as important as the scriptural laws and in some instances far more crucial.[1]

We still practice this today. We build fences to keep ourselves from committing certain sins. Soon these fences — instead of the sins they were designed to guard against — become the issue. We elevate our rules to the level of God's commandments.

When my children were barely teenagers, our family went on vacation to a different part of the country to enjoy the beach and the ocean. Since my Navy days, I have had a fascination for the ocean and its waves, so I was eager to take the family to the beach. When we got there, however, I discovered the beach was swarming with scantily clad young women. (I'm not talking about ordinary swimsuits. When I say scanty, I mean scanty.)

Now like Job, I had "made a covenant with my eyes not to look lustfully at a girl" (Job 31:1). I know I have not been as diligent as Job to stay faithful to that covenant, but at least I work at it. After about twenty minutes of continuously diverting my eyes, I said to my wife, "You and the kids stay as long as you like. I'm going to the car."

Why did I do that? Because I knew myself well enough to know that after a while my commitment to visual purity would wear thin. I knew that — given the continual temptations passing before me — in due time, I would succumb to the temptation to indulge a lustful look "just once" (which, of course, it never is). So I built a "fence" for myself that day. I left the beach.

Now suppose, because of my experience, I concluded that going to the beach would always lead to sin. I could have said to my son, "You are not to go to the beach anymore." I could have begun to look down my religious nose at others who went to the beach. I would have built a permanent fence: "Thou shalt not go to the beach." In due time that fence would have had almost the same force in my thinking as the Ten Commandments, especially as I would use it to judge or influence others.

That is the way a lot of manmade "dos and don'ts" originate. They begin as a sincere effort to deal with real sin issues. But very often we begin to focus on the fence we've built instead of the sin it was designed to guard against. We fight our battles in the wrong places; we deal with externals instead of the heart.

If I had said to my son, "You may not go to the beach," I would have failed him. He could have concluded that it was a sin to go to the beach (though he wouldn't understand why), and nothing would have been said about looking lustfully at the girls at school, or a dozen other places for that matter. Now that fence I could have built for my son (though I'm happy I didn't) may sound ridiculous to you, but I have seen almost the same fence built with the exact same neglect of the real issue.

Incidentally, the next time my wife and I went to the beach it was in another part of the country. We stayed almost a week and had a thoroughly enjoyable time. So please don't draw the conclusion: "Thou shalt not go to the beach."

When I was growing up, I was not allowed to go to the local pool halls. As I look back, I'm sure my parents did not want me to come under the influence of the unsavory characters who frequented those halls. So they built a fence to keep that from happening: "Don't go into those pool halls." The problem was I didn't understand why, so I grew up thinking it was a sin to play pool (don't laugh, I really did). Imagine my consternation when I moved to a Christian conference center and saw a beautiful antique pool table in the recreation room and godly men playing pool.

Should we scrap our fences, then? Not necessarily. Often they are helpful; sometimes they are necessary. Some years ago I realized I was craving ice cream to the point where I was not exercising responsible self-control. I had some every night at dinner and another dish at bedtime. So I built a fence. I asked my wife to no longer keep a regular supply of ice cream on hand. Only after my craving had been dealt with did we begin to have ice cream occasionally.

I think my parents' pool hall fence was appropriate. But there is a lesson in my experience for all parents: Don't focus on the fence. If you erect a fence for your children — for example, in regard to certain movies or television programs — be sure to focus on the real issues, not the fence. Take time to explain and re-explain the reason for the fence.

If you decide, as my parents did, that you don't want your children going to the local pool hall, explain why. Distinguish between playing the game itself — which has neither negative nor positive moral value — and the atmosphere you are trying to protect them from.

For all of us, it may be good to have some fences, but we have to work at keeping them as just that — fences, helpful to us but not necessarily applicable to others. We also have to work at guarding our freedom from other people's fences.

Some of the fences in our respective Christian circles have been around a long time. No one quite knows their origin, but by now they are "embedded in concrete." Although it may cause conflict if you violate one, you must guard your freedom. To paraphrase Paul, "Stand firm in your freedom, and don't let anyone bring you into bondage with their fences."

I'm not suggesting you jump over fences just to thumb your nose at the people who hold to them so dearly. We are to "make every effort to do what leads to peace and to mutual edification" (Romans 14:19). Use discretion in embracing or rejecting a particular fence. But don't let others coerce you with manmade rules. And ask God to help you see if you are subtly coercing or judging others with your own fences.

## DIFFERING OPINIONS

A second area of legalism arises from believers holding differing opinions about certain practices. If "fences" have been around since the days of the Pharisees, the issue of differing opinions has been around at least since the days of the apostle Paul. He devoted an entire chapter of the book of Romans to this brand of legalism. In Romans 14:1, Paul called this problem "disputable matters" or, as I have called it, differing opinions.

The crux of the problem is stated well by Paul in verse 5: "One man considers one day more sacred than another; another man considers every day alike. Each one should be fully convinced in his own mind." People simply have different opinions about various issues. One person sees no problem in a certain practice; another person considers that practice to be sinful.

Most often these differing opinions arise from our family, or geographical, or perhaps, church cultures. I know that a certain practice that was offensive to the church I grew up in was not even an issue in a church I attended in California, whereas the California Christians would have been scandalized by one prominent practice back in Texas. Yet neither practice is addressed in the Bible.

Where do these cultural convictions come from? They develop in various ways. Some have their origin in a "fence" someone erected a long time ago, and no one knows what the original problem was. Others originated in the individual experience of some Christian who began to lay his personal convictions on others.

Charles Swindoll told of a missionary family who literally were forced off the mission field over peanut butter.[2] They were sent to a location where peanut butter was not available, so they asked friends back in the States to occasionally send them some.

The problem was that the other missionaries considered it a mark of spirituality *not* to have peanut butter. The newer missionary family considered this a matter of differing opinions, so they continued to receive and enjoy their peanut butter. But the pressure from the other missionaries to conform became so intense, the newer family finally gave up and left the mission field.

How could something like this — that probably seems petty and foolish to us — have happened? I imagine it developed something like this: A missionary family who greatly enjoyed peanut butter went to this particular mission field. Upon discovering there was no peanut butter available locally, they faced a choice of doing without it or asking friends or relatives in the States to send it to them. As they considered their options before the Lord, they came to the conclusion that doing without peanut butter was a small sacrifice to make for being on the mission field. Though, like the apostle Paul, they had a "right" to peanut butter, they chose not to use that right (see I Corinthians 9:1-12). They did it as "to the Lord" (Romans 14:6).

If my theory of this issue's origin is correct, I personally find their thinking quite acceptable, perhaps even applaudable, in that circumstance. That's Paul's whole point in Romans 14. If they decided to give up peanut butter as to the Lord, who am I to belittle or ridicule them? Paul said the man whose faith allows him to eat peanut butter must not look down on him who does not (Romans 14:3).

So what went wrong? If the original missionary family made a sincere decision to give up peanut butter as to the Lord, how did it eventually become a divisive issue among missionaries? Again, I'm speculating. It probably happened because one family elevated the particular leading of God for them to the level of a spiritual principle, which they then applied to everyone: "If God has 'led' us to give up peanut butter on the mission field, surely that is His will for everyone else."

Whether I have speculated correctly on the reasons behind

this story or not makes no difference. Even if they are not true in this particular instance, they have been true in scores of others. As Christians we can't seem to accept the clear biblical teaching in Romans 14 that God allows equally godly people to have differing opinions on certain matters. We universalize what we think is God's particular leading in our lives and apply it to everyone else.

When we think like that we are, so to speak, "putting God in a box." We are insisting that He must surely lead everyone as we believe He has led us. We refuse to allow God the freedom to deal with each of us as individuals. When we think like that, we are legalists.

We must not seek to bind the consciences of other believers with the private convictions that arise out of our personal walk with God. Even if you believe God has led you in developing those convictions, you still must not elevate them to the level of spiritual principles for everyone else to follow. The respected Puritan theologian John Owen taught that "only what God has commanded in his word should be regarded as binding; in all else there may be liberty of actions."[3] If we are going to enjoy the freedom we have in Christ, we must be alert to convictions that fall into the category of differing opinions. We must not seek to bind the consciences of others or allow them to bind ours. We must stand firm in the freedom we have in Christ.

## SPIRITUAL DISCIPLINES

Earlier I mentioned our various lists of "dos and don'ts." We've looked at some typical "don'ts": don't go to the beach, don't play pool, don't eat peanut butter. If this list seems humorous to you, and you're wondering how anyone could have such foolish notions, consider that your own list could look just as foolish to someone else. But foolish or not is not the issue. The issue is that God has not appointed any of us to be the "moral policeman" of other believers.

SESSION SIX: Called to Be Free

Notes and Observations

But what about the "dos"? By the "dos" I'm thinking particularly of activities I call spiritual disciplines: having regular private devotions, studying the Bible, memorizing Scripture, meeting with a group Bible study, or faithfully attending a weekly prayer meeting.

Let me clearly say that I'm not out to disparage these disciplines at all. They are all good and helpful, and I seek to practice many of them myself. But spiritual disciplines are provided for our good, not for our bondage. They are privileges to be used, not duties to be performed. To take off on a familiar quotation from Jesus, "Spiritual disciplines were made for man, not man for spiritual disciplines" (see Mark 2:27).

We can become just as legalistic about our "dos" as we can about the "don'ts." In fact, newer believers coming into our fellowship from totally unchristian backgrounds usually don't have many cultural "don'ts." But the spiritual disciplines are fertile ground for legalistic thinking.

They can easily become a performance measurement by which we gauge whether to expect God's blessing or not. If I've been doing pretty well, having a regular quiet time, studying my Bible, and so on, then I'm hopeful about God's blessing. But if I've not been doing so well—haven't "been faithful" as we say—then, I might as well go back to bed.

We get even more legalistic about spiritual disciplines with others. We try subtle (or maybe not so subtle) coercion by communicating ever so slightly that a person who isn't practicing the same disciplines we are isn't "committed." Or we don't allow a person into our "in" group if he or she is not doing what we do. Again we think God should lead everyone else in spiritual growth as He does us.

I do think we should actively promote spiritual disciplines. They are absolutely necessary for growth in our Christian lives. And since ours is a largely undisciplined age, many believers are losing out on the benefits of those disciplines that could help them grow to maturity in Christ. But we should promote them

171

as benefits, not as duties. Perhaps we should stop talking about being "faithful" to have a quiet time with God each day, as if we were doing something to earn a reward. It would be better to talk about the *privilege* of spending time with the God of the universe and the importance for our own sake of being consistent in that practice.

If we are involved in a one-to-one discipling relationship, we must remember Paul's attitude when he wrote, "Not that we lord it over your faith, but we work with you for your joy, because it is by faith you stand firm" (2 Corinthians 1:24). In a one-to-one discipling relationship, we are there to serve, not to lord it over the other person. We should encourage the use of spiritual disciplines and do all we can to help the person succeed in them, but we should never require them as a condition of acceptance — either by God or by us. We must remember that the methods of spiritual disciplines are a means to the end, not the end themselves.

We need to teach grace before commitment, because, as we saw in session 4, grace understood and embraced will always lead to commitment. But commitment required will always lead to legalism.

## WHAT OTHERS THINK

Often we do not enjoy our freedom in Christ because we are afraid of what others will think. We do or don't do certain things because of a fear that we will be judged or gossiped about by others. But standing firm in our freedom in Christ means we resist the urge to live by the fear of what others think.

It is very instructive to me that, in Galatians, the Magna Carta of Christian freedom, Paul also said, "Am I now trying to win the approval of men, or of God? Or am I trying to please men? If I were still trying to please men, I would not be a servant of Christ" (1:10).

I had to learn this lesson the hard way.

As I said in session 2 (chapter 4), surprisingly soon after the death of my first wife, God brought into my life another godly lady — a single woman who had been a family friend for many years. As our friendship began to deepen into a romantic relationship, I became quite concerned about what people would think. I knew I would be violating the culturally accepted maxim of "don't make any major decisions the first year." At the same time, I sensed an inner compulsion in my spirit, which I felt was from God, to move ahead. My journal during those days records numerous times when I struggled with God over this issue. One day I wrote, "I wonder if God is pushing me along faster in this relationship than I want to go because of fear of what people will think."

I had put God in the box of our culturally accepted norm. Surely God wouldn't do anything in my life that would be unacceptable to my friends. God was actually doing a wonderful thing, but instead of fully enjoying His work of grace, I was struggling with Him because of what people might think.

If you are going to experience the joy of your freedom in Christ, you have to decide whether you will please God or people. I saw a cartoon one day that was a takeoff on one of Campus Crusade's Four Spiritual Laws. A wife, speaking to her husband, who was obviously a minister, said, "God loves you, and people have a wonderful plan for your life." That cartoonist captured a spirit that is widespread in evangelicalism. Other people want to tell you how you should live the Christian life, what you shouldn't do and what you should do. Often their ideas will not match how you feel God is guiding you.

I'm not advocating that we run roughshod over other people's convictions. We are called to a body, and we all need to live and minister as members of the body. But ultimately we are responsible to God, not other people. He is the One who puts us in the body as He pleases. He deals with each of us individually, putting each of us in circumstances tailored especially for our growth and ministry.

A friend of mine ministers to international students from a very different cultural and political background. For some reason, the best time of the entire week to meet with them in an evangelistic Bible study is during the Sunday morning worship service. My friend went to his pastor, explained the situation, committed himself to attending the Sunday evening service, but asked to be excused from the morning service with the pastor's approval and blessing. Fortunately, the pastor understood and heartily granted his approval of my friend's plan.

But what if some people in the congregation didn't understand? What if the Sunday school superintendent didn't understand why my friend was unavailable to teach the college age class? What are we to do in those situations? We are to exercise our freedom in Christ. If we believe God is guiding us in a certain direction, we have to obey God, not other people.

I learned something else through my romance experience. I realized I often had my own opinions of what other people should or should not do. I wouldn't try to influence their actions, but in my mind I would judge them — either approving or disapproving. So God "put the shoe on the other foot"; He exposed me to the possibility of other people not understanding what He was doing in my life. I learned the hard way to experience my own freedom in Christ and let other people experience theirs. We need to learn to let each other be free.

## CONTROLLERS

We've talked about some of the areas in which we practice legalism with each other and with ourselves: fences, differing opinions, spiritual disciplines, and fear of what others think. There are others. Expected attendance at all church meetings, or at the activities of our various parachurch organizations, is another fertile area for legalism. Another old bogey is "worldliness," which in the minds of some people can be seen in the amount of cosmetics a woman wears or the length of a man's hair.

Aggravating all of these areas is a class of people who have come to be known as "controllers." These are people who are not willing to let you live your life before God as you believe He is leading you. They have all the issues buttoned down and have cast-iron opinions about all of them. These people only know black and white. There are no gray areas to them.

They insist you live your Christian life according to their rules and their opinions. If you insist on being free to live as God wants you to live, they will try to intimidate you and manipulate you one way or another. Their primary weapons are "guilt trips," rejection, or gossip.

These people must be resisted. We must not allow them to subvert the freedom we have in Christ. Paul treated the legalism in the Galatian church as heresy, and he called down a curse on its perpetrators. I am not prepared to go that far with our present-day legalists/controllers, but I want to tell you their actions are no incidental matter. Their presence in our evangelical ranks is much more than a minor irritant, such as a fly buzzing around our heads. There are spiritual casualties all over our nation today because of the effects of legalistic controllers in their lives.

Controllers have been around a long time. Over three hundred years ago — in 1645 — the Puritan Samuel Bolton wrote these very instructive words on the issue of Christian freedom:

Let us never surrender our judgments or our consciences to be at the disposal and opinions of others, and to be subjected to the sentences and determinations of men. . . .

It is my exhortation therefore to all Christians to maintain their Christian freedom by constant watchfulness. You must not be tempted or threatened out of it; you must not be bribed or frightened from it; you must not let either force or fraud rob you of it. . . . We must not give up ourselves to the opinion of other men, though they be never so learned, never so holy, merely because it is their opinion. The apostle directs us to try all things and to hold fast that which is good (1 Thess. 5.21). It often happens that a high esteem of others in respect of their learning and piety makes men take up all upon trust from such, and to submit their judgments to their opinions, and their consciences to their precepts. This should not be so.[4]

Years ago someone said, "Eternal vigilance is the price of liberty." That is just as true in the spiritual as in the political realm. Freedom and grace are two sides of the same coin. We cannot enjoy one without the other. If we are to truly live by grace, we must stand firm in the freedom that is ours in Christ Jesus.

## SERVE ONE ANOTHER IN LOVE

Now that we have explored the issue of freedom as an expression of grace, we can quote the remainder of Galatians 5:13, "But do not use your freedom to indulge the sinful nature; rather, serve one another in love."

In a sense I have already dealt with Paul's cautionary note, in sessions 4 and 5. I deliberately delayed addressing the issue of Christian freedom until I had first dealt with the relationship of grace to the moral law of God. I wanted to show that the moral law, rightly understood, does not squelch grace or abridge our freedom in Christ.

We saw in chapter 6 that God's grace provides the only proper motive, as well as the only powerful motivation, to obey His commands. Our obedience, to be true obedience, must arise out of love for God and gratitude for His grace. We saw in chapter 7 that the moral law of God gives direction to our love. If I truly desire to express my love to Him, I need to know how to do that appropriately. Jesus gave us very simple directions (simple to understand, if not to practice): "If you love me, you will obey what I command" (John 14:15).

Then we saw in chapter 8 that, though the law gives direction, it provides no power to enable us to obey it. But God, by delivering us from the reign of sin and the law, and bringing us into His realm of grace, has provided the power in Christ and through His Spirit. So God by His grace has given us the right motive, the right rule or direction, and the needed power to live a life of love.

Only when we understand these basic truths are we in a position to respond to Paul's exhortation not to abuse our freedom, but instead, to serve one another in love. Here is a spiritual principle: *We cannot exercise love unless we are experiencing grace.* You cannot truly love others unless you are convinced that God's love for you is unconditional, based solely on the merit of Christ, not on your performance. John said, "We love because he first loved us" (1 John 4:19). Our love, either to God or to others, can only be a response to His love for us.

There are five words all beginning with the letter *L* that we need to keep in right relationship to one another. All five are either used or implied in Galatians 5:13-14. They are *law, liberty, love, license,* and *legalism.* (I have not used *license* up to now, and by that word I mean an abuse of our freedom in order to indulge our sinful nature.) We need to learn to live within the right relationships of law and love, law and liberty, and liberty and love. Only when we have those relationships in proper order will we avoid the traps of license on the one hand and legalism on the other. Grace keeps the law, love, and liberty in right relationship to one another.

In one southern state, a narrow two-lane highway has been built through a swampland by building up the road bed above the swamp. You must be extra alert not to drift off the road because there is no margin for error. If you go off the road, you do not end up on a grassy shoulder but rather submerged in a swamp.

As shown in the following illustration, the built-up roadbed represents grace that allows you to drive safely through the swampland of legalism and license.

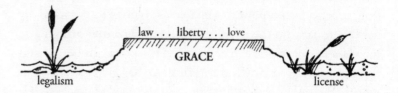

When you focus on grace in the fullness of its meaning, you will keep the law, liberty, and love in their proper relationship to one another. But if you focus on any one of them instead of on grace, you will invariably end up in the swamp of legalism or license.

What do I mean by the phrase, "grace in the fullness of its meaning"? An expression often used in a pejorative sense is *cheap grace*. The term denotes an attitude that, since God's grace is unconditional, I may live as I please; I may sin as much as I want because God will still love me and forgive me. That is the attitude of *license*. It results from focusing exclusively on liberty and denigrating God's law. To counteract this sinful attitude, some of us in Christian ministry have fallen into *legalism*. We have taught, either directly or implicitly, that God's grace is conditional, that there is a degree to which it is based on our performance. We have unduly focused on God's law and disparaged liberty.

But the reality is that there is no such thing as cheap grace. To us, the recipients, grace is not cheap; it is *unconditionally free*. But grace is not cheap to God either. Although grace is part of the essential nature of God, the extending of His grace to us cost Him the most expensive price ever paid, the death of His own dear Son.

So grace is never cheap. It is absolutely free to us, but infinitely expensive to God. That is what I mean by grace in the fullness of its meaning. Anyone who is prone to use grace as a license for irresponsible, sinful behavior, surely does not appreciate the infinite price God paid to give us His grace. But anyone who tends to use legalism as a hedge against license, just as surely forgets that grace cannot be earned by our behavior.

All of us need to diligently apply ourselves to learning to live under the reign of God's transforming grace. Then love, liberty, and the law will take their proper places in our lives, and we will avoid the swamplands of both legalism and license.

Notes and Observations

SESSION SIX

# Called to Be Free

(Chapter 9)

## STUDY QUESTIONS

### CENTRAL IDEA

As followers of Christ we are free. Free from the drive to earn God's favor by our actions. Free from the oppression of trying to live up to manmade religious rules and regulations. Free to let the Holy Spirit create in our lives something beautiful and pleasing to God.

### WARM-UP

What thoughts come to your mind when you hear the word freedom?

### EXPLORING GRACE

1.  a.  Read 2 Corinthians 3:17 and Galatians 5:1,13. Why do you think God wants us to realize the freedom we have in Christ?

    b.  What does freedom do for the human spirit?

    c.  Why do you suppose man is so quick to relinquish his freedom and revert to living by manmade rules and regulations that foster conformity?

2.  a.  Galatians 5:16-18 helps us understand how our freedom in Christ leads not to
        license but rather to a life led by the Spirit. How do you sense the leading of the
        Spirit in your life?

    b.  Give an example of a time recently when you felt the Spirit leading you — in a
        difficult decision, in the way you responded to a particular situation, or in the
        way you responded to a particular person.

3.  Many godly qualities will become dominant in our lives as we use our freedom
    to respond more and more to the Spirit. By God's grace, through the work of His
    Holy Spirit, these qualities are growing within us.

Below is a list of Christian character traits found in Galatians 5:22-23 and Colossians
3:12-15.

    a.  Share with the group the character traits you have seen in the lives of other
        members.

    b.  Which of these character traits do you think God is working to develop in
        your life?

| | | |
|---|---|---|
| compassion | love | kindness |
| joy | humility | peace |
| gentleness | patience | forbearance |
| goodness | forgiveness | faithfulness |
| thankfulness | self-control | |

4.   Knowing that the Spirit brings these godly qualities into our lives, what do you think your role is in this process?

5.   a.   Legalism that requires adherence to manmade rules is unfortunately quite common in churches today. Can you think of some examples that you have observed?

     b.   What are some of the natural results or effects of this kind of legalism?

6.   a.   In Romans 14:1-23 Paul clearly states that God allows equally godly people to have differing opinions on certain matters. Read these verses and then think of a modern parallel to the issue of eating meat.

     b.   How does Romans 14 help you better understand contemporary issues of differing opinions?

7.  We tend to be legalistic with each other when it comes to spiritual disciplines (prayer, Bible study, Bible reading, witnessing, fasting, and so forth). Due to our freedom in Christ, what do you believe should be our attitude toward these disciplines?

8.  a.  Sometimes we fail to enjoy the freedom we have in Christ because we are afraid of what others will think. Can you give an example of a time when you worried about what others would think when you were doing something you knew God had given you the freedom to do?

    b.  How did you handle the situation?

    c.  How would you handle it differently now?

## Closing Prayer

Focus on thanking God for the freedom you enjoy as followers of Jesus Christ. Ask the Lord to help you respond more to the working of the Holy Spirit in your lives.

## Going Deeper (Extra questions for further study)

1. Did your parents establish rules or put up "fences" that you did not understand? Give an example.

2. If you have children, how have you explained the reasons for your boundaries to your children?

### Pondering Grace *(For personal reflection)*

*A Christian man is the most free lord of all, and subject to none; a Christian man is the most dutiful servant of all, and subject to everyone.*

Martin Luther

*Only what God has commanded in his word should be regarded as binding; in all else there may be liberty of actions.*

John Owen

*Let us never surrender our judgments or our consciences to be at the disposal and opinions of others, and to be subjected to the sentences and determinations of men. . . . It is my exhortation therefore to all Christians to maintain their Christian freedom by constant watchfulness. You must not be tempted or threatened out of it; you must not be bribed or frightened from it; you must not let either force or fraud rob you of it.*

Samuel Bolton, *The True Bound of Christian Life*

# The Sufficiency of Grace

Read the following portion of *Transforming Grace*. In the margins, record observations, illustrations, or questions that come to mind as you read. Then answer the study questions that follow the reading.

---

## Chapter Ten: The Sufficiency of Grace

*But he said to me, "My grace is sufficient for you, for my power is made perfect in weakness." Therefore I will boast all the more gladly about my weaknesses, so that Christ's power may rest on me.*

2 CORINTHIANS 12:9

Notes and Observations

That life is difficult is a self-evident and universally recognized truth. The morning newspaper reported today that over 1,000 jobs were eliminated in our moderate-sized city over the past two months, making an already frail economy worse and leaving people without paychecks right at the Christmas season. As I write, several hundred thousand military personnel have been deployed to the Middle East, raising once again the terrible specter of war with its ever-increasing technological capability of widespread and wanton death and destruction. Returning to our local scene, a convicted murderer sits in our county jail waiting to hear if he will be sentenced to die for his crime.

We live in a fallen and sin-cursed world. Even Christians are not immune from the frustrating and often overwhelming circumstances of life resulting from that curse. I think of a couple who should be entering their retirement years, but cannot because they are still caring for a grown but partially dependent child. I am reminded of another friend who is faithfully caring for her husband, now stricken with Alzheimer's disease.

This morning I prayed for several families who are trying to cope with teenage and even grown children living in various stages of spiritual rebellion and estrangement from their parents. Only a block away, a mother with young children fights a seemingly futile battle with cancer. Not only are we as Christians not immune from such heartaches, it often seems we experience more of them than do the non-Christians around us.

But for almost two thousand years, multiplied thousands of believers have found comfort, encouragement, and the strength to endure from God's words to the apostle Paul, "My grace is sufficient for you" (2 Corinthians 12:9).

Paul was no stranger to adversity. Earlier in 2 Corinthians he had spoken of his troubles, hardships, distresses, beatings, imprisonments, riots, hard work, sleepless nights, and hunger (6:4-5). Yet one particular affliction apparently caused him more pain and grief than all the others combined. He referred to it as "a thorn in my flesh, a messenger of Satan, to torment me" (12:7).

We have no idea what Paul's "thorn in the flesh" was. It's pointless to speculate. Whatever it was, it was probably a natural hindrance to his ministry. We do know it was a Satanic attack (a messenger of Satan), but it was given to him at the direction of the God whom he loved and served with all his heart.

Paul had had a unique experience. As he described in the opening verses of 2 Corinthians 12, he had been caught up to the "third heaven," to God's paradise, and had heard inexpressible things — things he was not permitted to tell. This rapturous experience, apparently unique to Paul, could have caused him to be filled with pride had he been left to himself. But God in His infinite wisdom and love for Paul did not leave him exposed to that temptation. Paul himself described God's gracious bulwark against pride this way:

> To keep me from becoming conceited because of these surpassingly great revelations, there was given me a thorn in my flesh, a messenger of Satan, to torment me.

Three times I pleaded with the Lord to take it away from me. But he said to me, "My grace is sufficient for you, for my power is made perfect in weakness." Therefore I will boast all the more gladly about my weaknesses, so that Christ's power may rest on me. That is why, for Christ's sake, I delight in weaknesses, in insults, in hardships, in persecutions, in difficulties. For when I am weak, then I am strong. (2 Corinthians 12:7-10)

Notes and Observations

## DIVINE ASSISTANCE

I want to focus particularly on that crucial and blessed statement in 2 Corinthians 12:9, "My grace is sufficient for you," because it opens to us another dimension of God's grace we have not seen as yet in this book. To this point we have been studying the aspect of grace commonly defined as God's unmerited favor to us through Jesus Christ. In verse 9, as well as other Scriptures, we see grace used to mean *God's divine assistance to us through the Holy Spirit*. This divine assistance is actually the power of the risen Christ, but it is mediated to us by God's Spirit.

That grace has this meaning in various places of the New Testament seems to be recognized by almost all Bible commentators. John Calvin, for example, in his commentary on 2 Corinthians 12:9, said, "Here the word *grace* does not mean as elsewhere God's favour but is used by metonymy for [to indicate] the help of the Holy Spirit which comes to us from God's undeserved favour."[1]

Paul used *grace* in this same sense in 1 Corinthians 15:10 (a verse we will consider in chapter 11): "But by the grace of God I am what I am, and his grace to me was not without effect. No, I worked harder than all of them — yet not I, but the grace of God that was with me." Charles Hodge said of this passage,

> *The grace of God*, in this connection, is not the love of God, but the influence of the Holy Spirit considered

as an unmerited favour. This is not only the theological and popular, but also the scriptural sense of the word *grace* in many passages.[2]

A "popular . . . sense of the word grace" refers to the way we speak when we say something such as, "By God's grace I was able to love my disagreeable neighbor." We refer, of course, to God's enabling in an otherwise impossible situation. And we know that the aid we receive comes to us through the influence or help of His Spirit.

We can readily see this popular but biblical use of the word *grace* in a very familiar Scripture written by Paul, Philippians 4:12-13: "I know what it is to be in need, and I know what it is to have plenty. I have learned the secret of being content in any and every situation, whether well fed or hungry, whether living in plenty or in want. I can do everything through him who gives me strength."

If, in place of the words "through him who gives me strength," we substitute the words "by His grace," verse 13 would read, "I can do everything by His grace." Although the change of wording sounds strange to our ears because of the familiarity of this verse, we have not changed the theological statement at all. *"By His grace"* and *"through Him who gives me strength"* express an identical thought.

So we see that grace, as used in the New Testament, expresses two related and complementary meanings. First, it is *God's unmerited favor to us through Christ whereby salvation and all other blessings are freely given to us.* Second, it is *God's divine assistance to us through the Holy Spirit.* Obviously the second meaning is encompassed in the first because the aid of the Spirit is one of the "all other blessings" given to us through Christ. We distinguish these two aspects of grace, however, because the first focuses on God's grace as the source of all blessings, whereas the second focuses on God's grace expressed specifically as the work of the Holy Spirit within us.

## THE THORN IN THE FLESH

Paul needed grace, but he also needed the thorn in his flesh. Like us, he was susceptible to the temptation of pride, and the thorn was given to check that temptation. In fact, in the Greek text, the phrase translated in the New International Version "to keep me from becoming conceited" was repeated by Paul. The King James Version picks up this repetition with the following translation of verse 7: "And *lest I should be exalted above measure* through the abundance of the revelations, there was given to me a thorn in the flesh, the messenger of Satan to buffet me, *lest I should be exalted above measure*" (emphasis added).

As if to emphasize the need of the thorn, Paul twice stated the Lord's purpose in giving it to him. It was to keep pride at bay. Paul was a humble man. He considered himself "less than the least of all God's people" and the worst of sinners (Ephesians 3:8; 1 Timothy 1:15); yet he knew he was susceptible to pride, given the right circumstances. And the surpassing greatness of the revelations given to him could have been the right circumstances if God had left Paul to himself.

All of us are susceptible to pride. And pride stands in direct opposition to grace, for "God opposes the proud but gives grace to the humble" (James 4:6). Pride is often reflective of a self-righteous attitude. We begin to grow in the Christian life, and we see other believers who are not growing as we are. We are tempted to become proud of our spiritual growth. Or we see some Christian fall before temptation, and instead of being concerned, we become critical because of our own self-righteousness.

I remember my reaction when I heard that a friend — whom I considered to be very committed to Christ — was resigning from his Christian organization because he was divorcing his wife for another woman. I said to myself, *How could he do such a thing? I would never do that.* It seemed as if God spoke to me right then: "Oh, wouldn't you? Don't be so confident in yourself." I was sobered. I realized my "righteous indignation" and disappointment in my

189

friend was accompanied by a sinful attitude of self-righteousness. Pride can manifest itself in very subtle ways.

Most of us are familiar with the often used but very true expression, "There, but for the grace of God, go I." Perhaps we've even uttered it on occasion. But do we sincerely believe it? I think not. If we truly believed it, we would be far less judgmental, much more compassionate toward, and quick to pray for our brothers and sisters in Christ.

God had a beneficial purpose in giving the thorn, whatever it was, to Paul. And it *was* God who gave it, even though it was given through the instrumentality of Satan. Satan certainly had no interest in curbing Paul's temptation to pride; he would have wanted just the opposite. As in the case of Job, Satan undoubtedly wanted to drive a wedge between Paul and the Lord; he wanted Paul to turn against God. But just as God and Satan had different purposes in the affliction of Job, so God and Satan had different purposes for Paul's thorn in the flesh.

God never allows pain without a purpose in the lives of His children. He never allows Satan, nor circumstances, nor any ill-intending person to afflict us unless He uses that affliction for our good. God never wastes pain. He always causes it to work together for our ultimate good, the good of conforming us more to the likeness of His Son (see Romans 8:28-29).

God's purpose for Paul's thorn is clearly stated in the text: "to keep me from becoming conceited" (2 Corinthians 12:7). Sometimes God's purpose for allowing pain in our lives is clear; more often, it seems, it is not. In fact, frequently a great part of the pain is the sheer irrationality of it. God never explained to Job the purpose of his unbelievable pain. He left Job to suffer in the dark, so to speak. That is usually our experience.

Paul said the thorn was given to *torment* him. Other versions translate the verb as "harass," "buffet," or "afflict." The same verb is used in 1 Corinthians 4:11 where it is translated as "brutally treated." Paul was brutally treated by Satan. The apostle Peter said, "Your enemy the devil prowls around like a roaring lion looking for someone to devour" (1 Peter 5:8). The devil is cruel and vicious. He would devour us, if he could. He torments us to the full extent God allows. But, as was the case when Joseph's brothers sold him into slavery, though the devil intends to harm us, God intends it for good (see Genesis 50:20).

Paul's reaction to his thorn was one of deep anguish. He said, "Three times I pleaded with the Lord to take it away from me" (2 Corinthians 12:8). Although the thorn was always present, there were probably times when its pain, whether physical or emotional or both, was unusually severe. It is likely that on three of those occasions Paul was driven to cry out to God for its removal.

## THE PRIDE OF SELF-SUFFICIENCY

God never removed Paul's thorn, despite his anguished pleas. When Paul wrote these words, it had been fourteen years since he had received the surpassingly great revelations (see 2 Corinthians 12:2). During that time he had suffered many varied adversities. How could he have still needed the thorn to curb any temptation to become conceited? God had an even greater purpose for the thorn. He wanted Paul to experience the sufficiency of His grace. He wanted him to learn that the divine assistance of the Holy Spirit was all he needed. He wanted Paul to learn to lean continually on the Spirit for strength.

In earlier chapters we have seen that God's grace assumes our sinfulness, guilt, and ill-deservedness. Here we see it also assumes our weakness and inability. Just as grace is opposed to the pride of self-righteousness, so it is also opposed to the pride of self-sufficiency. The sin of self-sufficiency goes all the way back to the Fall in the Garden of Eden.

Satan's temptation of Eve was undoubtedly complex and many faceted. That is, it included what we would now consider a number of different temptations. But one of those facets was the temptation of self-sufficiency.

Satan said to Eve, "You will be like God, knowing good and evil" (Genesis 3:5). Mankind was created to be dependent upon God: physically, "in him we live and move and have our being" (Acts 17:28); and spiritually, Jesus said, "Apart from me you can do nothing" (John 15:5). God intended our dependence on Him to be conscious and continuous.

But Satan tempted Eve to assert her autonomy and self-sufficiency. As G. Ch. Aalders said, "That ideal of sovereign independence, which had been presented to her by the serpent, lured her on, 'and she took some [of the fruit] and ate it.'"[3]

Ever since the Fall, God has continually worked to cause His people to realize their utter dependence on Him. He does this through bringing us to the point of human extremity where we have no place to turn but to Him. One of the more dramatic and prolonged illustrations of this is found in His miraculous provision for the Israelite nation in the desert.

After living forty years in the desert, Moses recounted their experiences in the book of Deuteronomy. This is one of his more vivid recollections:

> Remember how the LORD your God led you all the way in the desert these forty years, to humble you and to test you in order to know what was in your heart, whether or not you would keep his commands. He humbled you, causing you to hunger and then feeding you with manna, which neither you nor your fathers had known, to teach you that man does not live on bread alone but on every word that comes from the mouth of the LORD. (8:2-3)

Note how Moses recalled the Israelites' utter extremity and total dependence on God:

- God humbled them.
- He caused them to hunger.

- He fed them with food they had never seen before.
- He taught them that man lives by the word that comes from God.

God humbled the people and *caused* them to hunger before He fed them. He deliberately brought them to the end of themselves. The description in Psalm 107:5 is apt: "They were hungry and thirsty, and their lives ebbed away." Then He fed them miraculously with food they had never tasted before. God wanted them to be acutely aware of the fact that *He* was feeding them; they were dependent on *His* provision every day. "Every word that comes from the mouth of the LORD" is not the revealed Word of Scripture but rather the commanding word of God's providence — "For he spoke, and it came to be; he commanded, and it stood firm" (Psalm 33:9).

P. C. Craigie's comments on this portion of Scripture help us see what God was doing to the Israelites:

> The wilderness tested and disciplined the people in various ways. On the one hand, the desolation of the wilderness removed the *natural props and supports* which man *by nature* depends on; it cast the people back on God, *who alone could provide* the strength to survive the wilderness. On the other hand, the severity of the wilderness period undermined the shallow bases of confidence of those who were not truly rooted and grounded in God. The wilderness makes or breaks a man; it provides strength of will and character. The strength provided by the wilderness, however, was *not the strength of self-sufficiency*, but the strength that comes from a knowledge of the living God. (emphasis added)[4]

On the very first page of the notebook I use during my morning devotions and prayer time, I have written these words from J. A. Thompson's commentary on this passage in Deuteronomy:

193

Already during the forty years of wandering God had taught Israel utter dependence on Him for water and food. Hunger and thirst could not be satisfied by human aid but only by God. The need for such divine provision in the hour of their extremity could not but humiliate the people. . . .

The provision of food, which Israel did not know previously, made plain the lesson that it is not mere food that gives life. Without the divine word the food itself may not be available. . . . Nothing was possible without Him, and even to eat they had to await His pleasure.[5]

Why do I review Dr. Thompson's comments almost every morning? I sense the need to constantly remind myself of my *utter* dependence on God in every area of life. I don't have to gather manna every morning; God has so graciously provided that the food I need for the day is already in the cupboard or the refrigerator. In those circumstances it is easy to forget our dependence on God. But the fact is I am just as dependent on God for water and food as were the people of Israel in the desert.

God provided for the Israelites through a continual miracle every day for forty years. He has provided for me and my family through His providential circumstances, also for many years. God wanted the Israelites to realize and remember their utter dependence on Him, so He used an extremity of need and a miraculous provision to capture their attention and teach them a lesson that is difficult to learn. Still, they forgot. How much easier is it, then, for us to forget when God is supplying our needs through ordinary, mundane ways.

It is even more difficult, however, for us to learn our dependence on God in the spiritual realm. A lack of money for food or to make the monthly mortgage payment gets our attention very quickly, and the need is obvious. The money is either available or it isn't. There's no pretending. But we can pretend in the spiritual realm. We can exist for months — going through the motions, perhaps even teaching Sunday school or serving as an elder or deacon — depending on nothing more than mere natural human resources.

The possible extremity of physical circumstances and my very real dependence on God to meet physical needs serves as a daily reminder of my spiritual dependence on Him. The physical dependence illustrates the spiritual dependence, reminding me of Jesus' words, "Apart from me you can do nothing." Dr. Thompson's words remind me that I am as dependent upon God as the Israelites were. My dependence may not be as obvious, but it is just as real and just as acute as if I had to wait daily for God to rain down manna from heaven. And if I am dependent in the physical realm, how much more dependent am I in the spiritual realm, where our struggle is not against flesh and blood, but against spiritual forces of evil (see Ephesians 6:12)?

## THE SUFFICIENCY OF GRACE

Before we can learn the sufficiency of God's grace, we must learn the *in*sufficiency of ourselves. As I have said, the more we see our sinfulness, the more we appreciate grace in its basic meaning of God's undeserved favor. In a similar manner, the more we see our frailty, weakness, and dependence, the more we appreciate God's grace in its dimension of His divine assistance. Just as grace shines more brilliantly against the dark background of our sin, so it also shines more brilliantly against the background of our human weakness.

We have looked at Paul's words in Romans 5:20: "But where sin increased, grace increased all the more." He could have just as aptly said in 2 Corinthians 12, "But where human weakness increased, grace increased all the more." That is essentially what he said in different words in verse 9: "But he said to me, 'My grace is sufficient for you, for my power is made perfect in weakness.' Therefore I will boast all the more gladly about my weaknesses, so that Christ's power may rest on me." *My power is made perfect in weakness.* On this Philip Hughes wrote,

> Indeed, the abject weakness of the human instrument serves to magnify and throw into relief the perfection of the divine power in a way that any suggestion of human adequacy could never do. The greater the servant's weakness, the more conspicuous is the power of his Master's all-sufficient grace.[6]

In this passage, God equates His grace with His power as specifically displayed in our weakness. This power infusing our weakness is a concrete expression of His grace: His power comes to our aid through the ministry of His Spirit in our lives. This is the mysterious operation of the Holy Spirit on our human spirit through which He strengthens us and enables us to meet in a godly fashion whatever circumstances we encounter.

Notice I said the Holy Spirit strengthens us and enables us to meet in a godly fashion *whatever circumstances* cross our paths. God's grace is not given to make us feel better, but to glorify Him. Modern society's subtle, underlying agenda is good feelings. We want the pain to go away. We want to feel better in difficult situations, but God wants us to glorify Him in those circumstances. Good feelings may come, or they may not, but that is not the issue. The issue is whether or not we honor God by the way we respond to our circumstances. God's grace — that is, the enabling power of the Holy Spirit — is given to help us respond in such a way.

God's grace is sufficient. The Greek verb translated "is sufficient" is the same one translated "will be content" in 1 Timothy 6:8: "But if we have food and clothing, we will be content with that." This helps us understand what *sufficient* means. Food and clothing refer to the necessities of life, not the luxuries. If we have the necessities we are to be content; that is, we are to realize they are sufficient. God may give us more from time to time, but we are to be content with the necessities.

So it is with God's grace in the spiritual realm. God always gives us what we need, perhaps sometimes more, but never less. The spiritual equivalent of food and clothing is simply the strength to endure in a way that honors God. Receiving that strength, we are to be content. We would like the "luxury" of having our particular thorn removed, but God often says, "Be content with the strength to endure that thorn." We can be confident He always gives that.

John Blanchard said, "So he [God] supplies perfectly measured grace to meet the needs of the godly. For daily needs there is daily grace; for sudden needs, sudden grace; for overwhelming need, overwhelming grace. God's grace is given wonderfully, but not wastefully; freely but not foolishly; bountifully but not blindly."[7]

There is a lesson about grace in the way God distributed the manna to the Israelites in the desert. Exodus 16:16-21 says,

"This is what the LORD has commanded: 'Each one is to gather as much as he needs. Take an omer for each person you have in your tent.'"

The Israelites did as they were told; some gathered much, some little. And when they measured it by the omer, he who gathered much did not have too much, and he who gathered little did not have too little. Each one gathered as much as he needed.

Then Moses said to them, "No one is to keep any of it until morning."

However, some of them paid no attention to Moses; they kept part of it until morning, but it was full of maggots and began to smell. So Moses was angry with them.

Each morning everyone gathered as much as he needed, and when the sun grew hot, it melted away.

Three times the text mentions that each person could gather "as much as he needed." There was an ample supply of manna for everyone. No one need go hungry because everyone could gather as much as he needed. Not only was there an ample supply, God in some mysterious way saw that no one had an overabundance, regardless of how much manna he gathered: "He who gathered much did not have too much, and he who gathered little did not have too little." Furthermore, the gathering was to be a day-to-day activity. They were to gather only what was needed each day — except on the day before the Sabbath. They were not allowed to store up for the future.

God's distribution of the manna illustrates the way He distributes grace. There is always an ample supply; no one ever need go without. But there is only as much as we need — and even that is on a day-to-day basis. God doesn't permit us to "store up" grace. We must look to Him anew each day for a new supply. Sometimes we must look for a new supply each hour!

This thought of God's ample but day-by-day supply of grace is beautifully expressed in the first stanza of Lina Sandell Berg's lovely hymn "Day by Day":

> Day by day and with each passing moment,
> Strength I find to meet my trials here;
> Trusting in my Father's wise bestowment,
> I've no cause for worry or for fear.
> He whose heart is kind beyond all measure
> Gives unto each day what He deems best
> Lovingly, its part of pain and pleasure,
> Mingling toil with peace and rest.[8]

Such a day-by-day parceling out of grace — and only as much as we need — may seem inconsistent with the abundant generosity of God we saw in earlier chapters. This is not the case at all. Rather, as we saw previously in this chapter, God continually works to keep us aware of our dependence on Him. We were created for a simple, childlike dependence on Him, but since the Fall we have tended to resist that dependence. God well knew this tendency when He gave this warning through Moses to the Israelites:

> You may say to yourself, "My power and the strength of my hands have produced this wealth for me." But remember the LORD your God, for it is he who gives you the ability to produce wealth, and so confirms his covenant, which he swore to your forefathers, as it is today. (Deuteronomy 8:17-18)

It is noteworthy that this warning occurs shortly after the reminder in verses 2-3, which we already studied. There the Israelites were reminded of their days of extremity and very obvious dependence on God for their daily food. But God warned them that, even after forty years of such conscious dependence, the day would come when they would look around at their bountiful supply of food and say, "My power and the strength of my hands have produced this wealth for me."

Such a self-sufficient attitude is obviously detrimental to our relationship with God, so He works to keep that from happening. He allows our respective thorns in the flesh to remain, giving us grace sufficient to cope with them only day by day. From time to time He brings extraordinary crises into our lives, as He did when Paul was forced to say, "We were under great pressure, far beyond our ability to endure, so that we despaired even of life. Indeed, in our hearts we felt the sentence of death. But this happened that we might not rely on ourselves but on God, who raises the dead" (2 Corinthians 1:8-9). Despite his ever-present thorn, Paul was brought to a crisis extremity to learn anew to rely not on himself but on God.

Whether it is the continuing thorn in the flesh or the extraordinary crisis that sometimes occurs, both are intended by God to keep us conscious of our human weakness and our dependence on Him, so that we might experience the sufficiency of *His* grace and the adequacy of *His* power. As John

Calvin said, "For men have no taste for it [God's power] till they are convinced of their need of it and they immediately forget its value unless they are continually reminded by awareness of their own weakness."[9]

Paul's attitude toward his weakness was vastly different from our usual modern response. We abhor weakness and glory in self-sufficiency and manmade accomplishments. Even Christians flock to hear the sports superstar or the popular entertainer give his or her testimony, simply because of that person's fame and status. How many of us would make any effort to hear a man who said, "I will boast all the more gladly about my weaknesses. . . . I delight in weaknesses. . . . For when I am weak, then I am strong"?

I think of how I have struggled with my own weaknesses instead of delighting in them. I think of the disappointment of failing to reach important goals, of humiliations suffered that were too painful to ever share with anyone, of somewhat minor but very annoying lifetime physical infirmities. Only in the last few years have I realized what a significant contribution those disappointments, heartaches, and frustrations — especially in their cumulative effect — have made on my walk with God and my service for Him. I think I am only beginning to understand a little bit the validity of Paul's statement, "When I am weak, then I am strong."

Sometimes when I am introduced as a speaker, I cringe inwardly as the person introducing me waxes eloquent about my accomplishments. I sit there and think, *What if they knew the other side of the story? Would they all get up and leave?* Yet ironically, it is the other side of the story, the humiliations and heartaches, the failures and frustrations — not the successes and accomplishments — that have qualified me to be there to speak. Those difficult times have driven me to the Lord. I'll be honest. It wasn't that I wanted to lean on God; I had no other choice. But I am finally learning that in weakness I find strength — His strength.

Philip Hughes said, "Every believer must learn that human weakness and divine grace go hand in hand together."[10] Paul had learned that lesson well. He said, "Therefore I will boast all the more gladly about my weaknesses so that Christ's power may rest on me" (2 Corinthians 12:9). Paul had learned that God's grace is indeed sufficient; His divine enabling through the power of the Holy Spirit would sustain him in the midst of the torments of his thorn, and in the depths of other weaknesses, insults, hardships, persecutions, and difficulties (verse 10).

As we noted earlier, it had been fourteen years since Paul received those surpassingly great revelations. If we assume the thorn was given to him at about the same time, and that the three instances when he pleaded for its removal occurred soon afterward, we can say that Paul had had almost fourteen years to prove the sufficiency of God's grace.

Paul was no ivory tower theologian. He did not write from the comfortable confines of a minister's study or a counselor's office (nor, for that matter, does any competent pastor or counselor today). Paul wrote from raw experience because he "had been there." The anguish he experienced was real anguish, and the grace he received was real grace. It was not theoretical, nor make-believe, nor merely "whistling in the dark" to keep up his courage. No, Paul experienced a very concrete expression of God's love and power as the Holy Spirit ministered comfort and encouragement to him in the midst of affliction.

Paul was not the first of the biblical writers to tell of the sufficiency of God's grace. Jeremiah, a prophet of God who endured much hardship and affliction could say,

> I remember my affliction and my wandering,
>     the bitterness and the gall.
> I well remember them,
>     and my soul is downcast within me.

> Yet this I call to mind
>> and therefore I have hope:
>
> Because of the LORD's great love we are not
>> consumed,
>> for his compassions never fail.
> They are new every morning;
>> great is your faithfulness.
>> (Lamentations 3:19-23)

Even Job, in the midst of suffering and despair, when he acknowledged he could not find God anywhere (see Job 23:8-9), could still say, "But he knows the way that I take; when he has tested me, I will come forth as gold" (verse 10).

Perhaps the most frequent and dramatic utterances of the sufficiency of God's grace in the midst of human frailty and affliction occur in the psalms. Consider, for example, David's testimony in Psalm 13:

> How long, O LORD? Will you forget me
>> forever?
>> How long will you hide your face from
>> me?
> How long must I wrestle with my thoughts
>> and every day have sorrow in my heart?
>> How long will my enemy triumph over
>> me?
>
> Look on me and answer, O LORD my God.
>> Give light to my eyes, or I will sleep in
>> death;
> my enemy will say, "I have overcome him,"
>> and my foes will rejoice when I fall.

But I trust in your unfailing love;
>   my heart rejoices in your salvation.
I will sing to the LORD,
>   for he has been good to me.

In this psalm, David recounted his experience of passing from the depths of despair to the heights of rejoicing. What enabled him to make such a dramatic transition? Although God's grace is not explicitly mentioned, we may be sure it was indeed the grace of God at work in him.

Asaph, another of the psalmists, experienced a different kind of thorn. He compared his experience as a godly man with that of the wicked and became discouraged. He said,

>   For I envied the arrogant
>   >   when I saw the prosperity of the wicked. . . .
>   This is what the wicked are like —
>   >   always carefree, they increase in wealth.

>   Surely in vain have I kept my heart pure;
>   >   in vain have I washed my hands in
>   >   >   innocence. (Psalm 73:3,12-13)

But then he discovered the grace of God and could say,

>   "Yet I am always with you;
>   >   you hold me by my right hand. . . .
>   My flesh and my heart may fail,
>   >   but God is the strength of my heart
>   >   and my portion forever. (verses 23,26)

The testimonies of God's power made perfect in human weakness do not end with the completion of the canon of Scripture. Down through the centuries men and women of God have experienced and borne witness to the sufficiency of His grace. One of the more beautiful expressions of this is found in the well-known poem of Annie Johnson Flint, "He Giveth More Grace":

> He giveth more grace when the burdens grow
> greater;
> He sendeth more grace when the labours
> increase;
> To added afflictions he addeth his mercy,
> To multiplied trials, his multiplied peace.
>
> When we have exhausted our store of
> endurance,
> When our strength has failed ere the day is
> half done;
> When we reach the end of our hoarded
> resources,
> Our Father's full giving is only begun.
>
> His love has no limits, his grace has no
> measure,
> His power has no boundary known unto men;
> For out of his infinite riches in Jesus,
> He giveth, and giveth, and giveth again.[11]

I urge you to read this poem slowly, reflectively, and prayerfully. Apply its message to your own burdens, afflictions, and trials. Ask God to make its truths real to you in your particular situation.

## APPROPRIATING GOD'S GRACE

God said to Paul, "My grace is sufficient for you." God, who is "the God of all grace" (1 Peter 5:10), is the giver of grace, but that does not mean we Christians are passive recipients of it.

Rather, we are to appropriate His grace.

Paul urged Timothy to "be strong in the grace that is in Christ Jesus" (2 Timothy 2:1). Grammatically, the verb is in the imperative mood; that is, it expresses a command or request. Paul wanted Timothy to *do* something; he wanted Timothy to appropriate God's grace and be strong in it.

Timothy apparently had a problem with timidity. In the same letter Paul had already said, "God did not give us a spirit of timidity" and "So do not be ashamed to testify about our Lord, or ashamed of me his prisoner" (2 Timothy 1:7-8). And to the Corinthian believers Paul had written, "If Timothy comes, see to it that he has nothing to fear while he is with you" (1 Corinthians 16:10). Timothy had a problem with timidity, and Paul wanted him to deal with it by appropriating the grace of God, "Be strong in the grace that is in Christ Jesus."

In session 8 (chapter 12) we will explore how we actually appropriate the grace of God. At this point I want to call your attention only to the necessity of our doing it, to the fact that we are not simply passive recipients of God's grace. Just as the Israelites had to gather day-by-day the manna God graciously provided, so we must appropriate day-by-day the grace that is always sufficient for every need.

There is one more truth I want us to see from Paul's words to Timothy. Timothy needed moral strength because he was prone to timidity. So Paul wrote, "Be *strong* in the grace that is in Christ Jesus." What is your greatest need just now? Is it contentment in a very difficult situation? Paul would say to you, "Be content in the grace that is in Christ Jesus." Is it patience or forbearance in very trying circumstances? Then be patient in the grace that is in Christ Jesus. Is it moral purity in a romantic relationship? Then be pure in the grace that is in Christ Jesus. Whatever your need at this time, you too can experience the reality of God's words to Paul: "My grace is sufficient for you, for my power is made perfect in weakness."

God's grace is sufficient. It is sufficient for *all* your needs;

it is sufficient regardless of the severity of any one need. The Israelites never exhausted God's supply of manna. It was always there to be gathered every day for forty years. And you will never exhaust the supply of God's grace. It will always be there every day for you to appropriate as much as you need for whatever your need is.

---

## Chapter Eleven: The Least of All God's People

*Although I am less than the least of all God's people,*
*this grace was given me: to preach to the Gentiles*
*the unsearchable riches of Christ.*
EPHESIANS 3:8

Writing a book is a formidable and daunting task, involving a lot of hard work. One of the most prolific writers of our time, Charles Swindoll described the process this way: "blood, sweat, tears, sleepless nights, lengthy stares at blank sheets of paper, unproductive days when everything gets dumped into the trash, and periodic moments when inspiration and insight flow."[12]

My own difficulty is further compounded because, as my wife said to me, "You do choose some of the more difficult subjects to write about." But as difficult as it is to seek to handle the Word of God correctly and present His truth accurately, it is even more humbling to realize that, though I try to, I have not lived up to the truth I am writing about.

I well remember the days when I was working on my first book, *The Pursuit of Holiness.* The more I studied and wrote about the subject of personal holiness, the less holy I saw myself to be. Some mornings, while shaving, I would look in the mirror and burst out laughing. I would say to myself, "Who do you think you are to be writing a book on holiness? You ought to be reading one yourself. But write one? No way!"

The only thing that gave me courage to continue was a verse

of Scripture that would always come to my mind, Ephesians 3:8, which says, "Although I am less than the least of all God's people, this grace was given me: to preach to the Gentiles the unsearchable riches of Christ." I realized I really did *not* deserve to write on such an awesome subject as holiness, but that I was doing so by the grace of God — by His free, unmerited, unearned, and undeserved favor.

Since that experience with my first book, Ephesians 3:8 has become a "life verse" for me — a verse of Scripture I go back to continually for encouragement. In fact, I doubt if a single week goes by when I don't have occasion to fall back on the realization that I am in the Christian ministry, not because I deserve to be, but because of God's free, unmerited favor.

Paul's testimony of receiving his office as a minister of the gospel purely by the grace of God was a very personal statement. Paul never ceased to be amazed that God chose him, the foremost persecutor of the church, to be the apostle to the Gentiles and to proclaim to them the unsearchable riches of Christ. In 1 Corinthians 15:9, he said, "For I am the least of the apostles and do not even deserve to be called an apostle, because I persecuted the church of God."

Not only did Paul consider himself the least of the apostles, to the Ephesians he referred to himself as "less than the least of all God's people." The expression "less than the least" is actually a "superlative comparative" word coined by Paul to express the depth of his genuine amazement that God would call him to be an apostle. Alfred Marshall translated Paul's coined word as *leaster*,[13] while F. F. Bruce translated it as *lessermost*,[14] both of which are coined English words seeking to accurately and literally translate Paul's emotional expression.

## THE UNWORTHY APOSTLE

Paul freely acknowledged that he received his apostleship purely as a result of God's undeserved favor. God then used Paul's testimony to encourage me at a time when I most keenly felt my complete unworthiness to write on the subject of personal holiness. The question, however, is this: To what extent can we use Paul's very personal testimony and my own experience to establish a scriptural principle regarding Christian ministry? Is all ministry, whether it be teaching a children's Sunday school class, or witnessing individually to inmates at the local prison, or preaching to thousands of people each Sunday, performed by the grace of God by people who are unworthy to be doing it?

Harry Blamires had an incisive answer to that question:

> In the upshot there is only one answer for the preacher who wonders whether he is worthy to preach the sermon he has composed or for the writer who wonders whether he is worthy to write the religious book he is working on. The answer is: Of course not. To ask yourself: Am I worthy to perform this Christian task? is really the peak of pride and presumption. For the very question carries the implication that we spend most of our time doing things we are worthy to do. We simply do not have that kind of worth.[15]

Of course, it matters little what Harry Blamires or Jerry Bridges thinks unless our thinking accords with Scripture. So what does the Bible say to this question? In Romans 12:6 Paul said, "We have different gifts according to the grace given us." Paul was referring to spiritual gifts given to every believer to enable us to fulfill the ministry or service God has appointed for us in the body of Christ.

But note that Paul said these spiritual gifts are given according to the grace of God, not according to what we deserve. The Greek word for a spiritual gift is *charisma*, which means "a gift of God's *grace*," whether it is the gift of eternal life as in Romans 6:23 or the gift of a spiritual ability for use in the body.

Dr. Gordon Fee has some helpful insight on the connection

of *grace* and *gifts*. In his comments on 1 Corinthians 1:4, which says, "I always thank God for you because of his grace given you in Christ Jesus," Dr. Fee said,

> The specific basis of Paul's thanksgiving in their case is God's "grace given you in Christ Jesus." Commonly this is viewed as a thanksgiving for grace as such, i.e., the gracious outpouring of God's mercy in Christ toward the undeserving. However, for Paul *charis* ("grace") very often is closely associated with *charisma/charismata* ("gift/gifts") and in such instances refers to concrete expressions of God's gracious activity in his people. Indeed, the word "grace" itself sometimes denoted these concrete manifestations, the "graces" (gifts), of God's grace.[16]

Peter wrote in a similar fashion as Paul: "Each one should use whatever gift he has received to serve others, faithfully administering God's grace in its various forms" (1 Peter 4:10). Peter and Paul are saying the same thing. The spiritual gifts we have, and the ministries we perform are gifts of God's grace. None of us deserves the gifts he or she has been given. They are given to us by God's undeserved favor to us through Christ.

This means the most "worthy" and the most "unworthy" of all Christians both receive their gifts and their ministries on the same basis. The "unworthy" person surely does not deserve his gift, but neither does the most "worthy." They both receive them as unmerited favors from God.

I put quotation marks around worthy and unworthy in the above paragraph, because in reality there is no such distinction in God's sight. In His sight, we are all totally and permanently bankrupt spiritually. Paul's statement, "There is no difference, for all have sinned and fall short of the glory of God" (Romans 3:22-23), is just as true for believers as for unbelievers.

We never earn our privileges of ministry because of our hard work or faithfulness in previous service to God. I taught adult Sunday school for many years in a small church before God launched me into a much wider sphere of ministry. But I did not earn an enlarged ministry through my "faithful" teaching; rather, it was a gift of God's grace.

We are so accustomed to thinking of spiritual gifts in terms of abilities to minister that we lose sight of the ordinary meaning of the word. A gift is something given to us; something we don't earn. But even our ordinary meaning fails to adequately convey the biblical sense. We tend to give gifts to people who, even though they have not earned them, in some sense deserve them because of their relationship to us or because they have done us a favor of some kind. But God gives spiritual gifts to people who do not deserve them. None of us deserves to be in God's service, whether it's teaching a children's Sunday school class or serving on some faraway mission field.

It is an awesome thing to attempt to speak on behalf of God. Yet that is exactly what we do when we teach or preach or write. It matters not whether our audience is one person or fifty thousand, whether they are kindergarten pupils or graduate theological students. Any time we say or write something that we hold out to be biblical truth, we are putting ourselves in the position of being God's spokesman.

Peter said, "If anyone speaks, he should do it as one speaking the very words of God" (1 Peter 4:11). I suspect that most people who read this book do teach the Scriptures occasionally if not regularly. Do we appreciate the awesomeness of our responsibility, to be speaking on behalf of God? Do we consider the accountability that comes with being entrusted with the divine message?

Paul himself was keenly conscious of his immense responsibility when he said, "Unlike so many, we do not peddle the word of God for profit. On the contrary, in Christ we speak before God with sincerity, like men sent from God" (2 Corinthians 2:17). He said he spoke like a man sent from God, but he also said he spoke before God, or in the sight of God.

That is, God not only sent him, but observed him.

One Sunday as I stood up to teach my adult Sunday school class, to my dismay, I realized the president of our denominational seminary was sitting in the class. To make matters worse, he also happened to be the professor of homiletics (the art of preaching). I was sure he was critiquing everything I said, both in content and delivery. Now if the presence of a seminary president in my class was an awesome experience, how much more awed should I be when I realize I speak, or write, in the very presence of God and on His behalf.

What, then, will give us the courage to undertake or continue to teach the Scriptures or, for that matter, to exercise any other spiritual gift? The answer is the heartfelt conviction that we have our ministry by God's grace. Again, as Paul said, "Therefore, since through God's mercy we have this ministry, we do not lose heart" (2 Corinthians 4:1).

It was a sense of God's mercy that gave Paul courage or, as he expressed it, caused him not to lose heart. Mercy is God's grace expressed specifically toward people who are viewed by Him as guilty, condemned, and helpless. It is generally expressed in terms of relieving the misery due to their sin. But God not only relieved Paul's misery, He elevated him to the office of apostle and gave him the ministry of proclaiming the riches of Christ.

But Paul never lost sight of his own unworthiness, even when exercising his office of apostleship. He never forgot he held that office by God's mercy. Here we see the biblical relationship between a sense of one's utter unworthiness on the one hand, and the courage to undertake a ministry for God on the other. To lose sight of our unworthiness is to risk exercising our gifts and fulfilling our ministries in a spirit of presumptuous pride, as if God were fortunate to have us on His team. But to focus too much on our unworthiness, to the neglect of God's grace, will effectively immobilize us for His service. That attitude is also an expression of pride because we are still focusing on ourselves and our worthiness or unworthiness, as if God

211

were dependent on some innate quality within us to equip us for His service.

Remember we did not declare temporary spiritual bankruptcy. Our bankruptcy is total and permanent. The only worthiness we have for entrance into God's kingdom is in Christ. The only worthiness we have with which to come before God is in Christ. And the only worthiness we have to qualify us for ministry is in Christ. If we are to progress in any aspect of the Christian life, we must look outside ourselves and only to Christ. It is in Him that the grace of God is so abundantly poured out on us.

## THE INADEQUATE APOSTLE

Paul was conscious throughout his entire ministry of his utter unworthiness to be a servant of Christ. We have seen how he expressed this sense of unworthiness in Ephesians 3:8 and 2 Corinthians 4:1. We again see him expressing it in 1 Corinthians 15:9-10:

> For I am the least of the apostles and do not even deserve to be called an apostle, because I persecuted the church of God. But by the grace of God I am what I am, and his grace to me was not without effect. No, I worked harder than all of them — yet not I, but the grace of God that was with me.

Paul freely admitted he did not deserve to be an apostle but that he was one by the grace of God — that is, by God's unmerited favor. In verse 10, however, we see Paul making a subtle, natural transition of thought as he frequently does. The word *grace* in his expression, "But by the grace of God I am what I am," can be taken in the context to mean either God's unmerited favor or God's enabling power. Looking back to his acknowledgment of unworthiness in verse 9, his statement would appear to mean, "I am unworthy to be an apostle, but by God's unmerited favor I am one."

Looking forward to the remainder of verse 10, however, where Paul was speaking about the effects of God's grace on his ministry, it would appear to mean, "By God's enabling power I am an effective apostle." I believe both of these meanings of grace are incorporated in Paul's statement. He was not giving us a technical treatise on grace and distinguishing its finer shades of meaning. Rather, Paul was speaking from his heart, and he was saying God's grace was sufficient for both his unworthiness and his inadequacy. When he said, "But by the grace of God I am what I am," he was saying, "I am an apostle as a result of God's unmerited favor shown to me and as a result of God's enabling power at work in me." And even the working of God's power is itself an unmerited favor from Him.

Like Paul, you and I need both aspects of grace to minister, because, also like him, we are neither worthy nor adequate. We need both. A school board interviewing men and women for the position of school principal should look for evidence of sterling character (worthiness) and professional competence (adequacy). Some candidates might be worthy but not competent; others competent, but not worthy. The school board must insist on both.

But God insists on neither. Instead He glories in calling into His service people who are neither worthy nor adequate. He makes them worthy in Christ alone, never in themselves. Then He makes them adequate through the mighty working of His Spirit within them.

Listen to how Paul expressed this last thought in Colossians 1:28-29: "We proclaim him, admonishing and teaching everyone with all wisdom, so that we may present everyone perfect in Christ. To this end I labor, struggling with all his energy, which so powerfully works in me." Paul found his worthiness in the worthiness of Christ and his adequacy in the power of Christ.

In 2 Corinthians 2:14-17, Paul spoke of his ministry of the

gospel, which in its eventual effect leads either to life or death. To those who believe, it leads to life; but to those who reject it, it leads to death. The eternal consequences of proclaiming such a gospel led Paul to exclaim, "And who is equal to such a task?" (verse 16).

You share the gospel informally with a neighbor, or perhaps in a more direct fashion when you are engaged in some evangelism program. In each case you are the smell of death or the fragrance of life to those with whom you share. Who is equal to such a task? You stand on Sunday morning before a class of junior high boys and girls. It seems to be almost insignificant; yet I have heard many adults give testimony of the life-changing influence on them of a childhood Sunday school teacher. Who is equal to such a task? You meet individually with a young person for basic discipleship training. He later goes to the mission field and translates the New Testament for a primitive tribe, which in turn evangelizes a neighboring tribe. Who is equal to such a task?

Paul answered this question just a few sentences later when he said, "Not that we are competent in ourselves to claim anything for ourselves, but our competence comes from God" (2 Corinthians 3:5).

Note that Paul said, "Not that we are competent in ourselves." If you feel incompetent in God's service you are in good company. Paul felt that way also. If there is anyone in the history of the church who could have relied on his own God-given endowments, surely it would have been Paul. He was a brilliant theologian, a gifted evangelist, a tireless church planter, and a sound missionary strategist. He was also adept at cross-cultural ministry ("To the Jews I became like a Jew, to win the Jews.... To those not having the law [the Gentiles] I became like one not having the law" [1 Corinthians 9:20-21]). Yet Paul, with all his abilities, said we are not competent in ourselves.

We are not competent, but God makes us competent. That is what Paul was saying in 1 Corinthians 15:10: "His grace to me was not without effect. No, I worked harder than all of them [the other apostles]." God's grace in its concrete expression of divine power was effective in Paul. In fact it was so effective that Paul could say he worked harder than all the other apostles. That is quite a statement and, at first glance, seems to put Paul in a position of unconscionable boasting. I used to be troubled by this statement. It seemed to be excessive boasting and quite out of character with Paul's obviously genuine humility. But I have come to realize Paul was not boasting. Rather, he was exalting the grace of God. He was saying that God's grace at work in him was so effective it caused him to work harder than all of them. The grace of God motivated him, enabled him, and then blessed the fruits of his labors.

But then, perhaps realizing he could be misunderstood, Paul added, "Yet not I, but the grace of God that was with me." Perhaps John Calvin helps us best understand Paul's intent when he wrote:

> For having said that something was applicable to himself, he [Paul] corrects that and transfers it entirely to God; entirely, I insist, and not just a part of it; for he affirms that whatever he may have seemed to do was in fact totally the work of grace. This is indeed a remarkable verse, not only for bringing down human pride to the dust, but also for making clear to us the way that the grace of God works in us. For, as though he were wrong in making himself the source of anything good, Paul corrects what he had said, and declares that the grace of God is the efficient cause of everything. We should not imagine that Paul is merely simulating humility here. He is speaking as he does from his heart, and because he knows that it is the truth. We should therefore learn that the only good we have is what the Lord has given us gratuitously; that the only good we do is what He does in us; that it is not that we do nothing ourselves,

215

but that we act only when we have been acted upon, in other words under the direction and influence of the Holy Spirit.[17]

Lest we lose sight of the human element in Calvin's emphasis on grace, I want to call your attention to one statement near the end of the quotation: "that it is not that we do nothing ourselves, but that we act only when we have been acted upon." Colossians 1:29, which we already looked at briefly, brings out the scriptural view of our working by His grace: "To this end I labor, struggling with all his energy, which so powerfully works in me."

The word *struggling* connotes great intensity, "to put forth every effort, involving toil."[18] So in 1 Corinthians 15:10, there is no hint of inactivity or turning it all over to the Lord. Paul said he worked hard. But he worked hard because God's grace worked effectively within him. Nor is there the suggestion that God and Paul worked together in the sense of a partnership. God did not do the evangelizing or church planting. Paul did that. But he did it because God's grace — that is, God's power through the Holy Spirit — was at work in him.

R. C. H. Lenski shed light on the relationship of God's grace to Paul's efforts: "It would, however, be a mistake to picture God's grace and Paul's efforts as two horses together drawing a wagon, . . . for the two are not coordinate. Paul's effort is, in the last analysis, due to God's grace, and it is put forth only as long as the Holy Spirit rules, guides, and leads him."[19] To which I would want to add, "and enables him."

The Holy Spirit must not only prompt, guide, and enable us, He must also bless our efforts if they are to have any effect. Paul recognized this truth when he said, "I planted the seed, Apollos watered it, but God made it grow. So neither he who plants nor he who waters is anything, but only God, who makes things grow" (1 Corinthians 3:6-7).

Paul and Apollos could both work extremely hard. They could do so in humble, conscious dependence on God's grace.

And yet they could fail to see any results from their labors because they, of themselves, could not change hearts. Only God can make things grow. Only He can cause the Word to take root and grow in the heart of that little girl in your Sunday school class. Only He can open people's hearts to respond to the gospel. Only He can cause that person you are seeking to disciple to respond to your challenge and instruction.

God's grace must work in the heart of the other person as well as work through us to minister to that person. So we must depend on His Spirit to work in us and through us, and we must also depend on Him to work in the hearts of those we are seeking to minister to.

Within the scope of this and the previous chapter we have seen that in ourselves we are *weak*, *unworthy*, and *inadequate*. We really are! We are not denigrating ourselves when we recognize this truth. We are simply acknowledging reality and opening ourselves to the grace of God. As we do this we can expect to experience His grace working mightily in our lives for, to para-phrase James 4:6, "Although God opposes the proud, He *does* give grace to the humble." James 4:6 is both a warning to the proud and a promise to the humble. That is, to those who genu-inely acknowledge they are weak, unworthy, and inadequate, God does promise to give grace.

## SUFFICIENT GRACE

God's grace is sufficient for our weakness. Christ's worth does cover our unworthiness, and the Holy Spirit does make us effec-tive in spite of our inadequacy. This is the glorious paradox of living by grace. When we discover we are weak in ourselves, we find we are strong in Christ. When we regard ourselves as less than the least of all God's people, we are given some immense privilege of serving in the kingdom. When we almost despair over our inadequacy, we find the Holy Spirit giving us unusual ability. We shake our heads in amazement and say with Isaiah,

"LORD, . . . all that we have accomplished you have done for us" (Isaiah 26:12).

The contrast between human weakness and divine power is vividly illustrated in Isaiah 41:14-15. This particular passage is set in the context of a lengthy message of encouragement to the downtrodden nation of Israel. Verses 14-15 read:

> "Do not be afraid, O worm Jacob,
>    O little Israel,
> for I myself will help you," declares the
>    LORD,
>       your Redeemer, the Holy One of Israel.
>
> "See, I will make you into a threshing sledge,
>    new and sharp, with many teeth.
> You will thresh the mountains and crush
>    them,
>       and reduce the hills to chaff."

God addresses the nation as "O worm Jacob, O little Israel." The designation *worm* is not used by God in a disparaging sense, but rather calls attention to the weakness and helplessness of the nation, as does the term "O little Israel." The metaphor of a worm is well chosen to express their weakness, because few things are more helpless and exposed to being trodden under foot than a worm. But the humbling designation as a worm and as little serves only to magnify the greatness of the encouragement God gives the nation: "Do not be afraid," "I myself will help you," and "I will make you into a threshing sledge, new and sharp, with many teeth."

The promise of the overall passage is that Israel, weak and downtrodden though she may be, will in due time prevail over her enemies because the Lord Himself will help her. He will not only help her, He will make Israel herself into a threshing sledge that devours her enemies. The ancient threshing machine was a sledge of thick planks armed with iron or sharpened stones as teeth to thresh the grain. God promises that, just as the threshing sledge breaks up the heads of grain, so "worm" Jacob will devour her enemies.

The imagery of the passage is a study in contrast between the weakness of Israel and the mighty acts she will perform with God's help. Dr. Joseph Alexander, a renowned professor at Princeton Theological Seminary in the mid-nineteenth century, said concerning this passage, "The image presented [of the threshing sledge] is the strange but strong one of a downtrodden worm reducing hills to powder, the essential idea being that of a weak and helpless object overcoming the most disproportionate obstacles, by *strength derived from another*" (emphasis added).[20]

That is a picture of the grace of God at work: a weak and helpless object overcoming disproportionate obstacles by strength derived from another. God makes us weak, or rather He allows us to become painfully conscious of our weakness, in order to make us strong with His strength.

Some years ago when God opened up for me a wider Bible teaching and writing ministry, I felt drawn to Isaiah 41:14-15. Even though the promise was given to the nation of Israel, I sensed God was allowing me to make a personal application, that He would indeed make me into a threshing sledge, a harvesting instrument in His hand. But I also sensed that God required, as a condition of the promise, that I accept the description of "worm Jacob, little Israel," not in a denigrating sense, but as a realization of my own personal weakness and helplessness.

I go back to that condition and promise almost every time I teach the Word of God or sit down to write. I do not do this in the sense of rubbing a good luck charm, but rather to acknowledge my own inability to accomplish anything for God and to lay hold of His promise to give me the power to minister for Him. God seems to keep saying to me, "As long as you are willing to acknowledge you are as weak and helpless as a worm, I will make you strong and powerful like a threshing sledge, with new, sharp teeth."

The gracious paradox of divine strength working through human weakness as taught in Scripture has been recognized through the centuries by the great teachers of the church. The respected Puritan theologian John Owen, for example, said,

> Yet the duties God requires of us are not in proportion to the strength we possess in ourselves. Rather, they are proportional to the resources available to us in Christ. We do not have the ability in ourselves to accomplish the least of God's tasks. This is a law of grace. When we recognize it is impossible for us to perform a duty in our own strength, we will discover the secret of its accomplishment. But alas, this is a secret we often fail to discover.[21]

## SACRIFICIAL GRACE

Effective Christian ministry, whether it is to one person or thousands, inevitably involves sacrifice. The Greek word we use to designate a minister is also the word used for servant. Thus a minister of the gospel is a servant, not only of God, but of those to whom he ministers. That is why Paul could very naturally say, "For we do not preach ourselves, but Jesus Christ as Lord, and *ourselves as your servants* for Jesus' sake" (2 Corinthians 4:5, emphasis added).

To minister effectively, we need not only the strength and ability to minister but also the heart and disposition of a servant. We must have the sacrificial attitude Paul had when he said, "We loved you so much that we were delighted to share with you not only the gospel of God but our lives as well, because you had become so dear to us" (1 Thessalonians 2:8). Paul gave himself without reservation to the people to whom he preached. Not only did he give unstintingly of his time and energy, but he also became "all things to all men"; he freely adapted himself to them, that he might win them for Christ.

Such a ministry does indeed require a sacrificial attitude, enabling us to put the needs of others before our own and causing us to lay down our lives in a sense to serve others. The question is then, "How do we get such a sacrificial spirit?" To answer that, let's look at a sort of "case study" of God's grace at work in an unusual way in the hearts of the Macedonian Christians.

Chapters 8 and 9 of 2 Corinthians have become the classic Scripture passage on the subject of Christian giving. In fact, it is difficult to teach on giving without drawing on principles from those chapters. It is not my purpose now to explore those principles, but rather to use the background situation of the passage to illustrate how we gain a sacrificial spirit by the grace of God.

Paul wanted to challenge the Corinthian Christians to give generously toward the need of the poorer believers in Jerusalem. To do this he held up as an example the generosity of the Macedonian churches. Here is what he said:

> And now, brothers, we want you to know about the grace that God has given the Macedonian churches. Out of the most severe trial, their overflowing joy and their extreme poverty welled up in rich generosity. For I testify that they gave as much as they were able, and even beyond their ability. Entirely on their own, they urgently pleaded with us for the privilege of sharing in this service to the saints. (2 Corinthians 8:1-4)

The generosity of the Macedonian churches was indeed remarkable. Their giving to the believers in Jerusalem was not out of an abundance, but rather, out of their own poverty. They themselves could well have qualified as beneficiaries of other people's giving. They gave, not according to their ability, but beyond their ability, in disregard of their own needs. Paul said they *pleaded* with him for the privilege of sharing in the offering he was collecting for the poor Jewish believers in Jerusalem. And all this for people whom they had never seen nor met.

What was the secret of such an outpouring of generosity? We have no reason to believe the Macedonians as a people were more inclined to generosity than any other people. And people as a whole do not tend to be generous in giving to the needs of others. Consider, for example, that in the United States, one of the most affluent nations in history, our giving to charitable and religious causes averages one or two percent of our income.

Paul said the Macedonians' secret was the grace of God (verse 1). Here is another occasion where Paul uses *grace* to mean a working of the Holy Spirit in the lives of believers. The sense is not that of God's unmerited favor considered as the source of blessing, but rather the working of His Spirit as a concrete expression of that favor.

Charles Hodge commented on 2 Corinthians 8:1,

> The liberality of the Corinthians was due to the operation of the grace of God. The sacred writers constantly recognize the fact that the freest and most spontaneous acts of men, their inward states and the outward manifestations of those states, when good, are due to the secret influence of the Spirit of God, which eludes our consciousness.[22]

So it was the grace of God operating in them through the Holy Spirit, not the superiority of their own character, that caused such an abundant outpouring of generosity from the Macedonians. God did not leave them to the resources of their own human nature — which is not naturally generous — but intervened in their hearts by the power of His Spirit to create this amazing generosity.

The question might arise, "Why didn't God create this same generosity in the hearts of the Corinthian Christians?" The answer is that is what He was doing at that time through Paul.

There is no doubt that God has the power to intervene directly and sovereignly in the hearts of people when He chooses to do so. Paul's conversion on the Damascus road is an incontrovertible case in point. And in 2 Corinthians 8, Paul said, "I thank God, who put into the heart of Titus the same concern I have for you" (verse 16). Apparently God worked directly in Titus's heart.[23]

But God's more usual way of working in the hearts of His people is through natural means. In the case of the Corinthians, it was through the exhortation and encouragement of Paul. (Although we have no record of it, we can reasonably assume God used Paul in the lives of the Macedonians also.) The Corinthians did respond positively, as evidenced by Paul's statement in Romans 15:26: "For Macedonia and Achaia were pleased to make a contribution for the poor among the saints in Jerusalem." (Achaia being the province where Corinth was located.)

Having looked at our "case study" of God's grace at work in the Macedonians, let's now return to the question, "How do we get the sacrificial spirit we need to serve God and other people?" The answer is, by the grace of God.

In regard to God's grace given to the Macedonians, which resulted in abundant generosity, Philip Hughes wrote, "There is no question of human resources, but only of divine grace; and that same grace was available to the Christians in Corinth."[24]

That same grace is also available to you and me to enable us to be generous in giving of ourselves, which is after all the concrete expression of a sacrificial spirit. We saw in chapter 10 that Paul said to Timothy, "Be strong in the grace that is in Christ Jesus" (2 Timothy 2:1). In 2 Corinthians 8–9, he was effectively saying to the Corinthians, "Be generous in the grace that is in Christ Jesus." And to us he would say, "Serve sacrificially in the grace that is in Christ Jesus." Again, we will consider how to appropriate this grace in session 8 (chapter 12), but for now, we need to be encouraged to realize that God's grace is both sufficient and effective. We can, by His grace, fulfill whatever ministry He has given us to do in the body of Christ.

# THE REWARD OF GRACE

We have seen in this chapter that every aspect of our ministry, whether it be an obscure ministry to one person or a public ministry to thousands, is by the grace of God. We are unworthy to minister, but God considers us worthy through Christ. We are inadequate to minister, but God makes us adequate through the powerful working of His Holy Spirit. We are not naturally given to self-sacrifice, but God gives us that spirit by His grace. *All is of grace.* No human worthiness or adequacy is required or accepted.

Such a strong, but I believe biblical, emphasis on God's grace apart from human worth or adequacy does lead to the question of the relationship of grace and rewards. Doesn't God promise rewards to His faithful servants? Didn't Paul himself teach that we must appear before the judgment seat of Christ to receive what is due us? If all our efforts are the results of God's grace, what room is left for "faithful service"?

God does promise rewards, and we must all appear before the judgment seat of Christ (see Matthew 25:21; 2 Corinthians 5:10). But these rewards are rewards of grace, not of merit. We never by our hard work or sacrificial service obligate God to reward us, for as Paul said in Romans 11:35, "Who has ever given to God, that God should repay him?"

If all our service to God is made possible by His undeserved favor and made effective by the power of His Spirit, then we have really brought nothing to Him that we did not first receive from Him. The Puritan Samuel Bolton said, "If there was anything of man's bringing, which was not of God's bestowing, though it were never so small, it would overturn the nature of grace, and make that of works which is of grace."[25] But it is all of God's bestowing. Every thought, word, or deed emanating from us that is in any way pleasing to God and glorifying to Him has its ultimate origin in God, because apart from Him, there is nothing good in us (see Romans 7:18).

Even the good works we bring to God are in themselves

defective, both in motive and performance. As we saw in session 5 (chapter 8), it is virtually impossible to purge our motives completely of pride and self-gratification. And we can never perfectly perform those good works. The best we can do falls short of what God requires, but the truth is, we never actually do the best we can, let alone what would meet God's perfect standard.

That is why Peter spoke of our "offering spiritual sacrifices acceptable to God through Jesus Christ" (1 Peter 2:5). Our best works are acceptable to God only because they are made acceptable by the merit of Jesus Christ. But God *does* accept them through Christ; He accepts them on the basis of His grace.

Ernest Kevan quoted one of the Puritans on the imperfection of our works as follows:

We do not do all that is commanded but come short of our duty, and that which we do is imperfect and defective in respect of manner and measure; and therefore in justice deserves punishment, rather than reward: and consequently the reward, when it is given, is to be ascribed to God's undeserved mercy and not to our merit.[26]

Finally, we must go back to the parable of the workers in the vineyard, which we studied in session 2 (chapter 4) and session 3. You will remember that, in the verses immediately preceding the parable, Jesus promised a reward "a hundred times as much," or ten thousand percent. God's rewards to us will not only be of grace, but will indeed be gracious — that is, generous beyond all measure.

So the grace of God in our service to Him does not negate rewards but rather makes them possible. As R. C. Sproul said, "But the blessing Christ promised, the blessing of great reward, is a reward of grace. The blessing is promised even though it is not earned. Augustine said it this way: Our rewards in heaven are a result of God's crowning His own gifts."[27]

This is the amazing story of God's grace. God saves us by

His grace and transforms us more and more into the likeness of His Son by His grace. In all our trials and afflictions, He sustains and strengthens us by His grace. He calls us by grace to perform our own unique function within the body of Christ. Then, again by grace, He gives to each of us the spiritual gifts necessary to fulfill our calling. As we serve Him, He makes that service acceptable to Himself by grace, and then rewards us a hundredfold by grace.

In Romans 1:17, Paul spoke of the gospel as revealing "a righteousness that is by faith from first to last" — that is, from beginning to end. This is also an appropriate term for grace, for faith is no more than the response to and appropriation of the grace of God. So the entire Christian life is a life lived under grace from first to last, from beginning to end, all "to the praise of his glorious grace, which he has freely given us in the One he loves" (Ephesians 1:6).

# The Sufficiency of Grace

## (Chapters 10 and 11)

## STUDY QUESTIONS

### CENTRAL IDEA

God's grace enables us to persevere and grow despite any and all obstacles. God gives each of us the grace we need to fulfill the ministry and service He has given to us to bring glory to His Name.

### WARM-UP

Give an example from the past week when God's grace was sufficient to enable you to meet some challenge.

### EXPLORING GRACE

1. In 2 Corinthians 12:2-10 we find a powerful passage about suffering and the sufficiency of God's grace. Read this passage and then answer the following questions.

   a. What explanations does Paul give for why his physical suffering is not removed?

   b. Why do you suppose we don't always get a clear explanation of why we are allowed to suffer certain things?

   c.   Why can God express His power in our lives better through our weaknesses than through our strengths?

2.   Think of a weakness in your own life. It could be a physical problem, an emotional weakness, or difficult circumstances. In what specific ways have God's power and grace become real in your life through this trial?

3.   About trials, James says that we are to "welcome them as friends" (James 1:2, PH). Read James 1:2-4.

   a.   What do you think James means by welcoming trials as friends?

   b.   Why does he encourage us to have this kind of attitude?

4.   a.   Do you tend to feel closer to God when your life is relatively trouble-free or when you have problems? Why do you think this is the case?

b. Is it necessary for us to experience troubles to be close to God? Why or why not?

c. What can a person who has a pretty easy life do to get close to God, short of praying for trials?

5. In the story of the Israelites' wanderings in the wilderness we see the total dependence of man upon God in a dramatic way. Read Deuteronomy 8:2-3.

a. Why do you think it seems so easy for us today to fall into the sin of thinking we are self-sufficient?

b. Why is it a sin to think we are self-sufficient?

c. Whether we realize it or not, we depend on God for far more than our physical needs. Is it easier for you to fall into an attitude of self-sufficiency in physical things or in spiritual things? Why do you suppose that's so?

6. In Romans 12:4-8, Paul explains that we each have different spiritual gifts. The Lord gives us these for the purpose of fulfilling the ministry or service He has given us. Look also at the list of spiritual gifts in 1 Corinthians 12:4-11.

   a. What spiritual gifts do you see evidence of in the lives of other group members?

   b. It is often easier to see the spiritual gifts of others than to see our own gifts. Nonetheless, we should be aware of the gifts God has given us so that we can put ourselves in positions where those gifts can be used. What spiritual gift(s) do you think God has given to you?

   c. Share a time when you were aware of God using your spiritual gift(s) in a specific situation.

7. Read 1 Corinthians 15:9-10 and Ephesians 3:8.

   a. What was Paul's perspective on his own ability to fulfill the job God had given him to do?

b.  What service or ministry has God given to you? (This could include raising your family, teaching Sunday school, being available for a friend in need, sharing the gospel with a neighbor, etc.) If you have trouble answering this question, spend some time in prayer, asking God to show you ways you can begin to serve Him right where He has placed you.

c.  How do Paul's words help encourage you in whatever God is asking you to do?

8.  Look at the following verses. How do they drive home the point that it is God who enables us in everything we do?

*   Isaiah 26:12

*   1 Corinthians 3:6

*   2 Corinthians 3:4-6

*   Colossians 1:28-29

9.  As believers we will stand before the Lord and receive rewards by God's grace based upon how we have lived this life. All of our growth and strength for service come from God. All the fruit of our labors is the result of God's grace. We must labor. God doesn't do that for us. But we must labor in dependence on His grace to enable us. Read 1 Corinthians 3:7-15, 2 Corinthians 5:10, and Ephesians 6:7.

    a.  What is the basis of the rewards we receive as Christians?

    b.  What happens to the Christian whose labors have had no eternal value?

    c.  What is the purpose of these rewards? See Revelation 4:9-11.

10. a.  In what area of your life do you sense the greatest need to experience of God's grace?

    b.  What barriers do you think you might be using to prevent God from working in your life?

## CLOSING PRAYER

Read aloud the poem by Annie Johnson Flint found in the "Pondering Grace" section. Then express your needs to the Lord and acknowledge His sufficiency. Confess your need to respond more to His working in your lives.

## GOING DEEPER (Extra questions for further study)

1. Read Philippians 4:4-13.

   a. What is the secret to being content that Paul refers to in verse 12?

   b. Have you learned to live by this secret in your own life? What specific things can you do to go deeper in living according to the principles Paul spells out in this passage?

2. What attitudes do the men in these passages display toward God in the midst of their suffering?

   • Psalm 13

   • Psalm 73:1-3,13-17,23-28

   • Lamentations 3:19-33

3.   What do the following verses say about how God works in our trials?

•   Genesis 50:20

•   Romans 8:28-29

### Pondering Grace (For personal reflection)

*The wilderness tested and disciplined the people in various ways. On the one hand, the desolation of the wilderness removed the natural props and supports which man by nature depends on; it cast the people back on God, who alone could provide the strength to survive the wilderness. On the other hand, the severity of the wilderness period undermined the shallow bases of confidence of those who were not truly rooted and grounded in God. The wilderness makes or breaks a man; it provides strength of will and character. The strength provided by the wilderness, however, was not the strength of self-sufficiency, but the strength that comes from a knowledge of the living God.*

 P. C. Craigie, The New International Commentary on the Old Testament: The Book of Deuteronomy

*For men have no taste for [God's power] till they are convinced of their need of it and they immediately forget its value unless they are continually reminded by awareness of their own weakness.*

John Calvin, *Calvin's New Testament Commentaries*

*Day by day and with each passing moment,*
*Strength I find to meet my trials here;*
*Trusting in my Father's wise bestowment,*
*I've no cause for worry or for fear.*
*He whose heart is kind beyond all measure*
*Gives unto each day what He deems best*
*Lovingly, its part of pain and pleasure,*
*Mingling toil with peace and rest.*

Lina Sandell Berg

*So [God] supplies perfectly measured grace to meet the needs of the godly. For daily needs there is daily grace; for sudden needs, sudden grace; for overwhelming need, overwhelming grace. God's grace is given wonderfully, but not wastefully; freely but not foolishly; bountifully but not blindly.*

John Blanchard, *Truth for Life: A Devotional Commentary on the Epistle of James*

*He giveth more grace when the burdens grow greater;*
*He sendeth more grace when the labours increase;*
*To added afflictions he addeth his mercy,*
*To multiplied trials his multiplied peace.*

*When we have exhausted our store of endurance,*
*When our strength has failed ere the day is half done;*
*When we reach the end of our hoarded resources,*
*Our Father's full giving is only begun.*

*His love has no limits, his grace has no measure,*
*His power has no boundary known unto men;*
*For out of his infinite riches in Jesus,*
*He giveth, and giveth, and giveth again.*

Annie Johnson Flint

# Appropriating God's Grace

Read the following portion of *Transforming Grace*. In the margins, record observations, illustrations, or questions that come to mind as you read. Then answer the study questions that follow the reading.

---

### Chapter Twelve: Appropriating God's Grace

*For we do not have a high priest who is unable to sympathize with our weaknesses, but we have one who has been tempted in every way, just as we are — yet was without sin. Let us then approach the throne of grace with confidence, so that we may receive mercy and find grace to help us in our time of need.*
HEBREWS 4:15-16

Notes and Observations

Several years ago a friend approached me about taking another assignment in The Navigators. I was quite happy in my existing situation, and the prospective job did not appeal to me at all. However, I told my friend I would consider it and pray about it. As I sought God's guidance, I assumed He would agree that the prospective ministry was not appropriate for me.

To say the prospective job did not appeal to me is actually an understatement. As I considered all the pros and cons of making a change, I listed five major reasons on the con side and none on the pro side. The more I thought about my friend's request, however, the more I had an uneasy sense that God wanted me to accept it. At the same time, the more I thought about the new job, the more I shrank from it. I found myself in a not uncommon dilemma of not wanting to do what I thought might be God's will for me. What was I to do?

The inner struggle between my personal desires and what I thought might be the will of God continued for several days and, in fact, grew in intensity. One evening I told God I wanted to do whatever His will for me was, but that I simply did not have the spiritual ability to say yes. I told Him I had reached the limits of my commitment to do whatever He asked me to do. I could go no further unless He enabled me to do so.

As I continued to wrestle with this dilemma, the words of John 12:24 in the King James Version came to mind, "Verily, verily, I say unto you, except a corn of wheat fall into the ground and die, it abideth alone: but if it die, it bringeth forth much fruit." The passage seemed appropriate for the occasion, for, to me, this prospective assignment would indeed involve a "dying" to my own desires for my family and ministry.

But the verse also reminded me of a biblical principle: "Dying" is a prerequisite to fruitfulness. Furthermore, Jesus actually assures us in the passage that if we "die," we will produce fruit. As I thought about the truth Jesus was teaching, I gained the spiritual strength to say yes. I was able to say, "God, the prospects of this assignment only look grim to me, but You have promised that if I 'die' in this situation, I will bring forth 'much fruit.' I don't see how this could possibly happen, but I believe Your promise and so I say yes." As it later turned out, that assignment was not God's will for me. Apparently He simply used that exercise as a means of spiritual growth I needed at the time.

My purpose for recounting that personal incident, however, is to illustrate how we appropriate God's grace — that is, God's power — to enable us to respond to the various circumstances and challenges that constantly come to us. Perhaps the idea of *appropriating* the grace of God is a new thought to you, and you're not quite sure what I mean. The basic meaning of the word is "to take possession of," and that is what we do when we appropriate God's grace. We take possession of the divine strength He has made available to us in Christ. To use an analogy, we draw on an inexhaustible bank account, the account of God's grace. Now there are times when the Holy Spirit works in a sovereign way in our lives, apart from any appropriating activity on our part, but more often He expects us to act to appropriate His grace. To this end, He has provided four principal means of doing so: prayer, His Word, submission to His providential workings in our lives, and the ministry of others.

## THE THRONE OF GRACE

The first avenue of appropriating God's grace is simply to ask for it in prayer. In the above situation, as I realized I had reached the limits of my commitment, I ceased asking God for guidance and began to ask for the grace — that is, the spiritual ability — to say yes to what I thought was His will. In Hebrews 4:15-16, we are invited, or more accurately, we are encouraged to go to God in prayer asking for the grace we need. The passage says,

> For we do not have a high priest who is unable to sympathize with our weaknesses, but we have one who has been tempted in every way, just as we are — yet was without sin. Let us then approach the throne of grace with confidence, so that we may receive mercy and find grace to help us in our time of need.

The throne of grace is a figurative expression for God seated on His throne as the God of all grace. It is obviously not the throne itself but God on the throne who will give us His grace in time of need. In Revelation 6:16-17, God is portrayed sitting on His throne as the God of wrath and judgment. The people who see Him in that setting will call for mountains and rocks to fall on them to hide them from His face and His wrath.

The prophet Isaiah saw God seated on His throne as the God of infinite majesty and holiness. Isaiah was awestruck and cried out, "Woe to me! . . . I am ruined! For I am a man of unclean lips, and I live among a people of unclean lips, and my eyes have seen the King, the LORD Almighty" (6:5). But in

Hebrews 4:16, we see, not a throne of wrath, nor even a throne of infinite majesty and holiness, but a throne of grace. We are encouraged to come to this throne, not with terror because of His wrath nor with awed fear because of His holiness, but with *confidence* because of His grace. God is indeed the infinitely holy God, high and exalted as Isaiah saw Him, and He will one day manifest Himself as the God of wrath to those who have spurned Him. But to us who are His children, He is the God of grace seated on His throne of grace.

We need to remember that it was God Himself who presented Jesus as the atonement for our sins, as the One who satisfied the justice of God and by that satisfaction turned aside God's wrath from us. And because of Jesus' atoning sacrifice, God's throne is no longer a throne of judgment and wrath for us, but it is now a throne of grace.

God, whom Paul described as living in "unapproachable light" (1 Timothy 6:16), now encourages us to enter "the Most Holy Place," His very throne room, and "draw near to God" (Hebrews 10:19-22).

This invitation is a striking contrast to the restrictions that existed under the Mosaic dispensation of the Old Testament. Under that system, *only* the high priest was allowed to enter the Most Holy Place of the temple, and then *only* once a year and *never* without the blood of the atonement (see Hebrews 9:7). Now *all* believers may enter the Most Holy Place in heaven, at *all* times, through the blood of Jesus, which was shed once for all (see Hebrews 10:19). Not only may we enter, we are encouraged to enter, to come into the very presence of God, and to come with confidence because we come by the blood of Jesus.

When we come to God's throne, we need to remember He is indeed the God of all grace. He is the landowner who graciously gave a full day's pay to the workers who had worked only one hour in the vineyard. He is the God who said of the sinful nation of Israel even while they were in captivity, "I will rejoice in doing them good" (Jeremiah 32:41). He is the God who remained faithful to Peter through all his failures and sins and made him into a mighty apostle. He is the God who, over and over again, has promised to never leave us, nor forsake us (see Deuteronomy 31:6,8; Psalm 94:14; Isaiah 42:16; Hebrews 13:5). He is the God who "longs to be gracious to you" (Isaiah 30:18), and He is the God who is for you, not against you (see Romans 8:31). All this, and more, is summed up in that one statement, the God of *all* grace.

As we approach the throne of grace, we find that Jesus, our Great High Priest, has gone before us and is, even as we come, already interceding for us (see Hebrews 7:24-25). Jesus is described by the writer of Hebrews as being able to sympathize with our weakness. The double negative, "For we do not have a high priest who is unable to sympathize with our weaknesses" (4:15), is equivalent to a very strong positive assertion: "We *do* have a high priest who *can* sympathize with us." As Dr. John Brown, a nineteenth-century Scottish theologian wrote, "The truth is, He not only can be touched [with our weaknesses], but cannot but be touched. The assertion is not, It is possible that He may sympathize; but, It is impossible that He should not."[1]

Jesus can sympathize with our weaknesses because He "has been tempted in every way, just as we are — yet was without sin." The word translated as *sympathize* means far more than the popular meaning, to feel sorry for. It is the capacity for sharing or understanding the feelings of another person. This feeling can be felt only by a person who has experienced the same or similar trials and who, consequently, understands what the other person is going through and has a desire to relieve the other's distress.

Dr. John Brown said,

It is pity; but it is something more than pity: it is the pity which a man of kind affections feels towards those who are suffering what he himself has suffered. . . .

241

The Son of God, had He never become incarnate, might have pitied, but He could not have sympathized with His people. To render Him capable of sympathy, it was necessary that He should become *man* that He might be susceptible of suffering, and that He should actually be a sufferer that He might be susceptible of sympathy.[2]

I suspect, however, that many of us, especially when we are experiencing physical or emotional pain, question whether or not Jesus suffered in the same way we are suffering. After all, He never experienced prolonged unemployment or had a child die in an auto accident or endured the debilitating effects of a crippling disease or watched a spouse die slowly and painfully from cancer. The biblical text does not assert that Jesus suffered in all these ways. It says, "We have one who has been tempted in every *way*, just as we are — yet was without sin" (4:15, emphasis added). That is, Jesus was tempted, or tried, in all the various *ways* human nature is afflicted. He was born into poverty and experienced rejection from His own family, reproach by the leaders of His day, desertion by His friends, and excruciating physical pain on the cross. And the absence in Scripture of any reference to Joseph after Luke 2 leads to a reasonable inference that Jesus lost His legal, earthly father before He was thirty.

Above all, He suffered the ultimate trial, which you and I will never have to experience: being forsaken by His heavenly Father (Matthew 27:46). Sometimes you and I *feel* forsaken in the midst of trial (David felt that way in Psalm 13:1), and that sense of divine abandonment is the hardest part of the trial. But Jesus actually *was* forsaken by God and knew it. Truly, He was "a man of sorrows, and acquainted with grief" (Isaiah 53:3, KJV). So Jesus does fully understand and sympathize with us in our times of trials. We can be sure, whatever the nature of our hurts, they are not new to Him. Because Jesus can enter into our hurts and does sympathize with us, we can approach God's throne with confidence, without being ashamed to lay our weaknesses before Him. He understands and He cares.

We are encouraged to come to the throne of grace where we have a sympathetic High Priest already interceding for us, "so that we may receive mercy and find grace to help us in our time of need" (Hebrews 4:16). We often use *mercy* and *grace*, as referred to God, interchangeably as synonyms, and some Bible commentators understand their use that way in this passage.

Though the two words are very close in their meaning, they are usually distinguished as follows: "[God's] goodness, exercised toward the unworthy, is called grace; toward the suffering, it is called pity, or mercy."[3] Louis Berkhof further elaborated on mercy as follows: "It may be defined as *the goodness or love of God shown to those who are in misery or distress, irrespective of their deserts.*"[4] Then, I understand the term *grace* in Hebrews 4:16 to mean that particular expression of grace we have been considering in the previous session: divine enabling through the help of the Holy Spirit.

Thus, we approach the throne of grace needing first mercy, because we come as ones in misery or distress. God in His mercy then gives us grace — that is, divine enabling through His Spirit — to help us in our time of need. We are thus enabled to cope with whatever adversity, trial, or dilemma we face in a godly manner.

I have analyzed Hebrews 4:15-16 rather extensively because we need to understand how to appropriate the grace of God through prayer. I believe all of us need to grasp more fully what it means to come to the throne of grace. We need to grasp in the depth of our souls what it means that we *do* have a High Priest, Jesus, who is able and disposed to sympathize with our weaknesses. Above all, we simply need to *go* to the throne of grace to find the grace to help in time of need.

That is what I did in the incident I recounted at the beginning of this chapter. I went to the throne of grace and told God I did not have the ability to respond to what I thought was His will for me at the time. I asked Him for the spiritual strength to say yes to Him. The disciples went to the throne of grace when Peter and John had been commanded by the Jewish rulers not to speak or teach at all in the name of Jesus. They prayed, "Now, Lord, consider their threats and enable your servants to speak your word with great boldness" (Acts 4:29). They went to God's throne of grace, and they asked for grace, specifically the grace to speak boldly for Christ in the face of tremendous opposition.

## THE WORD OF GRACE

The grace we receive from God, then, is the aid of the Holy Spirit. We do not understand just how the Holy Spirit interacts with our human spirit, but we do know He most often uses His Word. That is, He brings to our mind some Scripture or Scriptures, particularly appropriate to the situation. He may do this through one of our pastor's sermons, through a Christian book we are reading, through the encouraging words of a friend, or through our own reading or study of Scripture. In my case, since I have memorized so many Scriptures over the years, He often brings to my mind a memorized verse. This is what He did when through John 12:24 I realized that only through "dying" to my own plans and desires would I be fruitful. Having called our attention to the right Scripture, He then enables us to apply it to our situation, as He did for me with John 12:24.

In Acts 20:32, Paul said to the Ephesian elders, "Now I commit you to God and to the word of his grace, which can build you up and give you an inheritance among all those who are sanctified." Earlier in verse 24, Paul had referred to the gospel of God's grace, the good news of salvation through faith in Christ Jesus. In verse 32, however, he referred to "the word of his grace, which can build you up." The reference here is to the ongoing use of Scripture in our daily lives to build us up in the Christian faith. But Paul specifically called it "the word of his grace," the Word through which we come to understand and appropriate God's grace in our daily lives.

The Bible is not merely a book about God; it is a book from God. "All Scripture is God-breathed," said Paul (2 Timothy 3:16). The Bible is God's self-revelation to us of all He wants us to know about Himself and His provision for our salvation and our spiritual growth. It is God's only objective, authoritative communication to us.

If we are to appropriate the grace of God then, we must become intimate friends with the Bible. We must seek to know and understand the great truths of Scripture: truths about God and His character, and truths about man and his desperate need of God's grace. We need to get beyond the "how-tos" of Scripture — how to raise children, how to manage finances, how to witness to unbelievers — and all other such utilitarian approaches to Scripture. Such practical instruction from the Bible regarding our daily lives is indeed valuable, but we need to go beyond that.

Our practical age has come to disparage a firm doctrinal understanding of Scripture as being of no practical value. But there is nothing more practical for our daily lives than the knowledge of God. David's chief desire was to gaze upon the beauty of God (see Psalm 27:4) — that is, His holiness and sovereignty, His wisdom and power, and His faithfulness and unfailing love. Only in Scripture has God revealed to us the truths about His person and His character.

But the Bible is more than merely objective truth; it is actually life-giving and life-sustaining. The words of Scripture are "not just idle words for you — they are your life" (Deuteronomy 32:47). Growth in the grace of God — whether that be His divine favor to the unworthy, or His divine enabling to the needy — requires growth in our assimilation of the Word of God. In the biological realm, assimilation is the process by which nourishment is changed into living tissue. In the spiritual realm, it is the process by which the written Word of God is absorbed into our hearts and becomes, figuratively speaking, living spiritual tissue.

How do we know God's grace is sufficient for our particular "thorns"? How do we come to a proper understanding of what it means to live or minister "by the grace of God"? How do we learn about the "throne of grace" where we receive mercy and find grace to help us in our time of need? Where do we learn that God is the gracious landowner who gives us far, far more than we deserve? The answer to all these questions is the Scriptures. That is why Scripture is called the Word of His grace. God uses Scripture to mediate His grace to us. R. C. H. Lenski said, "God and the Word of his grace always go together; God lets his grace flow out through that Word."[5]

This close connection between God and the Word of His grace is illustrated in Romans 15:4-5, "For everything that was written in the past was written to teach us, so that through endurance and the encouragement of the Scriptures we might have hope. May the God who gives endurance and encouragement give you a spirit of unity among yourselves as you follow Christ Jesus." Verse 4 tells us that we receive endurance and encouragement from Scripture. Yet verse 5 says God gives endurance and encouragement. Endurance and encouragement are provisions of God's grace "to help us in our time of need." As we go to the throne of grace asking for it, God does provide. But He usually provides through Scripture.

If we are to appropriate the grace of God, then, we must regularly expose ourselves directly to the Word of God. It is not enough to only hear it preached or taught in our churches on Sundays, as important as those avenues are. We need a regular plan of reading, study, and yes, even memorization. Bible study and Scripture memorization earn no merit with God. We never earn God's blessing by doing these things, any more than we earn His blessing by eating nutritious food. But as the eating of proper food is necessary to sustain a healthy physical life, so the regular intake of God's Word is necessary to sustain a healthy spiritual life and to regularly appropriate His grace.

I strongly advocate Scripture memorization. In our warfare

against Satan and his emissaries, we are told to take "the sword of the Spirit, which is the word of God" (Ephesians 6:17). Charles Hodge commented on this statement:

> In opposition . . . to all the suggestions of the devil, the safe, simple, and sufficient answer is the word of God. This puts to flight all the powers of darkness. The Christian finds this to be true in his individual experience. It dissipates his doubts; it drives away his fears; it delivers him from the power of Satan.[6]

We might say, in the language of our present study, it provides the believer grace to help in time of need.

In order to take up God's Word as a sword, we must have it at hand, in our hearts. We must be like the psalmist who said, "I have hidden your word in my heart that I might not sin against you" (Psalm 119:11). To hide God's Word in our hearts is to store it or treasure it in our hearts against a time of future need. It is akin to our expression "to save for a rainy day." This principle of storing up God's Word has a much wider application than only keeping us from sin, especially as we tend to think of a more narrow description of sin as sexual immorality, lying, stealing, and the like. The Word, stored in the heart, provides a mental depository for the Holy Spirit to use to mediate His grace to us, whatever our need for grace might be.

Within the week that this chapter was written, I had a significant experience of this myself. A phone call from a distant city brought some very disturbing news about someone I am close to. I went to bed that night feeling as if I had just received an emotional "kick in the stomach." The next morning, however, I awakened with 1 Peter 5:7 going through my mind: "Cast all your anxiety on him because he cares for you." As I was getting dressed, the verse kept going through my mind, and I was given grace by God's Spirit to believe that He did care in this specific situation. I was thus able to cast that particular anxiety on Him, because I had received grace to help in time of need through His Word.

That one specific incident comes to mind because it is so recent. But it is only one in a series of incidents occurring frequently in my life — and I'm sure in the lives of all other believers who store up God's Word in their hearts. As F. F. Bruce said in his commentary on Ephesians 6:17, "The divine utterance, the product of the Spirit, lends itself readily to the believer who has laid it up in his heart for effective use in the moment of danger against any attempt to seduce him from allegiance to Christ."[7] In a footnote to that statement, Bruce refers specifically to Psalm 119:11.

So, if you desire to appropriate God's grace, you must have the sword of the Spirit — the Word of God — available in your mind for the Spirit to use. In fact the structure of Ephesians 6:17 provides a very instructive insight into the interaction between the Holy Spirit and the believer. Paul said we are to take the sword of the Spirit. That is something we must do. And yet it is the Spirit's sword, not ours. He must make it effective. The bare quoting of Scripture does not make it effective in our hearts, only the Spirit can do that. But He will not make His sword effective unless we take it up.

Often God's Word is not made effective immediately. In fact, there are many times when I struggle over an issue for a period of days, mulling over several pertinent passages of Scripture and crying out for grace, before the Holy Spirit finally makes them effective and gives His grace, helping in time of need. The Spirit of God is sovereign in His working, and we cannot squeeze Him into the mold of our spiritual formulas — for example, pray for grace, quote some verses, and receive a guaranteed answer.

God not only has His own ways of working, but also His own timetable. Sometimes He grants grace to help almost immediately as He did in my most recent experience with 1 Peter 5:7. At other times, He allows us to struggle for days, perhaps even weeks or months, before we receive the grace to help. But regardless of the delays He may impose on us, we must continue to come to the throne of grace believing His promise to grant grace to help, and we must continue to resort to appropriate Scripture until He makes it effective in our hearts. It is our responsibility to take up the sword of the Spirit; it is His prerogative to make it effective.

## SUBMISSION TO GOD

The third means God uses to administer His grace to us is our submission to His providential working in our lives. The apostle Peter said,

> All of you, clothe yourselves with humility toward one another, because,
>
> > "God opposes the proud
> > but gives grace to the humble."
>
> Humble yourselves, therefore, under God's mighty hand, that he may lift you up in due time. (1 Peter 5:5-6)

God gives grace to the humble, to those who humble themselves under His mighty hand of providence. Our tendency is not to humble ourselves but to *resist* the workings of His mighty hand. At best we fret and murmur and worry even as we cry out for deliverance. At worst we become angry or even rebellious against God. In so doing, we have become proud, and "God opposes the proud"; that is, He actually sets Himself in array against us.

If we are to appropriate God's grace, we must humble ourselves, we must submit to His providential working in our lives. To do this we must first see His mighty hand behind all the immediate causes of our adversities and heartaches. We must believe the biblical teaching that God is in sovereign control of all our circumstances, and whatever or whoever is the immediate cause of our circumstances, God is behind them all.

Job and Joseph are examples of those who saw the hand of God in their circumstances. In one day the Sabeans stole Job's oxen, and the Chaldeans carried off his camels and murdered his servants. Lightning burned up his sheep, and a mighty wind struck the house of his oldest son, killing all his children Later Job himself was afflicted with painful sores from the soles of his feet to the top of his head. Job's response at the loss of his children and his possessions was, "The LORD gave and the LORD has taken away" (Job 1:21). And with respect to his own affliction he said, "Shall we accept good from God, and not trouble?" (2:10).

Quite apart from Job's humble reaction toward God, we should note first that he ascribed his sufferings to the hand of God. He saw beyond the actions of evil men and the disasters of nature to the sovereign God who controlled those events. And the inspired writer who recorded the trials of Job, at the close of his account, said, "They [his relatives and friends] comforted and consoled him [Job] over all the trouble *the LORD had brought upon him*" (42:11, emphasis added). Even though the writer had himself reported the malicious activity of Satan in Job's life at the beginning of the narrative, he still ultimately ascribed Job's troubles to the Lord.

Joseph, when he finally revealed his identity to his wicked brothers who had sold him into slavery, saw beyond their evil acts and said, "So then, it was not you who sent me here, but God" (Genesis 45:8). He recognized that God in His sovereignty used even the heinous sins of his brothers to accomplish His purpose. So, you and I, if we are to appropriate God's grace in our times of need, must see His sovereignty ultimately ruling in all the circumstances of our lives. And when those circumstances are difficult, disappointing, or humiliating, we must humble ourselves under His mighty hand.[8]

Not only must we see God's mighty hand behind our

circumstances, we must also see it as the hand of a loving Father disciplining His children. We lose a lot of comfort in times of trials because we tend to view them as evidences of God's desertion of us rather than evidences of His Fatherly discipline and care. Hebrews 12:7, however, says, "Endure hardship as discipline; God is treating you as sons." The writer of Hebrews did not qualify hardship. He did not suggest that *some* hardship is God's discipline, while some may not be. He simply said endure hardship — all of it — as God's discipline. You may be sure that whatever hardship comes into your life from whatever immediate source, God is in sovereign control of it and is using it as an instrument of discipline in your life.

Further, the writer of Hebrews, in the previous sentence, had said this discipline is a proof of God's love, "because the Lord disciplines those he loves" (verse 6). He offers this, not as a word of warning, but as a word of encouragement (verse 5). The purpose of God's discipline, according to Hebrews, is "that we may share in his holiness" (verse 10), that we may be conformed in our character to His character.

Discipline may be either corrective or remedial. It may be sent for the purpose of correcting some sinful attitude or action, or to remedy some lack in our character. In either case, it is administered by our heavenly Father in love, not in wrath. Jesus has already borne the wrath of God in our place, so all adversities that come to us, come because He loves us and designs to conform us to the likeness of His Son.

Samuel Bolton said,

God has thoughts of love in all He does to His people. The ground of His dealings with us is love (though the occasions may be sin), the manner of His dealings is love, and the purpose of His dealings is love. He has regard, in all, to our good here, to make us partakers of His holiness, and to our glory hereafter, to make us partakers of His glory.[9]

It is difficult for us to see God's hand of love in the adversities and heartaches of life because we persist in thinking, as the world does, that happiness is the greatest good. Thus we tend to evaluate all our circumstances in terms of whether or not they produce happiness. Holiness, however, is a greater good than happiness, so God arranges and orchestrates circumstances to produce holiness before happiness. He is more concerned about our eternal than our temporal welfare and more concerned about our spiritual than our material welfare. So all the trials and difficulties, all the heartaches, disappointments, and humiliations come from His loving hand to make us partakers of His holiness.

John Newton expressed this intent of God in our trials and afflictions in his hymn "Prayer Answered by Crosses":

I asked the Lord that I might grow
    In faith and love and every grace,
Might more of his salvation know,
    And seek more earnestly his face.

'Twas he who taught me thus to pray;
    And he, I trust, has answered prayer;
But it has been in such a way
    As almost drove me to despair.

I hoped that, in some favoured hour,
    At once he'd answer my request,
And by his love's constraining power
    Subdue my sins, and give me rest.

Instead of this, he made me feel
    The hidden evils of my heart,
And let the angry powers of hell
    Assault my soul in every part.

Yea, more, with his own hand he seemed
    Intent to aggravate my woe,
Crossed all the fair designs I schemed,
    Blasted my gourds, and laid me low.

Lord, why is this? I trembling cried;
    Wilt thou pursue this worm to death?
This is the way, the Lord replied
    I answer prayer for grace and faith.

These inward trials I now employ
    From self and pride to set thee free,
And break thy schemes of earthly joy,
    That thou may'st seek thy all in me.[10]

But it is not enough to see God's mighty hand behind the immediate causes of all our adversities, nor to see it as the hand of a loving Father disciplining His children. I have seen the doctrine of the sovereignty of God in the Scriptures for so many years that I instinctively see His hand behind every circumstance. And I have come to the place where I acknowledge, almost reluctantly sometimes, that all hardship is God's discipline, either corrective or remedial. The rub comes in *submitting* to it. Sometimes we resist it. But if we are to appropriate God's grace in our trial, we must first submit to His hand, which brought the trial.

God gives grace *only* to the humble, to those who are not only humble toward other people, but are humble, or submissive, under His mighty hand. John Lillie expressed this idea so well. He said, "'*Humble yourselves, therefore,*' receiving in silent, meek submission whatever humiliation it [God's hand] may now lay upon you. For this is your time of trial, and, when paternal rod meets thus with the child-like spirit, will be surely followed by another time of healing and joy." Then Dr. Lillie added an important word of exhortation: "See that you do not frustrate the gracious purpose of God and lose the blessing of sorrow. Rather make that purpose yours also."[11]

After the death of my first wife, a friend sent me a sympathy card on which she had copied the following verse, apparently from an ancient hymn, which I have now put in my notebook to meditate on frequently when I pray:

> Lord, I am willing
> To receive what You give,
> To lack what You withhold,
> To relinquish what You take,
> To suffer what You inflict,
> To be what You require.

We must have that spirit if we are to humble ourselves under God's mighty hand and receive the grace He has promised to give.

But there is still one more essential element in this exercise of humbling ourselves under His mighty hand. We must not only submit, we must also do so in faith that He will lift us up in due time. The "due time" is when the adversity has accomplished its purpose. As the prophet Jeremiah said,

> For men are not cast off
> by the Lord forever.

> Though he brings grief, he will show
> compassion,
> so great is his unfailing love.
> (Lamentations 3:31-32)

God will not leave His heavy hand of adversity on us one moment more than is necessary to accomplish His purpose: "For he does not willingly bring affliction or grief to the children of men" (verse 33).

The humbling of ourselves under God's mighty hand always leads to exaltation. Sometimes this may consist in the removal of whatever affliction God has brought into our lives and the restoration of peaceful circumstances, perhaps even more prosperous circumstances than before. This happened in the case of Job: "The LORD blessed the latter part of Job's life more than the first" (Job 42:12). At other times, though the circumstances are not changed, as in the case of the death of a loved one, the heaviness and painful grief or agony are removed. This happened in the case of Paul's thorn. He was given grace to accept his thorn.

How are we to obtain such faith when it often seems to us God has forgotten us? The answer lies in 1 Peter 5:7: "Cast all your anxiety on him because he cares for you." *God cares for you.* Even though He is disciplining you, He cares for you. As we have already seen, discipline is an indication of His care. But His care goes beyond necessary discipline. Even as He disciplines you, He shares in your pain. Isaiah described God's attitude toward Israel, "In all their distress he too was distressed" (Isaiah 63:9). The same can be said of God's attitude toward you. In all your distress He too is distressed.

Because God cares for you, you can cast your anxiety on Him. Do not get these thoughts reversed. The text does not say, "*If* you cast your anxieties on Him, He will care for you." His care is not conditioned on our faith and our ability to cast our anxiety on Him; rather, it is because He *does* care for us that we can cast our anxiety on Him.

Even at this point, we need the help of the Holy Spirit to do this. Even with all the assurance this whole passage provides us, its truth sometimes fails to reach our hearts. Sometimes we have to pray for the grace to humble ourselves under His mighty hand and the grace to believe that He does in fact care for us. Sometimes we must pray as did the father who came to Jesus asking Him to heal his son. When Jesus said to him, "Everything is possible for him who believes," the father exclaimed, "I do believe; help me overcome my unbelief!" (Mark 9:23-24).

## MINISTERS OF GRACE

The fourth principal means by which God ministers His grace to us is through the ministry of other believers. This truly is a primary means God uses, because He has ordained that in the body of Christ all the members "should have equal concern for each other" (1 Corinthians 12:25). Of course, this is to be a reciprocal ministry. We should be channels of grace to one another.

Let me deliberately misuse a statement of Scripture to make a point: This is one area where most of us feel it is indeed "more blessed to give than to receive" (Acts 20:35). That is, we are more inclined to be ministers of grace to others than to allow others to be ministers of grace to us. Our problem is we are reluctant to be transparent and vulnerable to each other. We men especially don't like to admit we have problems. That is perceived as a sign of weakness.

We want to appear as if we have life under control. We want to appear as if we are successfully dealing with temptations to sin, and as if we are successfully dealing with the difficult circumstances of life. We are just as unwilling to let others know we have been passed over for promotion at work as to admit we are having lustful thoughts about the secretary in the next office.

The times when we need an extra measure of God's grace are often the times when we are most reluctant to let other people know we need it. This leads to an important principle regarding the ministry of grace. Each of us needs to cultivate a small group of friends with whom we can be transparent and vulnerable. This might be on an individual or small group basis. But we need a few people — including our spouse, if we have one — with whom we feel free to share our failures, hurts, and sorrows. The Puritans used to ask God for one "bosom friend" with whom they could share absolutely everything. That is a good goal for us today.

We saw in the section "The Word of Grace" that we should

store up God's Word in our hearts against a time of future need. We also should "store up" a few bosom friends against the day when we need them to be God's ministers of grace to us.

Usually when we think of the ministry of grace to one another, we think of the initiative being with the person who will be the minister. But the initiative is often with the one who has a need. We have to admit our need and give the other person "permission" to minister to us. We have to, in some way, communicate that we are not only willing to share our needs but are willing to be ministered to.

What are some ways in which we can ask others to be ministers of grace to us? In answering, we need to keep in mind that we are asking the person to be an avenue for God's Spirit to pour out His grace to us. We are asking the person, or persons, to help strengthen our contact with the Holy Spirit so that we can better receive the divine assistance He has promised to give. We are not asking, at this point, for practical assistance or human counsel. That may be appropriate at the right time. But for now, we are thinking of our need for grace, for God's divine power to come to help us in our time of need.

That being true, the first thing we need from others is prayer support. It is instructive how often Paul asked the recipients of his letters to pray for him, even when he did not seem to have extremely pressing needs. So certainly in our times of need we should ask others to pray for us. But, if they are to pray effectively for us, we must be willing to share what our real needs are.

The second thing we need is their help in accepting and applying Scripture to our specific needs. We might say, "Here is my problem. What Scriptures do you think might help me?" I realize this is a radical suggestion, because so often, when we are experiencing adversity, the last thing we want is for someone to give us a pat answer in the form of a Scripture verse. But if we have developed the kind of friendship where we can be transparent and vulnerable with one another, then we are not going to be giving each other pat-answer type responses.

Third, we can ask the other person to be a minster of grace to us by helping us see our situation with a better, more objective, perspective. We all know our tendency to magnify problems, or perhaps put the worst construction on events affecting us. The other person can be the Holy Spirit's agent to help us see our circumstances more objectively. That better perspective may help us to more readily humble ourselves under God's hand.

You will recognize that, in this section on ministers of grace, I have not introduced anything beyond the basic avenues of prayer, God's Word, and submission to God's providence. This is as it should be. All another person can do is facilitate our own contact with the Holy Spirit. All another can be is an avenue of God's grace. We have nothing to offer each other just from ourselves.

We also need to keep in mind, as I have mentioned, that ministering grace is a two-way street. If you were to look up in a concordance the expressions *one another* and *each other*, you would see how strongly the New Testament writers emphasize ministering to one another. We are to pray for one another, encourage one another, teach and admonish one another, spur one another on, carry each other's burdens, share with one another, and so on. Truly the body of Christ should be constantly alive with this reciprocal ministry to one another.

But let's keep our focus for now on ministering grace to one another, that is, being an agent available for the Holy Spirit to use to convey His grace to someone else. We have considered briefly how we may reach out to others and allow them to be ministers of grace to us. This in itself takes some grace, and we may need to pray, "Lord, help me to be transparent and open to my friend, even though doing so seems humiliating to me right now. And make my friend a minister of Your grace to me."

Since this is a reciprocal ministry, however, let's now consider some ways by which we can be ministers of grace to others. All of us, if we are exploiting this avenue of God's grace, should find ourselves at various times on both the receiving and the giving end. To borrow a principle of reciprocity from Paul's teaching on giving, "At the present time your plenty will supply what they need, so that in turn their plenty will supply what you need" (2 Corinthians 8:14).

How, then, can we be ministers of grace to others? Well, obviously in the same three basic ways they can be ministers to us: prayer, the Word of God, and help in submitting to God's providence. But there is a crucial difference between receiving and giving. In receiving we must *give* permission to the other person to share Scripture with us and to help us submit to God's providence. In giving, we must *receive* permission. Usually this means we must first *earn* the right to minister to the person through a relationship of mutual sharing, openness, and trust that we have already established.

The one area where we do not need to give or receive permission is, of course, in praying for one another. But even here, another individual cannot pray for your specific needs if you have not been willing to share them. There are some difficult or tragic events, such as the death of a loved one, the loss of a job, or a crippling disease or accident, that result in certain obvious needs we can pray for. But even in these areas, each of us responds to those events in ways distinctive to us, and in these areas of individual response we need to share and receive specific prayer requests with the close circle of friends we have cultivated.

Prayer is probably the most important way we can be a minister of grace to someone else. We have already considered God's gracious invitation to approach the throne of grace to receive mercy and find grace to help us in our time of need. But sometimes brothers or sisters in Christ are so discouraged about their adversity and God's seeming silence over a prolonged period, they just don't have the spiritual strength even to approach the throne of grace. To them the doors of heaven are shut and God just doesn't seem to "be there." At these times we need to "carry" that person to the throne of grace by our prayers.

This type of ministry is beautifully illustrated in the literal carrying of the paralytic man to Jesus as recorded in Mark 2:1-12. This is one of the few events in Jesus' ministry recorded in all three of the synoptic gospels. The story is familiar to most of us. We admire the faith and tenacity of the man's friends who, when they could not bring him in to Jesus through the door of the house, went up on the roof, and after making a hole in it, lowered the man through the roof to where Jesus was.

Let's consider some often overlooked facets of the story. The man was completely paralyzed, at least unable to walk. As such he would have been a dead weight to his friends, unable even to cooperate with them as they carried him on his mat. The mat was probably a thin, straw-filled mattress, which the man on being healed could easily pick up and carry out with him. So the mat itself was likely limp, providing no stability to aid the man's friends. In every respect, the paralytic lying helplessly on his mat was an awkward, heavy burden to be carried. But the paralytic's friends were undeterred by either the awkwardness of their burden or the obstacle of the crowd. They persisted until they brought him before Jesus.

Sometimes one of our friends or loved ones becomes a spiritual paralytic. The affliction or trial he or she has undergone has virtually immobilized the person spiritually. He is unable to help himself. Not only that, but the spiritual "mat" he is lying on — that is, faith in God and trust in His promises — is no more than the equivalent of a thin, straw-filled mattress. If you try to encourage him through Scripture, he will look at you blankly and tell you Scripture just doesn't mean anything to him anymore. He has tried to claim God's promises, but nothing "works." God just isn't there.

This person has become an awkward, heavy spiritual burden. You cannot pray with him, you can only pray for him. But just as the paralytic's friends persisted until they brought him to Jesus, so we too must persist in bringing this person to the throne of grace until God heals him spiritually.

Notes and Observations

Of course, the spiritual paralytic is an extreme case. More often than not, the person to whom we are called to be a minister of grace can still go to the throne of grace himself. But we are still called to rally around that person in prayer. God can, and often does, answer our individual prayers, but the general tenor of Scripture is that God desires we support each other in prayer.

Beyond prayer, we must in some way receive permission to be a minister of grace to the person in need. One of the best ways we can do this is to demonstrate that we care. The first thing the person requiring grace needs from you is the assurance and demonstration that you care. We want to help that person come to the place where he or she can cast that hurt on God, truly believing God *does* care. So often, though, our perception of God's care is derived from our more tangible perception of other people's care. If we see care demonstrated in our friends, it is easier for us to believe God cares. It shouldn't be this way; we should not gauge the care of God by the care of fallible, sinful human beings. But we do. And often, God wants us to be the tangible evidence of His care.

How can we demonstrate that we care? Obviously the first thing we must do is to make contact. If you live in the same city, invite the person to lunch or coffee, or in some way establish personal contact. Based on my own experience after the death of my first wife, and confirmed by several friends who have lost loved ones, this is where we so often fail each other. Apparently because we feel awkward and don't know what to say, we don't say anything. In fact, we may even avoid the hurting person. One friend, whose wife died some months after mine, said to me, "Jerry, where are my friends?" Another told me of someone, who was one of his best friends, avoiding him after the death of a child.

If you have failed to make contact because you didn't know what to say, allow me to offer a suggestion. Just tell the person, "I know you must be hurting badly, and I don't know what to say, but I just want you to know I care." Then, if appropriate you could add, "If it would help, I'd like to have lunch [or whatever] with you, and just listen to you. I'd like to know how you are really doing."

Above all, do not ask the person merely in passing at church or somewhere else "How are you doing?" Though you may not intend this, it communicates to the hurting person that you are expecting the typical cultural response, "Oh, just fine!" Speaking as one who has "been there," this is taken as more of an indication that you don't care than that you do.

When you have demonstrated to the person that you do care — be sensitive to determine when the other person believes this — you can begin to ask gently probing questions, such as, "How are you and God getting along during this tough time?" "Are you able to get any comfort from the Scriptures, or are they just dead to you right now?" Ask questions in a way that communicates you won't be shocked by negative answers.

The sharing of Scripture with a person who is deeply hurting requires a great deal of sensitivity. We must be careful that we do not appear to be "preaching" or giving glib answers to difficult problems. A good rule is to comfort others only with Scriptures that have comforted us in a similar situation. We also need to be sensitive to the person's receptivity of our sharing Scripture. I have found it helpful to write the other person a letter in which I share Scripture I think might be helpful. This doesn't require a response from the other person and consequently seems to be less intrusive than sharing face to face.

Ministering to one another in time of need is an important means by which the Holy Spirit mediates His grace to us. But, as I have already observed, this is to be a reciprocal ministry. Do you have one or more people who are ministers of grace to you? Have you earned the right through a regular caring relationship to be a minister of grace to others? We do need each other's help to appropriate the grace of God, for as Ecclesiastes 4:9-10 says,

Two are better than one,
　　because they have a good return for their
　　　　work:

If one falls down,
　　his friend can help him up.
But pity the man who falls
　　and has no one to help him up!

If you realize you do not have such a "grace ministry" relationship with one or more friends and are wondering how to develop it, let me offer a few suggestions. First, we must admit we need it. Some of us, especially we men, are reluctant to admit such a need. Self-sufficient independence seems to be a hallmark of western culture. But if you have read to this point in our grace study, you probably have realized and acknowledged that none of us is self-sufficient — even in our personal, private relationship with God. He has made us in such a way that we need one another.

Second, ask God to lead you to the specific people with whom you can develop such a mutual relationship. As you pray, consider the various people within your sphere of acquaintances who might be possibilities. If you are looking for a one-to-one relationship, invite that person to breakfast or lunch or something similar, and see if the "chemistry" is there, that is, if you sense a mutual comfortableness with one another in sharing personal needs, goals, spiritual lessons, and so on. If you are looking for a small group environment, invite two or three friends who might be interested to get together and explore the formation of such a group.

Don't be surprised, however, if God answers your prayer for a friend or friends in an unexpected way. He may well bring into your life someone whom you have not thought of as a possibility. You may be looking for someone whom you consider a spiritual "giant" to be your mentor and counselor. God may

Notes and Observations

provide someone who seems to be the equivalent of "worm Jacob" (Isaiah 41:14) as we discussed in session 7 (chapter 11).

As you begin to develop your relationship, you will often struggle within yourself about what you are willing to share. Again, this is especially true of us men because of our reluctance to admit we have needs. But speaking as one who is prone to be this way, my encouragement to you is this: Unless you sense a definite check from the Lord in your spirit, just "suck in your breath" and plunge in. I think you will be surprised how understanding your friend or small group will be, and how they will begin to open up and share their own struggles with you.

But don't just share your struggles, and above all, don't just commiserate with one another. Remember, we are to be ministers of grace to each other. We are to seek to be avenues of the Holy Spirit to help the other person appropriate the grace of God. Praying with and for one another, sharing applicable portions of Scripture, and helping each other submit to God's providential dealings with us, must characterize our times together.

During the time David was hiding from Saul, who was trying to kill him, he fled to the cave of Adullam. While there he wrote Psalm 142, a cry of distress to God. Verse 4 is one of the most plaintive cries in all of human literature:

> Look to my right and see;
>     no one is concerned for me.
> I have no refuge;
>     no one cares for my life.

Does that describe the way you sometimes feel? Do you think no one is concerned for you, no one cares for you? If so, you need one or more friends who will be ministers of grace to you. And very likely, you need to be such a minister of grace to someone else.

## Chapter Thirteen: Garments of Grace

*Therefore, as God's chosen people, holy and dearly loved,*
*clothe yourselves with compassion, kindness, humility,*
*gentleness and patience. Bear with each other and*
*forgive whatever grievances you may have against*
*one another. Forgive as the Lord forgave you. And*
*over all these virtues put on love, which binds*
*them all together in perfect unity.*
COLOSSIANS 3:12-14

One day, driving back to the office from an appointment, I was grappling with some difficult circumstances in my life and feeling a bit sorry for myself. But as I drove, I tried to focus my mind on some portions of Scripture and reflect on them rather than on my problems. As I did this, I thought of Colossians 3:12-14, the Scripture text at the beginning of this chapter.

I had memorized this passage years ago and had reviewed it and reflected on it many times, but that day I saw the passage in a new way. Always before, when reflecting on the passage, my mind had gone directly to the character traits we are to put on: compassion, kindness, humility, gentleness, patience, forbearance, and love. I had never paid attention to the apostle Paul's introductory phrase: "Therefore, as God's chosen people, holy and dearly loved." To me Paul was saying nothing more than, "Since you are Christians, act like Christians." I saw his emphasis to be solely on Christian duty, the traits of Christ's character I should seek after.

But that day the Holy Spirit caused my mind to focus on the two words "dearly loved." It was as if He said to me, "Jerry, you are feeling sorry for yourself; but the truth is, you are dearly loved by God." Dearly loved by God. What an incredible thought! But it is true, and that afternoon the Holy Spirit drove home to my heart the wonderful truth with such force that my self-pity was completely dispelled. I continued on to our office rejoicing in the fact that, despite my difficult circumstances, I was dearly loved by God.

Of course, the main thrust of Paul's teaching in this passage is that we are to clothe ourselves with Christlike virtues, what I call "garments of grace." But he grounds his exhortation on the grace of God — on the fact that we are chosen by Him, holy in His sight, and dearly loved by Him. It is difficult, perhaps impossible, for us to show compassion or patience to someone else if we are not sure God is patient with us — or, worse, if we don't sense the need for God to be patient with us. So these garments of gracious Christian character can only be put on by those who are consciously experiencing God's grace in their own lives.

Having experienced God's grace, we are then called on to extend that grace to others. The evidence of whether we are living by His grace is to be found in the way we treat other people. If we see ourselves as sinners and totally unworthy in ourselves of God's compassion, patience, and forgiveness, then we will want to be gracious to others.

God's grace is indeed meant to be a transforming grace. As Paul said in Titus 2:11-12, "For the grace of God that brings salvation has appeared to all men. It teaches us to say 'No' to ungodliness and worldly passions, and to live self-controlled, upright and godly lives in this present age." The grace of God brings salvation, not only from the guilt and condemnation of sin, but also from the reign of sin in our lives. It teaches us to say "No" to ungodly character traits, but also to say "Yes" to godly character traits. God's grace teaches us to clothe ourselves with "garments of grace."

Paul listed eight different character traits in Colossians 3:12-14 with which we are to clothe ourselves. I did a detailed study on most of these traits, as well as others, in an earlier book *The Practice of Godliness*, so I will not cover that material again.[12] Instead, I want to focus on five character traits that are particularly related to grace: gratitude, contentment, humility, forbearance, and forgiveness.

# GRATITUDE

The very first character trait that should flow out of experiencing God's grace is *gratitude* to Him. Everything we are and everything we do that is of any value, we owe to the grace of God. This, of course, begins with our salvation. The longer I live the Christian life, the more grateful I am for the salvation God gave to me when I was an eighteen-year-old college student.

Years ago I memorized Mark 8:36-37: "For what shall it profit a man, if he shall gain the whole world, and lose his own soul? Or what shall a man give in exchange for his soul?" (KJV). Initially, I memorized that passage to use in witnessing, to help point out how utterly important it is for a person to take the gospel offer seriously. But in recent years I have begun to meditate on those verses for my own benefit to help me realize what an infinitely priceless gift I have received in God's gracious gift of eternal life. As I think of the message of those verses, I visualize a balance scale with all the treasures of the entire world on one tray and eternal life on the other tray. The two trays are not balanced. Rather, the scale is bottomed out on the side of eternal life.

In the gift of eternal life, God has given us greater treasure than all the accumulated wealth of the whole world. Are we sufficiently grateful for this priceless gift? Do we take time to actually give thanks to God for the gift that cost Him so much? Are we as grateful today as we were the day we initially experienced the forgiveness of our sins and peace with God? If we are truly living by the transforming grace of God in our daily lives, gratitude for God's gift of eternal life through Jesus Christ will be a growing experience. We should have a greater sense of gratitude, and be more desirous of expressing that gratitude to God, today than the day we were brought out of the kingdom of sin into the kingdom of grace.

God has, of course, given us so much else in Christ. Have we grown in the Christian life so that we are a bit more mature

267

today than we were a year ago? Are we perhaps more loving and gentle today than we were a year ago? If so, where did this growth come from? It did not come from ourselves, because as Paul said, "I know that nothing good lives in me, that is, in my sinful nature" (Romans 7:18). There are only two moral forces within us: our sinful nature and the Holy Spirit empowering our new nature. If we are more Christlike today than a year ago, it is because of the work of the Holy Spirit within us, and this is by the grace of God.

Certainly, as we have seen in earlier chapters, we must clothe ourselves with Christlike virtues (Colossians 3:12-14), but these same virtues are elsewhere called the fruit of the Spirit (Galatians 5:22-23) — that is, the result of His work in us. One great paradox of the Christian life is that we are fully responsible for our Christian growth and at the same time fully dependent upon the Holy Spirit to give us both the desire to grow and the ability to do it. God's grace does not negate the need for responsible action on our part, but rather makes it possible.

What about ministry? Have we accomplished some specific work for God? As we have already seen, we must admit to God, "All that we have accomplished you have done for us" (Isaiah 26:12). There is nothing, absolutely nothing, we are or we have done that is worthwhile, that is not the result of God's Spirit working in us and through us.

I fear that often we Christians begin to think our spiritual growth and "success" in ministry is due, at least in large measure, to our own goodness and hard work. The irony is, the more committed and diligent we are, the more susceptible we are to that temptation. We face the same temptation in a spiritual sense that Israel faced in a material way when God warned them they would be prone to say, "My power and the strength of my hands have produced this wealth for me" (Deuteronomy 8:17).

Let us go on to the temporal blessings of life. Are we comfortably situated in a nice home with plenty of food in the cupboard and the refrigerator? Do we enjoy a reasonable degree of health? Do we have our own personal copy of the Bible (aside from the half dozen or so different translations some of us have)? Are we able to gather with other believers for worship and study of the Scriptures without fear of religious persecution?

All of these blessings come to us by God's grace, and all of them are occasions for gratitude and giving thanks to Him. It is interesting that some people use the expression "saying grace," for the prayer of thanksgiving at meal time. I have no idea of that expression's origin, but I suspect it was born out of a recognition that the food on the table was not only from God, but that it was there by His grace.

We actually ought to "say grace" continually throughout the day for the temporal and spiritual blessings that come our way so abundantly. I know many of us are going through some difficult times, and it's tough to have a grateful spirit. But if we will stop and consider, we will recognize that we are still recipients every day of the amazing grace of God. If we are truly growing in grace, gratitude—and its expression in actually giving thanks to God—will be an ever-growing characteristic in our lives.

## CONTENTMENT

Gratitude is a handmaiden of *contentment*. An ever-growing attitude of gratitude will certainly make us more content since we will be focusing more on what we do have, both spiritually and materially, than on what we do not have. But contentment is more than focusing on what we have. It is focusing on the fact that all we do have, we have by the grace of God. We do not deserve anything we have, materially or spiritually. It is all by His grace.

Discontent usually arises when we think we are not getting what we deserve, or when we think we are not getting as much as someone else. We have already seen the corrosive effect of discontent in the attitude of those who worked all day in the vineyard (see session 3). They were discontent and consequently unhappy,

269

because they felt they had earned more than the workers who were hired at the eleventh hour. How different from their attitude was Paul's who regarded himself not only as "the least of the apostles" but even as "less than the least of all God's people" (1 Corinthians 15:9; Ephesians 3:8). Paul truly regarded himself as an "eleventh hour" worker in God's vineyard, as one who was receiving a full day's wages, and more, for one hour's work.

Discontent is a sign that we are living by works, that we think we deserve more than we are getting, that in some way God isn't being fair to us. One of the more helpful passages of Scripture on this subject is Luke 17:7-10:

> Suppose one of you had a servant plowing or looking after the sheep. Would he say to the servant when he comes in from the field, "Come along now and sit down to eat"? Would he not rather say, "Prepare my supper, get yourself ready and wait on me while I eat and drink; after that you may eat and drink"? Would he thank the servant because he did what he was told to do? So you also, when you have done everything you were told to do, should say, "We are unworthy servants; we have only done our duty."

I'm sure this passage of Scripture offends many people's sense of fairness just as much as does the parable of the workers in the vineyard. The master of the servant seems completely selfish and callous to the needs of his servant. But Jesus was not commending the master, He was simply describing conditions as they existed. The issue was, given the culture of the day, who had a right to have expectations of whom? Clearly, the servant, when he had fulfilled his duties, had no right to expect either gratitude or consideration. He had simply done what he was supposed to do.

God is not selfish and callous like the master in Jesus' story. He is the generous and gracious landowner we saw described in the parable of the workers in the vineyard. But we *are* the servants of Luke 17:7-10. When we have done everything we were told to do — and who of us has come anywhere close to that standard? — we should still say, "We are unworthy servants; we have only done our duty."

If we want to live by what we deserve, God could say, "All right, let's first add up your debits, and then we'll think about your credits." Our problem is we don't recognize our debits. We don't recognize how far, far short we come every day in doing what we are supposed to do. And because of that, we tend to live by works instead of by grace in our daily relationship with God.

Paul said, "Godliness with contentment is great gain" (1 Timothy 6:6). All the wealth and prestige in the world with discontentment results in poverty of spirit. But contentment arising in our souls from living by grace — that is, from realizing we have not received what we actually deserve, but daily receive what we don't deserve — brings great wealth of spirit, even if we are living in poverty and obscurity.

I commend to you for meditation in respect to contentment Luke 17:10, which sums up Jesus' teaching in that story.

## HUMILITY

A person living by God's grace will also clothe himself with *humility*. Unfortunately this particular fruit of the Spirit is not eagerly sought after by most believers. Perhaps that is because it is often confused with self-depreciation, which denies there is any good or worth in us. To refer again to the illustration I used in session 7 (chapter 11) from Isaiah 41:14-15, this false notion of humility causes us to see ourselves only as "worm Jacob" and "little Israel" without at the same time seeing ourselves becoming mighty threshing sledges through God's grace at work in us.

But, as Charles Hodge so aptly said, "Christian humility does not consist in denying what there is of good in us; but in an abiding sense of ill-desert, and in the consciousness that

271

what we have of good is due to the grace of God."[13] Humility, then, gives credit where credit is due, namely to the working of the Holy Spirit in our lives. Pride, which is the opposite of humility, seeks to find within ourselves some innate goodness or even to ascribe to our own commitment or faithfulness the cause of any blessings of God in our lives. Pride might say, for example, "Because I have been faithful and obedient, God has blessed me"; whereas humility would say, "Because of God's grace at work in me, I have been motivated and enabled to be faithful and obedient."

Humility begins with God's grace and recognizes that the good in us in the form of Christlike character, and the good done by us in service to God and other people, is totally undeserved on our part and is due to the work of the Holy Spirit in our lives. But humility does not deny the evidences of His gracious work in us and through us. To do so would be to dishonor Him as much as to ascribe the cause and results of His working to ourselves.

Jesus not only said, "No branch can bear fruit by itself," but He also said, "If a man remains in me and I in him, he will bear much fruit" (John 15:4-5). To remain, or to use the word we are more familiar with, to abide in Christ is to set aside our own wisdom, strength, and merit in order to draw all from Him.[14] In other words, to abide in Christ is the same as to depend totally on God's grace, both in the realm of ability and in the realm of merit. But the point I want to make here is Jesus did say that when we abide in Him, when we depend on the grace of God, we will bear much fruit. So it is not honoring to God, nor is it a mark of true humility to refuse to see the good produced in us or through us. Humility, then, is a recognition that we are at the same time "worm Jacob" and a mighty threshing sledge — completely weak and helpless in ourselves, but powerful and useful by the grace of God.

We have been looking at humility in a vertical dimension — that is, in our relationship to God — recognizing that all the good we have and do is from Him. But there is a horizontal dimension of humility in relationship to other people. Pride, in relation to other people, is comparing ourselves with others and seeing ourselves as superior to them in some way—whether it be in character, conduct, or achievement. One of the worst forms of pride is spiritual pride, an attitude that I am more holy or righteous or faithful or obedient or more fruitful in evangelism than others.

Humility toward others, then, is once again a recognition that all we are and do that is of any worth is a gift of God's grace. Hence, humility turns the temptation to pride into an occasion for gratitude to God for what He has done in and through us.

There is another aspect of humility in relation to other people. Paul probably had this aspect in mind when he said in Colossians 3:12 that we should clothe ourselves with humility. According to R. C. H. Lenski, "The virtue admired by pagans [in Paul's day] was domination, powerful self-assertion, assuming a position above other men; hence . . . [humility] was despicable to the pagan mind, a poor, low mind that could not assert itself and lord it over anybody."[15] Unfortunately, this self-assertive, domineering attitude was not limited to Paul's day; it is still with us today and, even more unfortunately, is found among Christians.

But Jesus took the pagan meaning of humility and turned it upside down. He washed His disciples' feet—the usual task of the most lowly servant—and told His disciples they should follow His example (see John 13:1-15). He said, "For who is greater, the one who is at the table or the one who serves? Is it not the one who is at the table? But I am among you as one who serves" (Luke 22:27). Above all, Jesus laid aside His glory and became the ultimate servant, dying for us on the cross (see Philippians 2:5-11). By His actions, Jesus turned what was deemed a weakness by pagans into a strength and virtue for Christians. The person who wants to experience God's transforming grace in his or her life must be prepared to let the Holy Spirit transform self-assertiveness into Christlike humility and servanthood.

## FORBEARANCE

In his "garments of grace" list in Colossians 3:12-14, Paul put *forbearance* ("bear with each other") and *forgiveness* together. These two character traits should certainly be hallmarks of a person living by God's transforming grace. Forbearance is no longer a common word in most vocabularies. We tend to use the word *patience* in its place, as in "please be patient with me." Forbearance literally means "to put up with" and is translated that way several places in the New Testament.

For example, the Lord Jesus said in Matthew 17:17, "O unbelieving and perverse generation, . . . how long shall I stay with you? How long shall I *put up with* you?" (emphasis added). Paul spoke similarly when he wrote to the Corinthians, "I hope you will *put up with* a little of my foolishness; but you are already doing that" (2 Corinthians 11:1, emphasis added).

So when Paul said to "bear with each other," he was saying, "put up with one another," or as we would say, "be patient with one another." When we use "be patient" in this manner, we are saying to put up with or overlook the faults and thoughtless acts of others. One person is always prompt for appointments, another is habitually late. When they set a lunch date, the prompt person will very likely have to put up with twenty or so minutes of tardiness from the habitually late person.

But there are two ways we can put up with the faults and thoughtless acts of other people. One way is politely but grudgingly. A person says, "Excuse my lateness," and we smile and say, "Of course," while inwardly we are saying, "Why can't you be on time like I always am?" Such an attitude is born out of pride and is obviously not the way God intends that we put up with or be patient with one another.

The other way is to recognize that God has to constantly put up with our faults and failures. Not only are we faulty and thoughtless in our relationships with one another, more importantly, we are faulty and thoughtless in our relationship with God. We do not honor and reverence Him as we should. We prefer the entertainment of television to intimate fellowship with Him. But God is patient with us because of His grace. And to the extent that we consciously live in His grace, we will be patient with others. In fact, the definition of patience in our common use implies the latter, gracious way of putting up with the faults of others.

We all recognize that grudgingly "putting up with" is not true patience according to our common meaning. True patience holds no grudge, not even a minor, momentary one.

In Ephesians 4:2 Paul urges us to "[bear] with one another in love." The basis for our patience with one another is love. As Peter said in 1 Peter 4:8, "Above all, love each other deeply, because love covers over a multitude of sins." Love not only covers over a multitude of sins but also a multitude of faults in one another. But where do we get such a love? John answers this in 1 John 4:19: "We love because he first loved us."

As we saw in an earlier chapter, the object of the verb *love* in 1 John 4:19 is indefinite. John could be saying, "We love *God* because He first loved us"; or he could be saying, "We love *one another* because God first loved us." Perhaps John intended both meanings, although the context seems to indicate the latter. If so, he is saying the basis of our love for one another is God's love for us. This being true, the extent of our love for each other will be based on our consciousness of and appreciation of God's love for us. The more we have a heartfelt comprehension of God's love for us, the more we will be inclined to love others. And since love covers over a multitude of faults, the more we will be inclined to be patient with one another. So patience ultimately grows out of a recognition of God's grace in our lives. The more we are consciously living by grace, the more we will be patient with one another. Or to say it another way, if we are not patient with each other, we are not living by grace.

## FORGIVENESS

Paul said we are to go beyond being patient with one another; we are also to *forgive* each other. Forgiveness differs from forbearance in that it has to do with real wrongs committed against us. Forbearance or patience should be our response to unintentional actions due to the faults or carelessness of another. Forgiveness should be our response to the intentional or provocative acts of another, the instances when they attempt to or actually do harm us in some way.

In Colossians 3:13, Paul said, "Forgive whatever grievances you may have against one another." Paul's language seems to take for granted that such grievances will occur. As believers, all of us are still far from the Christlikeness we would like to have. So we not only offend our fellow believers unwittingly through our faults and failures, but we also sometimes offend deliberately. We need forgiveness not only from God but from one another. And we need to forgive one another as God forgave us.

Paul said, "Forgive as the Lord forgave you." We are to forgive because we have been forgiven. As F. F. Bruce said, "The free grace of the Father's forgiving love is the pattern for his children in their forgiveness of one another."[16] This thought takes us back to Jesus' parable of the unmerciful servant in Matthew 18:21-35. We considered this briefly at the end of chapter 3 in session 2, but I want to look at it in more detail now. For convenience the parable is reproduced here:

> Then Peter came to Jesus and asked, "Lord, how many times shall I forgive my brother when he sins against me? Up to seven times?"
>
> Jesus answered, "I tell you, not seven times, but seventy-seven times.

"Therefore, the kingdom of heaven is like a king who wanted to settle accounts with his servants. As he began the settlement, a man who owed him ten thousand talents was brought to him. Since he was not able to pay, the master ordered that he and his wife and his children and all he had be sold to repay the debt.

"The servant fell on his knees before him. 'Be patient with me,' he begged, 'and I will pay back everything.' The servant's master took pity on him, canceled the debt and let him go.

"But when that servant went out, he found one of his fellow servants who owed him a hundred denarii. He grabbed him and began to choke him. 'Pay back what you owe me!' he demanded.

"His fellow servant fell to his knees and begged him, 'Be patient with me, and I will pay you back.'

"But he refused. Instead, he went off and had the man thrown into prison until he could pay the debt. When the other servants saw what had happened, they were greatly distressed and went and told their master everything that had happened.

"Then the master called the servant in. 'You wicked servant,' he said, 'I canceled all that debt of yours because you begged me to. Shouldn't you have had mercy on your fellow servant just as I had on you?' In anger his master turned him over to the jailers to be tortured, until he should pay back all he owed.

"This is how my heavenly Father will treat each of you unless you forgive your brother from your heart."

As we consider the parable, note first that Jesus gave it in response to a specific question from Peter: "How many times shall I forgive my brother when he sins against me? Up to seven times?" The parable serves to reinforce Jesus' answer, "not seven times, but seventy-seven times."

The servant in the parable owed his master millions of dollars. When the master ordered that he and his family and all he had be sold to repay the debt, the servant stalled for time. He said, "Be patient with me, and I will pay back everything." The servant should have declared bankruptcy and pleaded for mercy; instead, he pleaded for time. He thought he could wipe out his huge debt, given sufficient time. But he owed an impossible sum. According to David Seamands, the annual taxes at that time from all the Palestinian provinces put together amounted to only $800,000.[17] Yet the servant owed millions of dollars. There was no way he could pay his debt.

This servant illustrates a person who is living by works. He foolishly thought he could work his way out of debt. But the master knew that only grace would suffice to meet the man's needs, so he freely forgave him and canceled the debt.

Despite experiencing such overwhelming forgiveness, this man refused to forgive a fellow servant who owed him only a few dollars. Instead, he ruthlessly demanded payment. The obvious message of the parable is that, whatever offense anyone has committed against us, it is trifling compared to the vast debt of our sins against God.

It seems that the unmerciful servant's unforgiving attitude arose out of his lack of understanding of grace. He wanted to repay his debt, or to use an earlier expression in this book, to pay his own way. In his mind he never declared total bankruptcy. That is why, even after receiving such gracious forgiveness himself, he treated his fellow servant so unmercifully. Had he recognized his own total bankruptcy, and consequently, the necessity for absolute grace on the part of his master, he probably would have behaved differently.

Many Christians behave like the unmerciful servant and for the same reason. Because they have not admitted their own total and permanent spiritual bankruptcy, they do not recognize the infinite extent of God's grace to them. They still see themselves as basically "good," and because of that, they expect everyone else to be "good" also, especially in relationship to them. Because they do not recognize their own continued bankruptcy before God, they insist that everyone else pay his own debts.

But the Christian living by grace recognizes his own spiritual bankruptcy. He sees the vast contrast between his sins against God of "several million dollars" and his neighbor's sins against him of only a "few dollars." And because of this, he both understands and responds to Paul's instruction, "Forgive as the Lord forgave you."

So we have come full circle and are now back where we began in session 1, recognizing our own spiritual bankruptcy. This is where we must begin and end if we are to experience the joy of living by God's transforming grace. So I invite you and urge you to lay aside any remnant of self-goodness you may think you still have. Admit your total spiritual bankruptcy, and drink deeply from the infinite grace of God. And then in deep awareness of what you have received, extend that same spirit of grace to others.

# Appropriating God's Grace

## (Chapters 12 and 13)

## STUDY QUESTIONS

### CENTRAL IDEA

God's grace is applied to our lives and made real in our experience through prayer, the Bible, submission to His sovereignty, and the ministry of other believers.

### WARM-UP

Describe a recent time when you experienced God's grace in a specific way. What did God use to give you this sense of His grace?

### EXPLORING GRACE

#### *Experiencing God's Grace Through Prayer*

1.  a.  Hebrews 4:14-15 encourages us to go to God in prayer, asking for the grace we need. What does this passage give as some of the reasons why we can approach God with confidence? (See also Hebrews 2:18.)

    b.  In what ways do you find any of those reasons encouraging?

2.  If we are to experience God's grace through prayer, we must pray. But even for Christians this often seems to be the last thing we get around to doing.

a.   Why do you think many Christians don't pray more?

b.   How do you feel about your prayer times at this point in your spiritual pilgrimage?

c.   What specific things do you think you need to do to improve your prayer life?

## God's Grace Applied to Our Lives Through His Word

1.   If we are to experience the grace of God, we must regularly expose ourselves to the Word of God. God can bring His Word to our attention in many ways, including:

- Friends
- Sermons
- Bible study
- Bible reading
- Christian books
- Bible memorization
- Christian radio and television

a.   Which of these are a part of a regular week for you?

b. Is there one area you believe you need to give more time to in your life? If so, which one?

2. a. Share a time when God used a particular Scripture passage in your life to speak directly to you.

b. By what means did you become aware of this passage at the time you needed it?

c. How did it help you in your particular situation?

### *Receiving God's Grace Through Humble Submission to Him*

1. To experience God's grace, we must humble ourselves and trust that God is in control regardless of the difficulty of our circumstances. Read 1 Peter 5:5-7.

a. What are we told to do in these verses?

b. What is the end result of our humility? When will we receive this end result?

c.  In what areas of your life is God teaching you to be more humble?

2.  a.  Describe the attitude of a person who refuses to submit to what God is allowing into his life.

b.  How is the grace of God restricted in this person's life?

c.  Have you ever experienced a time when your attitude created a barrier in your life to enjoying the grace of God? Share what you learned from this experience.

### *God's Grace Given to Us Through the Ministry of Others*

1.  There are three basic ways that we can help one another respond to the Holy Spirit in our lives and thus receive God's grace:

- Pray for and with each other.
- Share relevant verses with each other.
- Help each other submit to the providence of God in our lives.

a.  We must have close relationships with other people if we want God to use those people in these three ways in our lives. How do you cultivate close relationships in your life?

b.   Give an example of a time when someone used one of these three ways to minister God's grace to you.

2.   In order for God to use you to minister His grace to someone, that person must be receptive and open to your input. In the same way, we must communicate to others our willingness to let them minister to us.

a.   How good are you at letting others minister to you? Are you able to admit your needs to others?

b.   How good are you at reading the signals from others as to when you could be a minister of God's grace in their lives?

### *Appropriating God's Grace*

1.   a.   Of the four ways that God can make His grace real in our lives discussed in this lesson, which one do you think you have the biggest problem with?

b.   Take a few minutes to come up with a specific plan for how you will make yourself more available to God in that area this week.

## Closing Prayer

Pray the following prayer as a group. Read one sentence at a time. Allow enough time of silence between sentences for each person to talk to God about specifics in his or her life that relate to this prayer.

Lord, I am willing to receive what You give.

Lord, I am willing to lack what You withhold.

Lord, I am willing to relinquish what You take.

Lord, I am willing to suffer what You inflict.

Lord, I am willing to be what You require.

## Going Deeper (Extra questions for further study)

1. Colossians 3:12-14 gives us a list of qualities that are the result of God's grace at work in our lives.

   a. What do these verses say about how God thinks of us?

   b. How do the qualities listed in these verses enable us to be ministers of God's grace to others?

   c. Choose one of the qualities listed and commit to asking God every day for a week to increase that quality in your life.

2. Read Hebrews 7:25 and 1 John 2:1. How could the fact that Christ is interceding for you affect the way you pray?

3. a. What do the following verses teach us about God's sovereignty and the attitude we should have toward trials?

   • Genesis 50:20

   • Job 1:20-21

   • Job 2:9-10

   b. How does trusting God and seeing His hand ultimately ruling in the circumstances of our lives help us maintain an attitude of humility?

4. Ecclesiastes 4:9-12 gives us a poetic description of how much we need one another. What are some of the reasons why we need strong friendships within the fellowship of believers?

### Pondering Grace (For personal reflection)

*To pray is nothing more involved than to let Jesus come into our hearts, to give Him access with all His power to our needs. From this it is clear that success in prayer does not depend upon the assurance of the one who prays, nor upon his boldness, nor any such thing, but upon this one thing that he opens his heart to Jesus.*

O. Hallesby, *Prayer*

*Prayer is the exercise of drawing on the grace of God. Don't say — I will endure this until I can get away and pray. Pray now; draw on the grace of God in the moment of need.*

Oswald Chambers, *My Utmost for His Highest*

*If the majesty and grace and power of God are not being manifested in us (not in our consciousness), God holds us responsible. "God is able to make all grace abound." Be stamped with God's nature, and His blessings will come through you all the time.*

Oswald Chambers, *My Utmost for His Highest*

*God and the Word of his grace always go together; God lets his grace flow out through that Word.*

R. C. H. Lenski, *The Interpretation of The Acts of the Apostles*

## Prayer Answered by Crosses

*I asked the Lord that I might grow
    In faith and love and every grace,
Might more of his salvation know,
    And seek more earnestly his face.*

*'Twas he who taught me thus to pray;
    And he, I trust, has answered prayer;
But it has been in such a way
    As almost drove me to despair.*

*I hoped that, in some favoured hour,
    At once he'd answer my request
And by his love's constraining power
    Subdue my sins, and give me rest.*

*Instead of this, he made me feel
    The hidden evils of my heart,
And let the angry powers of hell
    Assault my soul in every part.*

Yea, more with his own hand he seemed
        Intent to aggravate my woe,
Crossed all the fair designs I schemed,
        Blasted my gourds, and laid me low .

Lord, why is this? I trembling cried;
        Wilt thou pursue this worm to death?
This is the way, the Lord replied
        I answer prayer for grace and faith.

These inward trials I now employ
        From self and pride to set thee free,
And break thy schemes of earthly joy,
        That thou may'st seek thy all in me.

John Newton

# Help for Group Leaders

The following pages are designed to help a discussion leader guide a group through this book. You can appoint one person to lead each session, or you can rotate leadership.

## GETTING STARTED

Choose a time and place to meet that is consistent, comfortable, and relatively free from distractions. If you meet in a home, make plans to deal with pets, ringing telephones, and other distractions.

### SET YOUR SESSION FORMAT.

Decide how long your sessions will be and map out a general plan for each gathering. Following is a sample format for a sixty-minute session.

- Ten minutes for settling in, opening prayer, and warm-up conversation. Refreshments can help people mingle, but don't let them consume too much of your time.
- Forty minutes for discussion of the study questions. Open your discussion by inviting group members to share their responses to the chapter(s) they read during the week. Then move into discussing the questions that followed the session's reading.
- Ten minutes for closing prayer time and closing comments. Before you end, call attention to the next session's readings and encourage group members to complete the study questions on their own.

### CUSTOMIZE THE MATERIAL FOR YOUR GROUP.

In this study guide, you'll find the following elements:

- *Text.* Group members should read this chapter or chapters before getting together.
- *Central Idea.* This states the main point of the session. It will be helpful to keep

this in mind while you prepare and during group discussions.

- *Warm-up.* This ice-breaker question will introduce the topic of discussion and help you and other group members connect at the beginning of the sessions.
- *Exploring Grace.* These questions help you grapple with the ideas in the text as you look at relevant Scripture passages. Group members should read and answer these questions before the group meets together.
- *Closing Prayer.* These suggestions are designed to help your closing prayer time relate to the lesson.
- *Going Deeper.* These are extra questions for additional study and discussion if time allows. You can draw from these questions if more material is needed or encourage group members to study them on their own as a follow-up after the session.
- *Pondering Grace.* These quotes are for personal reflection and for stimulating further thought. They may also help broaden the discussions.

Leaders should decide which questions and elements to cover during group time. You probably will not have time to discuss all questions in depth; focus on the ones that are most important for your group. When a question is about a Scripture passage, it will be helpful to read the passage together. When there are a number of passages, decide which ones to discuss during group time.

Please note that the number of sessions in the study guide doesn't correlate directly with the numbers of chapters in the book. Sometimes a session will combine chapters in one lesson. We created the study guide this way so as to compress the sessions into a shorter amount of time (eight weeks, if you do one session per week) than the book would allow (thirteen chapters). If you want to create a longer study, you might cover some sessions in two weeks instead of one.

## Plan your first session.

You may want to plan a potluck for your first meeting together. In this way, group members can get to know one another in the context of a meal, which is a good way to break down barriers. Then after dinner you can have your first session.

The content you cover in this session depends on which of the following options you choose.

*Option one: An eight-week study.* This is how we've set up this book. In this format, make sure each participant has a copy of this book prior to session 1. Encourage everyone to read the chapters and respond to the study questions for session 1 prior to your first meeting.

*Option two: A nine-week study.* In this option, you add an additional "opening week" to the study to use for distributing the books and getting acquainted with group members. In this session, have someone read the first two pages of the preface aloud as the group follows along. Encourage participants to point out insights or discoveries that stood out to them. Talk together about group members' experiences of living by grace. Can they identify with the author's statement that "most of us tend to base our personal relationship with God on our performance instead of His grace. . . . We are saved by grace but we are living by the 'sweat' of our own performance"? Pray together for open hearts and minds; for an awareness that God is present, engaged, and interested in your discussions; and for a spirit of mutual encouragement as you study and discuss the book during the coming weeks. Then assign the preparation under option one above for your next meeting — the real "session 1" of this study.

Whichever option you choose, be sure to set aside adequate time in the first meeting for people to share who they are. It is amazing how much more productive and honest a Bible discussion is when the participants know each other.

At some point in the evening (probably toward the end), go over the following guidelines. They help make a discussion more fruitful, especially when you are dealing with issues that truly matter to people.

- *Trustworthiness and respect.* No one should repeat what someone shares in the group unless that person gives express permission. Even then, discretion is imperative. Be trustworthy. Participants should talk about their own feelings and experiences, not those of others.
- *Attendance.* Each session builds on the previous ones, and you need each other. So, ask group members to commit to attending all sessions, unless an emergency arises.
- *Participation.* This is a group discussion, not a lecture. It is important that each person participate in some way.
- *Preparation.* Encourage everyone to read the material and answer the questions before the group meets. Your discussions will be more interesting if group members have prepared in advance. In addition, group members will get far more out of the study if they have spent time thinking about the questions and meditating on the Scriptures before meeting.

- *Honesty.* Appropriate openness is a key to a good group. Be who you really are, not who you think you ought to be.
- *Transformation.* The goal of this study is to come to know God's heart and character in a way that leads to transformation from the inside out. As you read and study, please allow God to take you past simply gaining knowledge to encountering Him in fresh ways.

## GENERAL HELPS

Below, we have provided general helps for leading your group, but we can't cover every situation you will encounter—such as a group that talks too much or a group that won't discuss at all. Talk with veteran leaders in your church when you need input and ideas. And remember: Your greatest help is always God's Holy Spirit, who has committed to living with you and doing life with you. He's an extraordinary teacher, and you can rely on His strength, wisdom, and problem-solving skills for your group.

### Preparing for a Session

Your aim as a leader is to prepare an environment that is conducive to growth. You want group members to feel comfortable with one another so they freely engage with the material and discussion.

*Pray for the group.* As the group leader, your most important preparation for each session is prayer. You will want to make your prayers personal, of course, but here are some suggestions for how to pray:

- Let God be the leader of the group. Ask Him to show you what portions and questions to emphasize and how to format the discussion. Invite God to give you input on your groups' unique needs each week.
- Ask the Holy Spirit to bring alive the truths you are studying, personalizing them for each group member.
- Pray that nothing will keep the group members from attending. Ask God to enable them to feel free to share their thoughts and feelings honestly and to contribute their unique gifts and insights.
- Pray for group members' private times with God this week. Ask God to be active in nurturing them.

- Ask for the Holy Spirit's guidance in exercising patience, acceptance, sensitivity, and wisdom as you talk with each other. Pray for an atmosphere of genuine love in the group, with each member being open to learning and change.
- Pray that your discussion will lead each of you to love the Lord more deeply, obey Him more closely, and demonstrate His presence more tangibly.
- Pray for insight as you go over the study materials and for wisdom as you lead the group so that you tap into God's desires for your time together.

*Study and customize the material.* After prayer, your most important preparation is to be thoroughly familiar with the material you will discuss. You will find it important to read the chapters that are covered by each session and to make sure you have answered all of the questions.

Decide which questions you want to discuss as a group. You may not have time to cover all the questions. Consider and ask God about which questions are most important for your particular group.

## LEADING A SESSION

Following are general guidelines for leading a group discussion. If you are a new leader, you can also ask an experienced group leader to mentor you.

*Invite God to be the leader.* Open each session with prayer, acknowledging that God is present with the group and that He has an "agenda" for the session. Surrender your plan for the time to Him and invite Him to work in and speak to group members.

*Work toward a relaxed and open atmosphere.* This may not come quickly, so be a model for the others of acceptance, openness to truth and change, and love. Develop a genuine interest in each person's remarks and expect to learn from them. Show that you care by listening carefully. Be affirming.

*Invite opening comments.* Open your discussion by inviting group members to share any responses, observations, or questions about the chapter(s) they read. If a group member brings up a point that will be discussed later in the session, affirm what a good point it is and mention that you'll be talking more about this later. This will help keep your discussion from getting sidetracked at the beginning.

*Pay attention to how you ask the questions.* Don't ask flatly, "What did you get for number 1?" Instead, by your tone of voice convey your interest and enthusiasm for the question and your warmth toward the group. The group will adopt your attitude. Read the questions as though you were asking them of good friends.

*Vary your approach as you move through the questions.* For some questions you might pose the issue to no one in particular and wait for responses. For others, you might direct the question to a specific individual, let him or her respond, and then encourage others to respond as well. As much as time permits, encourage unrushed, multiple responses. Sometimes you'll discover deeper levels of insight as one participant builds upon the thoughts of another.

*Expect variations or pauses in the discussion.* Sometimes a group won't respond as quickly as you'd like. If that happens:

- Be comfortable with silence. Let the group wrestle to think of answers. Don't be quick to jump in and rescue the group with your answers.
- Reword a question if the group members have trouble understanding it.
- If a question evokes little response, feel free to leave it and move on.
- Feel free to answer questions yourself occasionally. In particular, you might need to be the first one to answer questions about personal experiences. In this way you will model the depth of openness and thought you hope others will show. You can also model an appropriate length of response. Don't answer every question, but don't be a silent observer.
- If the discussion is winding down on a question, go on to the next one. It's not necessary to push people to see every possible angle.

*Ask only one question at a time.* Often, participants' responses will suggest a follow-up question to you. Be discerning as to when you are following a fruitful train of thought and when you are going off on a tangent.

*Be aware of time.* Don't spend so much time discussing that you run out of time for application and prayer. Your goal is not to have something to discuss but to become more like Jesus Christ.

*Encourage constructive controversy.* The group can learn a lot from struggling with the many sides of an issue. If you aren't threatened when someone disagrees, the whole group will be more open and vulnerable. Intervene, if necessary, to be sure that people are debating ideas and interpretations of Scripture, not attacking each other's feelings and character. If the group gets stuck in an irresolvable argument, say something such as, "We can agree to disagree here," and move on.

*Don't be the expert.* People will stop talking if they feel you are judging their answers or that you think you know best. Let God's words in the Bible be the expert, the final say. Let people candidly express their feelings and experiences.

*Don't do for the group what it can do for itself.* With a beginning group, you may have to ask all of the questions, do all of the outside research, plan the applications, etc. But within a few meetings you should start delegating various leadership responsibilities. Let members learn to exercise their gifts. Let them start making decisions and solving problems together. Encourage them to maturity and unity in Christ.

*Encourage people to share feelings as well as facts.* There are two dimensions of truth: the truth about how people feel, and the truth about who God is. People need to face both their real feelings and the real God.

*Summarize the discussion frequently.* Help the group see where the discussion is going.

*Let the group plan applications.* The action responses in this guide are suggestions. Your group should adapt them so they are relevant and life-changing for members. If group members aren't committed to an application, they won't do it. Encourage, but don't force.

*Allow freedom during your prayer times.* To close a meeting, you can have one person pray or open up the time for brief conversational prayers from anyone who wishes to pray aloud. (Tip: No one should ever feel pressured or obligated to pray aloud. It can help everyone relax if you assure them of this ahead of time.) You might use your prayer time to pray for group members' general needs, or suggest that you pray personally for each member regarding the insights and struggles they encountered with this session. Feel free to allow silence during prayer so that God has space to respond individually to group members' prayers.

## Reviewing After a Session

Use the following questions each week to help you improve your leadership next time.

1. How did you see God at work during your time together?
2. Did you have the right number of questions prepared? Should you add to the next session's questions or plan to cover fewer questions?
3. Did you discuss the major issues? If you missed major points, on your notes for next week mark the essential questions or points you want to cover and summarize.
4. Did you know your material thoroughly enough to have freedom in leading?
5. Did you keep the discussion from wandering?
6. Did everyone participate? Were people open? Was anyone overtalkative? Disruptive? Think about how you can handle these problems next week if they occur again, or ask another group leader for ideas.

7. Was the discussion practical? Did it lead to new understanding, new hope, repentance, change? If necessary, brainstorm some application questions that can help lead the group in this direction.

8. Did you begin and end on time? If necessary, put a clock or watch in plain sight in your meeting area so you can easily glance at it and keep track of time.

9. Did you give the group the maximum responsibility that it can handle?

10. What does God think of the time together?

11. How would He want to be your coach and mentor as you lead next week? If you're feeling inadequate in some area of leadership, how would He want to be strong for you and provide the power, wisdom, and expertise you need?

12. How does He want to affirm you for your investment in leading this group? Where is He proud of you and pleased with you, as a proud Father might be?

# Notes

## SESSION ONE: The Performance Treadmill

1. Stephen Brown, *When Being Good Isn't Good Enough* (Nashville, TN: Thomas Nelson, 1990), 108.
2. Harold S. Kushner, *When Bad Things Happen to Good People* (New York: Avon Books, 1981), 8.
3. The word translated as "rebellion" in the New International Version is translated as "transgression" in most other versions of the Bible. However, the word means a rejection of authority, so *rebellion* is a good word to use.
4. C. Samuel Storms, *The Grandeur of God* (Grand Rapids, MI: Baker, 1984), 124.
5. Storms, 125.
6. Abraham Booth, *The Reign of Grace* (repr., Swengle, PA: Reiner Publications, 1976), 40, 48.
7. Augustus M. Toplady, "Rock of Ages" (1776).

## SESSION TWO: Grace — It Really Is Amazing

1. Philip P. Bliss, "Hallelujah, What a Savior!" (1875).
2. Robert Lowry, "Nothing But the Blood" (1876).
3. Jay E. Adams, *From Forgiven to Forgiving* (Wheaton, IL: Victor Books, 1989), 18.
4. R. C. H. Lenski, *The Interpretation of St. Matthew's Gospel* (Minneapolis, MN: Augsburg, 1943), 758.
5. R. C. H. Lenski, *The Interpretation of St. Paul's Epistle to the Romans* (Minneapolis, MN: Augsburg, 1936), 385; and John Murray, *The New International Commentary on the New Testament: The Epistle to the Romans* (Grand Rapids, MI: Eerdmans, 1959), 208.
6. C. Samuel Storms, *The Grandeur of God* (Grand Rapids, MI: Baker, 1984), 125.
7. William Hendriksen, *A Commentary on the Gospel of John* (Edinburgh, Scotland: The Banner of Truth Trust, 1961), 88.
8. Hendriksen, 88–89.
9. John Newton, "Come My Soul, Thy Suit Prepare," *Trinity Hymnal* (Philadelphia, PA: The Orthodox Presbyterian Church, 1961), hymn 531.
10. R. C. Sproul, "Suffering and Merit?" *Tabletalk* 13, no. 1 (February 1989): 5.

## SESSION THREE: **Does God Have a Right?**

1. William Arnot, *Parables of Our Lord* (1865; repr., Grand Rapids, MI: Kregel), 214.

2. R. C. H. Lenski, *The Interpretation of St. Matthew's Gospel* (Minneapolis, MN: Augsburg, 1943), 758.

3. Philip E. Hughes, *The New International Commentary on the New Testament: Paul's Second Epistle to the Corinthians* (Grand Rapids, MI: Eerdmans, 1962), 36.

4. John Calvin, *Calvin's New Testament Commentaries*, vol. 10, *The Second Epistle of Paul the Apostle to the Corinthians and the Epistles to Timothy, Titus and Philemon*, eds. David W. Torrance and Thomas F. Torrance, trans. T. A. Smail (Grand Rapids, MI: Eerdmans, 1964), 21–22.

5. Martin Luther, quoted in Leland Ryken, "Puritan Work Ethic: The Dignity of Life's Labors," *Christianity Today*, October 19, 1979, 17.

## SESSION FOUR: **Compelled by Love**

1. Martyn Lloyd-Jones, *Romans: An Exposition of Chapter 6, The New Man* (London: The Banner of Truth Trust, 1972), 8.

2. Stephen Brown, "The Song of Grace (Part 1), 1 Peter 5:6-14," cassette (Key Biscayne, FL: Key Life Tapes, 1990).

3. Richard Gilbert, "Sola Gratia and Sanctification," *Modem Reformation*, September/October 1990, 7.

4. Charles Hodge, *Commentary on the Epistle to the Romans* (1886; repr. Grand Rapids, MI: Eerdmans, 1955), 384.

5. John Murray, *The New International Commentary on the New Testament: The Epistle to the Romans*, vol. 2 (Grand Rapids, MI: Eerdmans, 1965), 111.

6. Martin Luther, quoted in R. C. H. Lenski, *The Interpretation of St. Paul's Epistle to the Romans* (Minneapolis, MN: Augsburg, 1936), 746.

7. Ernest F. Kevan, *The Grace of Law* (Grand Rapids, MI: Baker, 1976), 63.

8. Abraham Booth, *The Reign of Grace* (repr., Swengel, PA: Reiner Publications, 1976), 201.

9. Charles Hodge, *An Exposition of the Second Epistle to the Corinthians* (London: The Banner of Truth Trust, 1959), 133.

10. Philip E. Hughes, *The New International Commentary on the New Testament: Paul's Second Epistle to the Corinthians* (Grand Rapids, MI: Eerdmans, 1962), 258.

SESSION FIVE: **The Proof of Love**

1. Charles Colson, *Loving God* (Grand Rapids, MI: Zondervan, 1983), 15.
2. Samuel Bolton, *The True Bounds of Christian Freedom* (1645; repr., Edinburgh, Scotland: The Banner of Truth Trust, 1978), 219.
3. Gordon J. Wenham, *The New International Commentary on the Old Testament: The Book of Leviticus* (Grand Rapids, MI: Eerdmans, 1979), 33, 35.
4. Arthur W. Pink, *The Doctrine of Sanctification* (Swengel, PA: Bible Truth Depot, 1955), 200.
5. Pink, 128.
6. William Hendriksen, *New Testament Commentary: Exposition of Paul's Epistle to the Romans* (Grand Rapids, MI: Baker, 1980), 404.
7. John Murray, *The New International Commentary on the New Testament: The Epistle to the Romans*, vol. 2 (Grand Rapids, MI: Eerdmans, 1965), 114.
8. Jerry Bridges, *The Pursuit of Holiness* (Colorado Springs, CO: NavPress, 1978).
9. William Hendriksen, *New Testament Commentary: Exposition of Philippians* (Grand Rapids, MI: Baker, 1962), 120.

SESSION SIX: **Called to Be Free**

1. William L. Coleman, *The Pharisees Guide to Total Holiness* (Minneapolis, MN: Bethany, 1977), 8–9.
2. This story is based on Charles R. Swindoll, *The Grace Awakening* (Dallas, TX: Word, 1990), 93.
3. Sinclair B. Ferguson, *John Owen on the Christian Life* (Edinburgh, Scotland: The Banner of Truth Trust, 1987), 154.
4. Samuel Bolton, *The True Bounds of Christian Freedom* (1645; repr., Edinburgh, Scotland: The Banner of Truth Trust, 1978), 220–221.

SESSION SEVEN: **The Sufficiency of Grace**

1. John Calvin, *Calvin's New Testament Commentaries*, vol. 10, *The Second Epistle of Paul the Apostle to the Corinthians and the Epistles to Timothy, Titus and Philemon*, eds. David W. Torrance and Thomas F. Torrance, trans. T. A. Smail (Grand Rapids, MI: Eerdmans, 1964), 161.
2. Charles Hodge, *An Exposition of the First Epistle to the Corinthians* (London: The Banner of Truth Trust, 1959), 317.

3. G. Ch. Aalders, *Bible Students Commentary: Genesis*, vol. 1, trans. William Heynen (Grand Rapids, MI: Zondervan, 1981), 102.

4. P. C. Craigie, *The New International Commentary on the Old Testament: The Book of Deuteronomy* (Grand Rapids, MI: Eerdmans, 1976), 185.

5. J. A. Thompson, *The Tyndale Old Testament Commentaries: Deuteronomy: An Interpretation and Commentary* (Downers Grove, IL: InterVarsity, 1974), 134–135.

6. Philip E. Hughes, *The New International Commentary on the New Testament: Paul's Second Epistle to the Corinthians* (Grand Rapids, MI: Eerdmans, 1962), 451.

7. John Blanchard, *Truth For Life: A Devotional Commentary on the Epistle of James* (Welwyn, England: Evangelical Press, 1986), 268.

8. Lina Sandell Berg, "Day by Day," trans. Andrew L. Skoog, *Praise! Our Songs and Hymns* (Grand Rapids, MI: Singspiration Music, 1980), 370.

9. Calvin, 161.

10. Hughes, 443.

11. Annie Johnson Flint quoted in Blanchard, 268.

12. Charles Swindoll, *The Grace Awakening* (Dallas, TX: Word, 1990), ix.

13. Alfred Marshall, *The New International Version Interlinear Greek-English New Testament* (Grand Rapids, MI: Zondervan, 1976), 764.

14. F. F. Bruce, *The New International Commentary on the New Testament: The Epistle to the Colossians, to Philemon and to the Ephesians* (Grand Rapids, MI: Eerdmans, 1984), 317.

15. Harry Blamires, *Recovering the Christian Mind* (Downers Grove, IL: InterVarsity, 1988), 32–33.

16. Gordon D. Fee, *The New International Commentary on the New Testament: The First Epistle to the Corinthians* (Grand Rapids, MI: Eerdmans, 1987), 37.

17. John Calvin, *Calvin's New Testament Commentaries*, vol. 9, *The First Epistle of Paul to the Corinthians*, eds. David W. Torrance and Thomas F. Torrance, trans. John W. Fraser (Grand Rapids, MI: Eerdmans, 1960), 317–318.

18. W. E. Vine, *An Expository Dictionary of New Testament Words* (Nashville, TN: Royal Publishers, Inc., n.d.), 424.

19. R. C. H. Lenski, *The Interpretation of St. Paul's First and Second Epistle to the Corinthians* (Minneapolis, MN: Augsburg, 1963), 644.

20. Joseph Addison Alexander, *Isaiah, Translated and Explained* (1867; repr., Minneapolis, MN: Klock & Klock Christian Publishers, Inc., 1981), 95.

21. John Owen, *Sin & Temptation*, abridged by ed. James M. Houston (Portland, OR: Multnomah, 1983), 99.

22. Charles Hodge, *An Exposition of the Second Epistle to the Corinthians* (London: The Banner of Truth Trust, 1959), 192.

23. For a more complete discussion of the sovereignty of God in the lives of people, see my book *Trusting God: Even When Life Hurts* (Colorado Springs, CO: NavPress, 1988), especially chapter 4, "God's Sovereignty Over People."

24. Hughes, 287.

25. Samuel Bolton, *The True Bounds of Christian Freedom* (1645; repr., Edinburgh, Scotland: The Banner of Truth Trust, 1978), 94.

26. Ernest Kevan, *The Grace of Law* (Grand Rapids, MI: Baker, 1976), 190. Kevan quotes verbatim from the Puritans, including their seventeenth-century spelling and pronunciation. I have modernized both for the convenience of the reader.

27. R. C. Sproul, "Suffering and Merit?" *Tabletalk* 13, no. 1 (February 1989): 5.

SESSION EIGHT: **Appropriating God's Grace**

1. John Brown, *An Exposition of Hebrews* (1862; repr., Edinburgh, Scotland: The Banner of Truth Trust, 1961), 232.

2. Brown, 231.

3. J. L. Dagg, *Manual of Theology* (1857; repr., Harrisonburgh, VA: Gano Books, 1982), 76.

4. L. Berkhof, *Systematic Theology* (London: The Banner of Truth Trust, 1941), 72.

5. R. C. H. Lenski, *The Interpretation of The Acts of the Apostles* (Minneapolis, MN: Augsburg, 1934), 853.

6. Charles Hodge, *A Commentary on the Epistle to the Ephesians* (1856; repr., Grand Rapids, MI: Baker, 1980), 389.

7. F. F. Bruce, *The New International Commentary on the New Testament: The Epistle to the Colossians, to Philemon and to the Ephesians* (Grand Rapids, MI: Eerdmans, 1984), 409–410.

8. For further treatment of the subject of God's sovereignty and suffering, I again refer you to my book *Trusting God: Even When Life Hurts* (Colorado Springs, CO: NavPress, 1988).

9. Samuel Bolton, *The True Bounds of Christian Freedom* (1645; repr., Edinburgh, Scotland: The Banner of Truth Trust, 1964), 25.

10. John Newton, "Prayer Answered by Crosses," quoted in John J. Murray, *Behind a Frowning Providence* (Edinburgh, Scotland: The Banner of Truth Trust, 1990), 15–16, 20–21.

11. John Lillie, *Lectures on the First and Second Epistle of Peter* (1869; repr., Minneapolis, MN: Klock & Klock Christian Publishers, 1978), 320.

12. Jerry Bridges, *The Practice of Godliness* (Colorado Springs, CO: NavPress, 1983).

13. Charles Hodge, *An Exposition of the First Epistle to the Corinthians* (London: The Banner of Truth Trust, 1959), 317.

14. Though I have not quoted him word for word, this definition of abiding in Christ is from Frederic Louis Godet, *Commentary on John's Gospel* (1886; repr., Grand Rapids, MI: Kregel, 1978), 855. This is the best definition of what it means to abide in Christ that I have come across.

15. R. C. H. Lenski, *The Interpretation of St. Paul's Epistles to the Colossians, to the Thessalonians, to Timothy, to Titus and to Philemon* (Minneapolis, MN; Augsburg, 1937), 170.

16. Bruce, 365.

17. David A. Seamands, *Healing for Damaged Emotions* (Wheaton, IL: Victor, 1981), 26.

# About the Author

Jerry Bridges is an author and Bible teacher. His most popular book, *The Pursuit of Holiness*, has sold over one million copies. He is also the author of *Trusting God*, *The Discipline of Grace*, *The Fruitful Life*, *The Gospel for Real Life*, and *Respectable Sins*. As a full-time staff member with The Navigators for many years, Jerry has served in the collegiate ministry and community ministries.

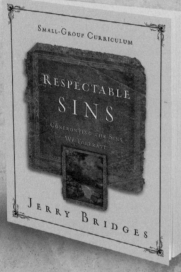
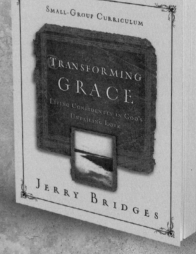